# MEN
# AT
# WAR

*Also by Luke Turner*

Out of the Woods

# MEN AT WAR

## LOVING, LUSTING, FIGHTING, REMEMBERING 1939–1945

## LUKE TURNER

WEIDENFELD & NICOLSON

First published in Great Britain in 2023 by Weidenfeld & Nicolson,
an imprint of The Orion Publishing Group Ltd
Carmelite House, 50 Victoria Embankment
London EC4Y 0DZ

An Hachette UK Company

1 3 5 7 9 10 8 6 4 2

A CIP catalogue record for this book is
available from the British Library.

ISBN (Hardback) 978 1 4746 1886 1
ISBN (eBook) 978 1 4746 1888 5
ISBN (Audio) 978 1 4746 1889 2

Typeset by Input Data Services Ltd, Bridgwater, Somerset

Printed in Great Britain by Clays Ltd, Elcograf S.p.A.

www.weidenfeldandnicolson.co.uk
www.orionbooks.co.uk

'Bless 'em all, bless 'em all, bless the long and the short
and the tall.'
British military song


'War is a prolonged passionate act, and we were involved in it.'
Elizabeth Bowen


'The Present is a room; the Past furnishes it, the Future lights it.'
Dan Billany

For Maximilian, in hope.

# CONTENTS

Never Served                          1
Boys and Their Toys                  16
Come and See                         31
Heavy Metal                          49
The Generation Game                  65
Private Normal                       78
Fight or/and/or Flight              101
Strength in Unity                   113
Dead Men's Beds                     132
They Don't Like It Up 'Em           145
Vile Bodies                         156
The Clap Trap                       172
Sodomy and Ignominy                 191
A Flame Without a Hearth            213
People Are People                   231
Breaking the Cage                   247
The Democracy of Death              262
Mr Thwaites Britain                 280
Aftermath                           306

Notes                           319
Acknowledgements                335
Credits                         339

# NEVER SERVED

A boy on his holiday scans the sky for the RAF jets that rip apart the murmur of the Norfolk coastline, now a distant dot among the summer clouds, now screeching so low he feels he might reach out and touch them.

A man in his mid-thirties who looks not unlike that small boy stamps his feet for warmth in the lookout of a luxury ocean liner, wrapped up against the cold Atlantic air, talking with a stranger about home and their different lives as together they scan the horizon for the dreaded plume of spray from the periscope of a German U-Boat.

A young Canadian peers through clear Perspex at the pale concrete slabs of a runway flickering ever faster past him before they disappear into the gloom as the bomber defeats gravity and lifts into the sky. This will be the final time he would know the earth.

A woman – who, against the standards of her day, does not consider herself a woman at all – stretches in a Cambridgeshire field, exhausted from the effort of haymaking. She runs a tough, calloused hand through Brylcreemed hair and looks up as the drone of bombers once more fills the harvest air.

Two men sit around an earth stove in an Italian POW camp, sharing out a Red Cross parcel to cook for themselves and three comrades. Together, they will write one of the love stories of the Second World War.

A normally suave officer clambers soaked to the skin onto a French harbour wall, machine-gun fire and explosions all around him. In a fit of rage he has never known before, he batters the prone form of a German soldier with the butt of his revolver.

In an orchard outside Bayeux, soon after D-Day, a wireless operator and a Mauritian soldier lie naked under the trees, engrossed in one another's bodies as apples ripen and artillery booms not far away.

Over London, the engine of a V-1 Doodlebug rocket ceases its pulsing and falls silent. In a West End theatre below, the audience dive under their seats, but a man who could not fight continues to move across the stage with a sensuous grace.

These are moments in time of the Second World War and its aftermath; one – the boy on the Norfolk beach – is not actually from the war at all but shaped entirely by its memory.

Throughout my childhood, the Second World War was my popular culture. While my peers were getting into pop music, fantasy comics, American wrestling, Hollywood films and football, I was seeking the war wherever I could. I'd ask for trips to air museums or the Royal Tournament. I watched every episode of *Dad's Army* and each Sunday, I'd scour the *Radio Times* for the afternoon's war film – *The Dam Busters, Ice Cold in Alex, The Eagle Has Landed, Reach for the Sky, Battle of Britain, 633 Squadron, The Guns of Navarone, A Bridge Too Far.* The plastic Airfix models that I painstakingly built in my bedroom took on a magical power, becoming strange objects that connected me to this past world so tantalisingly out of reach. I went through phases when I would become obsessed with different aspects of the war – often the Battle of Britain, but also the night raids over Germany or D-Day – and build kits accordingly. I'd repaint old models in different camouflage to represent their transfer to, say, the North African desert. Spitfires, Heinkel He 111, Messerschmitt Bf 109 and 110, Hurricane, Wellington, Lancaster, Typhoon, a couple of Mosquitos were hung with fishing line (less visible than thread) from my bedroom ceiling. I realise now that the solvent-heavy paints and glues of the time meant that I was probably slightly out of my tree when I imagined the feats of violence that my aircraft were to complete.

I didn't like to put the figures of the pilots and crew in my fighters and bombers. It didn't feel right to slap on blue paint for uniforms, a bit of brown for leather straps, a splurge of white mixed with red on the face for skin. They were all doomed, after all. When inevitably pins popped from the ceiling or fishing line unravelled and the models crashed to the floor, I'd paint cotton-wool red and black and stick it onto the broken plastic to represent flame and greasy smoke, then rehang them as if they were being shot down. I always felt guilty if it was an RAF aircraft ablaze. After the second or third crash, they were taken to the garden, stuffed with BBQ firelighters and ignited to trail black toxic smoke around the roses and raspberry canes as I made the sound of chattering machine guns and screaming engines.

Always lurking in my mind was the knowledge that these were machines of metal and wood designed at great expense and with extreme precision to keep a man's brain alive long enough that it might overwhelm and destroy another brain before it could do the same. Much as I found warplanes beautiful, this human aspect made me feel uneasy – I was aware what the modern jets that split the skies of the north Norfolk coast were for and how they connected with the bombers of the past that I'd gawp at in war museums or recreate in plastic. I wanted to focus only on the machines. One of my first artistic efforts was a picture book I drew one rainy day on one of those Norfolk holidays. Inspired by the jets thundering overhead, it told of the heroics of an RAF squadron but, instead of being flown by men, the aircraft had faces, spoke to one another, were the living beings themselves, like some strange hybrid of Thomas the Tank Engine and future autonomous drones.

Between the archetypes and heroes of war films and the plastic of my model kits was an absence and a silence. It was one made up of millions of men.

For years, I struggled to understand the poem that was as familiar as the Bible passages and hymns that were also etched into my young mind, the four lines repeated every Remembrance Sunday service:

> They shall grow not old,
> as we that are left grow old:
> Age shall not weary them,
> nor the years condemn.

As a child, I looked at veterans on telly, among family friends or at the men I knew at church who had been alive during the Second World War, and it seemed to me that they had always been old. Reading historical accounts of the war and seeing the ages of the men writing or being written about still gives me a jolt – Battle of Britain ace Richard Hillary, severely injured and a popular author by twenty-three – as do the endless neat stones in military cemeteries for aircrew, soldiers and sailors aged nineteen, twenty, twenty-one. When I thought of men in Lancaster bombers or on the beaches of D-Day, they were never just a few years older than me, as was actually the case, but always with white receding hair, crow's feet and wrinkles, wiry and shrivelled, or perhaps a little paunched. It is easier to process a fascination with war if it feels as if the men who died were already near death. There was no way of seeing them as they were.

That cringing awkwardness I felt and still feel when it comes to putting the crew in my model aircraft was also because those men were anonymous to me, like my grandad Percy or Great-Uncle Reg, both of whom had been in the war but died long before I was born. I knew them just as black-and-white photographs of a man in uniform. That was how, in childhood, I saw all the men of the Second World War, with nothing to go on save the characters from mainstream war films, photographs in memoirs and history books and grainy footage from the occasional documentary on the four terrestrial TV channels. They were flat, beyond comprehension.

During the pre-adolescent years, when the true workings of the human body and ideas of manhood are abstract and intangible, adults exist in another zone of experience and imagination. The reality of their lives is obscure and as children, we view them with a mixture of admiration and mystery. I loved chatting to a bloke at church about his model railway, but always held back from asking about his experiences at the Dunkirk evacuation in 1940. On one level, I was afraid of connecting my war obsession with the reality of human suffering, but it also felt taboo to pry into experiences that must have been so terrible to endure. I was not alone – a 2021 survey by British veterans' organisation SSAFA found that over 40 per cent of respondents regretted not speaking to their elderly relatives about their wartime experiences before they passed away. I grew up with the cultural narrative that they had made a huge sacrifice and when they came back, they didn't want to talk about it. I had no idea until years after he died, for instance, that my mum's cousin Raymond, a man whose gentle demeanour and pointy beard made him seem like a relic from the Edwardian era, and who ran a second-hand bookshop in Eastbourne, had been the navigator on a Beaufighter attack aircraft, flying dangerous missions against German and Italian shipping in the Mediterranean.

I suspect that I am not alone in hearing most of my war stories from women of that generation, primarily about the home front, rather than what happened overseas. My sole first-hand account of the conflict came from my granny, who talked about watching the Blitz over London from the slopes of Epping Forest. It was Granny who pointed out that I had put the wings of a polystyrene Spitfire on back to front. She shared tales of being evacuated to the Gloucestershire countryside, where my great-aunty would pause doing the washing-up, pick up a shotgun and start blasting at rabbits through the open window. I don't remember her ever talking about what my grandad Percy had got up to, and never wanted to ask. When you're a child, death seems so absolute and appalling that it is hard to enquire about a loved one who has gone, another layer in our national awkwardness about discussing our mortality and the past. I would only realise much later that the war very nearly ended our family before my dad was even born.

Granny's stories finished when she died suddenly in 1996. I still regret never recording her speaking about the war. As I got older, I craved new voices. When I moved to London in 2000, it was still a place scarred by the Second World War. The grand museums of Exhibition Road in Kensington and Tate Britain on the north bank of the Thames had ugly chunks torn out of their sharp stone walls by shrapnel from bombs. Before gentrification prompted a building boom in Hoxton, the area of east London where I lived, there were gaps in the streets, cellars opened to the sky and used as car parks, empty fireplaces hanging in thin air, even the remains of wallpaper and paint. My flat was in a post-war block that had replaced rows of terraces and our old neighbour, known as Nanny G, would recount her memories of what had brought about this profound change to London's topography. One day during the Blitz, she'd stood mesmerised by a German parachute mine as it floated gently down. It exploded, demolishing homes and knocking her out. She loved telling the story, in her rich Cockney accent, of what happened next. 'I came round and they was asking where I was from. 'OXTON I kept telling 'em. *Oxon*, they kept saying, *you're from Oxford? Nah, 'Oxton*. Took 'em days to work it out.' Hobbling along our concrete landing to the lift, Nanny G seemed superficially unscarred by these memories that had left their mark on the surrounding streets. The war had come and swept her early life away; where the house in which she had been born once stood there is now a park.

I look back at these fragments I had from Granny and Nanny G and realise that it's no wonder that into this vacuum of storytelling and knowledge flooded fantasy and exaggerated reality in the form of war films, comics, novels, toys and playground games of Brits and Yanks v Japs and Jerries.

In my early twenties, I bought a black shirt in a San Francisco thrift store, purely for the cut and the collar, intending to remove the US military eagle insignia on the shoulder when I got home. I ended up being chased down the street by a military veteran, screaming at me, 'Take it off, boy, you've never served!' I felt he had a point. To put on the uniform in which men took oaths to fight for their country, to wear a jacket of which the next garment from the sewing machines might have ended up tailored by bullets and soaked with blood, is an appropriation of sorts. I've always been suspicious of those parties and 'vintage' events – Blitz-themed, gin in teacups, bunting and nostalgia – that neglect to remember to lay on the risk of an air raid, weak beer, fugs of cigarette and pipe smoke and meagre snacks as part of the ticket price. I suppose you could still easily end the night with your pants full of VD, but it seems in terrible taste. Those of us who never served, the overwhelming majority, owe it to those who did to remember them with a far greater sensitivity and care than we have in recent years.

It's often said that in Britain we spend too much time going on about the war, but I'm not sure if we've had enough honest conversations that try to understand who these men actually were. These complicated, tricky people are known to us now only through old photographs or flickering black-and-white newsreel footage. They're rarely individuals but blurred splodges, or perhaps if in closer focus, mugging up for the camera, cigs and pipes clenched in propaganda grins. I think of a Royal Mail stamp issued for the seventy-fifth anniversary of D-Day in 2019, a collection of white faces peering out from identical uniforms. Mostly we just see the machines they were fleshy blobs within – bombers streaming contrails in European skies, tanks leading plumes of sand and dust across the Libyan desert, ships tossed like toys in the storms of the Atlantic. Often these same images are shown over and over again in TV documentaries, their power dulled by repetition and familiarity, even error. If these programmes used the wrong aircraft or tank to illustrate a historical moment, could I really trust what they said about the men, so often portrayed as simple heroes?

The military realities of the Second World War are still up for discussion. There are new stories to be found, existing narratives to re-examine. I can spend hours listening to podcasts like *We Have Ways*, where the nuances of the conflict are raked over and discussed by historian James Holland and comedian Al Murray, or following Twitter accounts that give detailed analysis of specific events in the wider history of the war. I've passed many an evening pouring over wartime reconnaissance imagery and comparing the locations on modern-day maps and aerial photographs, trying to understand which houses on my street were bombed, locate an anti-tank ditch in the woodland near where I live in north-east London or work out exactly where in a tiny French village an artillery barrage I'd been reading about in a novel-cum-memoir had landed. I see this as a form of digital archaeology and I'm sure I'm not alone in these cartographical investigations, a search for connection not in some voyeuristic fetishisation of destruction, but trying to understand how men like me might have felt and coped as terrible things happened in ordinary places. I suppose it's a layperson's attempt at a term I learned from the contemporary military historians on the *We Have Ways* podcast. 'Walking the ground' is the practice of visiting old battlefields to get a feel of the landscape in which the action happened. Spending time wandering fields where carnage was sown, examining folds in the terrain, woodlands and the siting of buildings might offer a deeper insight not just into military decisions made so long ago, but also how these impacted the lives and fates of individuals caught up in them. This is an exploration of the working of the military mind at the strategic, operational and tactical level on the battlefield, but it strikes me that we can do similar by walking the psychic terrain of the conflict. By this, I mean the lived experience of both the war and the years before and after, as captured in memoir, film, art, theatre, photography, novels, poetry and especially autofiction. So many novels of the Second World War closely follow and mirror the experiences of their writers, making them feel as valuable as veteran testimony. After all, I read about how contributors to the government's Mass Observation reports during the war would, when questioned about the events years later, put themselves closer to the action, or how veteran testimony and historical reports of D-Day changed over the years, even to be influenced by war films, often frustrating historians. Fiction gave former servicemen a licence to include harsher realities and personal narratives than might have been acceptable in straight autobiography or historiography. The private traumas and horrendous memories that the men of the Second World War carried with them have died with their bodies. These texts are all that we have left. They sit alongside what was created and recorded by the state – Mass Observation reports, Operational Record Books, unit war diaries, maps, orders, signals – all the admin on unlimited sheets of paper with which wars are fought as much as they are with guns and high explosive.

In recent years, with childhood a distant memory and the prospect of bringing new life into the world myself an increasing possibility, I felt that I needed to go through a process of self-examination to fully understand why I had been and, to be honest, still am, so crazily obsessed with the Second World War. The post-war generations have spent decades walking the ground of a war that is a cultural artefact as much as it was a geopolitical event. The Second World War wasn't just my popular culture, but that of the entire nation, arguably more enduring in its reach, and certainly its consequences, than the Beatles or the Rolling Stones. What applied to me, as an individual shying away from the brutal realities of wartime violence in favour of tales of machines and heroics, seemed also to be the case for my country.

The Second World War as it looms in the British psyche is a powerful weapon. It's no coincidence that as it moves beyond living memory, so the accompanying narrative has, lately, taken a turn for the jingoistic, caught up in febrile debates around our national myth and identity. It is used as a signifier for a past glory that might once again be attainable or a stick with which to beat younger generations. It can often feel as if Britain is stuck in some perpetual, childlike, simplistic obsession with the war that has prevented it from growing up and living in the present. Over my adult decades, the truth often felt lost behind football jingoism, belligerent rows over wearing a poppy and tired arguments that praised wartime leader Winston Churchill as an unimpeachable hero on one hand or grotesque warmonger and racist on the other. As the academic Thomas Colley points out in his book on how the British people understand war, the historiography is loose – now Churchill is praised as a war leader and his predecessor Chamberlain the weak appeaser of Nazism, but at the time, Chamberlain was lauded for seeming to have avoided a major European war, whereas Churchill's speeches were not always well-received.

The war is there as a vast hyper-object in the past, defining nearly every moment of the present, if you want it to. In a modern nation of civilians who largely exist in the comfort that they are unlikely ever to face war, this leaves its memory up for grabs. There is a nostalgia for a time when Britain stood 'alone' in the face of overwhelming odds, an idea not only debunked long ago by historians such as Angus Calder but also given short shrift by some at the time. Although *Punch*, a popular magazine in the early years of the war, was not averse to stirring up this sort of sentiment in the face of the military setbacks of 1940, after the fall of France, it printed a cartoon by Fougasse of two soldiers at some lonely picket, looking out to sea at a distant battleship. 'So our poor old Empire is alone in the world,' says one. 'Aye we are,' his comrade replies, 'the whole five hundred million of us.' Nevertheless, the narrative of a nation alone in 1940 was revived in the backdrop to Brexit, as was the British exceptionalism around Covid-19, in which time, with weary inevitability, politicians summoned the 'Blitz spirit' – that idea of a particularly British form of stoicism best represented by the slogan Keep Calm and Carry On – to get the nation through the crisis. Even that motto, devised by the Ministry of Information in 1939, comes with its own myth. Though it featured on 2.45 million posters, these were never widely distributed, and ended up being pulped as part of a recycling drive in the spring of 1940.

Hovering above all this – literally, when his picture was painted in London skies by hundreds of drones on New Year's Eve 2021– was Captain Tom Moore, the Second World War veteran who walked laps of his garden to raise £32m for the NHS. It was an incredible feat and touched a nerve in the public imagination, but it struck me as depressing that a veteran of the war was having to bail out the key institution that had been set up in the wave of hope and hunger for societal transformation at its end. It was particularly galling given that the same politicians who so loved to wheel out the memory of the war in Covid-19 boosterism were squandering billions of pounds of public money on, at best inefficient and at worst downright corrupt, healthcare procurement.

As noble as Captain Tom Moore's efforts appeared, the drone incarnation seemed appropriate for what he had become – an ephemeral portrait in lights of a hero then and a hero now. It was little different from so many of the cultural responses to the war that had emerged since 1945 in which lives had been presented in two dimensions, the conflict as dramatic fiction or infotainment. British men at war were frequently portrayed as accidental warriors, doing their bit because their time demanded it. When Prime Minster Boris Johnson praised 'the greatest generation of Britons who ever lived' on the seventy-fifth anniversary of VE Day in May 2020, he borrowed from the American writer Tom Brokaw, who in a bestselling book wrote that the US men and women of the 1940s were 'the greatest generation any society has ever produced'. I do not believe it undermines the sacrifice of those millions of men and women to say that such hyperbole creates a banality of generalisation. It does nothing to illuminate the complicated reality of their minds and bodies, but turns them into plastic icons for a form of ancestor worship.

I've always been fascinated by the power of Winston Churchill's speeches, how that deep and sonorous voice with a hint of a boozy lisp conveyed a defiance that, for the most part, was an effective means of geeing the country up to fight. I still find them moving today. At 2:54 p.m. on 13 May 1940, three days after the Germans attacked Luxembourg, the Netherlands, Belgium and France, Churchill made his first speech to the House of Commons since becoming prime minister. With the situation for Europe looking bleaker by the hour, he warned MPs that 'many, many long months of struggle and of suffering' were ahead if the country was to 'wage war against a monstrous tyranny never surpassed in the dark, lamentable catalogue of human crime' and eventually achieve victory. In this warning of the privations of total war, he offered up his side of the bargain: 'I have nothing to offer but blood, toil, tears and sweat.'

Here, Churchill was conjuring the essence of an idealised, British martial masculinity in the service of the state, to be squeezed out of every man in the struggle. Yet today, his powerful worlds breathe new life into the departing generation in a way that I had not foreseen when I was younger. Blood is more than a liquid shed for a cause. Sweat is not only released by toil, which in itself is not merely physical but emotional, including the work that needs to be done to recover from trauma. Tears are not merely those of that trauma or grief, but reconciliation, love and understanding. All four make up the elements of desire, the precious and individual life force so often denied in our assumptions of the 1940s. Men had not become biologically or hormonally any more complex during the long hangover since 1945.

Alongside my forays down internet wormholes, pouring over maps of the sites of airfields and battles, and reading military history, over the years I'd encountered gay and bisexual cultural figures who had been young men during the 1940s. These now kept coming to mind. It is these men, and more like them, that I have spent the last few years getting to know as I researched this book. Men like Peter de Rome, who, after the war, made gay erotic films on Super8; Micky Burn, the commando who appeared in a documentary about his life as a bisexual man; Colin Spencer, a teenager during the war who, afterwards, would spend his National Service in Germany treating soldiers with VD; Dudley Cave, a gay activist I learned about via a tweet from Peter Tatchell; Dan Billany, who wrote two astonishing novels, one a gay love story set in an Italian POW camp; and Wing Commander Ian Gleed, a pilot whose Mk 1 Hurricane sat in my stash of unbuilt model kits and whose surprising private life was revealed when I searched for information about the pilot named on the instruction sheet. These men don't just give an insight into the hidden histories of queer Britain but an incisive, analytical awareness of how the often exclusively male societies of the armed forces fucked and felt. Billany, in particular, had a keen understanding of the men he fought alongside, and how the military 'had usurped their bodies' yet could never entirely occupy their minds, feelings and desires.

The best observer is often the one who remains slightly hidden, at one step removed from those they are looking at. Gay and bisexual men, in the unique position of being legally judged and defined by their sexuality, can seem to me to be in tune with what it is to be a man in a way that heterosexuals sometimes aren't. The light shone through this prism became more acute in wartime, when gay and bisexual men were removed from the confines and rules of conventional civilian society and thrown into the moral upheaval of war. Yet I didn't want my focus to end there, forcing the gay and bisexual men at war into some kind of ghetto just as their time had. There were straight men too who were driven, to varying degrees, by a tangle of lust and shame, not fitting into conventional ideals of military masculinity. Their enthusiasm for the war ebbed and flowed, and a few did not even fight at all. Among their number are writers, poets, artists, dancers and working men who in 1945, or thereabouts, tried, as best they could, to return to their peacetime lives. Some never made it home. They were both ordinary and extraordinary. Some seem familiar to us today, others as if they are from another world. Mine is a civilian's-eye view of the war because that is what they had, these men who had answered their nation's call, had given their blood, toil, tears and sweat, only for our culture to forget them in favour of shallow, easy myths.

As the anxiety of Covid-19 and the hapless screeching of our politicians became almost too much to bear, building each new model kit – late at night, music on in the background – was a much-needed escape. I realised that my hobby had, as an adult, become ritualistic. I went online to chat with the knowledgeable and generous community of military history and modelling enthusiasts to work out the right markings for a particular aircraft. I gently washed the grey plastic parts in soapy water, fitted and glued them together, mixed the correct combination of colours and used my new airbrush to lay down primer and base layers, slowly building up the paint of their camouflage schemes. I protected this with a layer of Pledge floor polish before adding the transfers of RAF roundels and identification letters, then weathered the model with oil stains, dirt and dust to make it look as realistic as possible. I still couldn't bear to put the men in the cockpit.

# BOYS AND THEIR TOYS

One of my first toys was a gun, given to me not long after my birth in 1978 by, of all people, the Sunday school at Dad's church in Bradford. It never reached my cot. My parents, Dad a Methodist minister and Mum the daughter of a conscientious objector, didn't want me to play at war, or to have martial toys. They tell me now their efforts were in vain. I would pick up sticks and mime shooting with them. The aerials and antennae on my space Lego – a company that then had a pacifist policy of not making toy weapons – were repurposed as cannons and missiles. The sailing dinghies in my favourite book *Swallows and Amazons* turned into the ships of Nelson's Navy and the Hornblower novels. My model railway went to war, a kit of a Gloster Gladiator biplane crashed on the plaster of Paris hillside, and battles took place across the tracks. I would do anything I could to recreate the tools and machines of violence.

There's nothing new about the urge to play at war. Antonia Fraser, in *A History of Toys,* writes that 'as long as men go to war and armies exist children will want to play with soldiers'. She describes how in 1383 Charles V of France played with a wooden cannon – 'royal children, above all others, were given war-toys, because of the combative destiny which lay before them'. Toy soldiers belonging to children of the Roman Empire have been unearthed in archaeological sites from the Mediterranean to Britain, while ancient models of warships, complete with ramming prow and warrior crew, have been found in Greece. The historian Henry Harris writes that model soldiers have been part of human life for thousands of years and in his view were entirely gendered – 'as the doll was to the girl, so was the toy soldier to the boy'. Winston Churchill possessed a sense of destiny, a belief that everything he had done led to his eventual role as war leader. A self-conscious predestination comes in a telling passage in *My Early Life*, as he writes that he had 'embarked on a military career [. . .] entirely due to my collection of model soldiers.' His miniature army consisted of 1,500 soldiers, all British, who were thrown into conflict with the forces of his brother, Jack, who was only permitted to have 'coloured' troops and no artillery. The young Winston's dubiously and unfairly dominant force was arranged 'in the correct formation of attack' for inspection by his father, the Conservative politician Lord Randolph Churchill. Apparently impressed, father asked son if he wanted to go into the Army and the positive response was taken seriously. 'For years I thought my father with his experience and flair had discerned in me the qualities of military genius,' Churchill recalled, 'but I was told later that he had only come to the conclusion that I was not clever enough to go to the Bar. However that may be, the toy soldiers turned the current of my life.'

Whether or not this is mere personal myth, the late nineteenth-century aristocrat's son fitted the notion that children playing at conflict was a form of preparation for the real thing. Writing after the Second World War, Brigadier John Rawlings Rees, consultant psychiatrist to the Army and medical director of London's

Tavistock Clinic, analysed how the Army had tried to get the best out of its men by appealing to a sense of masculine adventure and excitement at the power of weaponry. During the early war years, new recruits arrived full of enthusiasm but found training so dull that their morale was impacted. Therefore, more 'realism' was introduced – he cites the example of how some instructors insisted that men know the names of all the parts of their weapons, as well as how to clean and reassemble them, before they were permitted to fire, something they found dull: 'No one would expect a small boy to be interested in his air gun until he had fired it; having done so he is quite keen to look after it, and the same holds true of an adult man.'

This blurring of the distinction between child's play and adult training for war was taken to a logical extreme by H. G. Wells, a pacifist who, along with his contemporaries Robert Louis Stevenson, G. K. Chesterton and Jerome K. Jerome, loved to play with toy soldiers. In 1913, he published *Little Wars*, a guide for battle with model soldiers aimed squarely at a male market – its subtitle was: 'A Game for Boys from twelve years of age to one hundred and fifty and for that more intelligent sort of girl who likes boys' games and books'. He described the spring-loaded replicas of actual artillery pieces that could knock down soldiers from the other side of the room as 'this priceless gift to boyhood', just as mass-produced plastic model aircraft and tanks were to the post-Second World War generations. *Little Wars* ends with utopianism. Wells argues that his war games were better than the 'Real Thing', with 'no smashed nor sanguinary bodies [. . .] no petty cruelties', a 'homeopathic remedy for the imaginative strategist' with no actual death and destruction. He suggested putting 'prancing' monarchs, patriots, adventurers, 'all the practitioners of Welt Politik', into one vast Temple of War with cellars full of little trees, forts, houses to be knocked down by 'unlimited' numbers of toy soldiers to 'let them lead their own lives there away from us'.

*Little Wars* was published in 1913. Could it have come out after the war that began the following year? In his introduction to the 1970 edition, Isaac Asimov wrote, 'Ah, for the innocence of 1913, when men could, in all honesty, think of war as an exercise for tin soldiers.' He wrote that, in the pre-First World War years, society missed the thrill of wars and sought to find a replacement in adventures with toys. Wells and Asimov touch on the paradox of war play – does it act as a sublimation of martial desires or does it inflame them? In the appendix to *Little Wars*, Wells writes of how army officers had been in touch to see if his game plan might be adapted for Kriegspiel, the war-gaming practice developed by the nineteenth-century Prussian military.

I think of Wells' idea of battles with toy soldiers instead of the Real Thing when I watch 'Goodbyeee', the tragic final episode of BBC comedy *Blackadder Goes Forth*, in which Captain Blackadder telephones British army commander General Sir Douglas Haig in an attempt to avoid 'the big push'. As he listens to the entreaties of the man who saved his life in the old Colonial wars, Haig knocks over ranks of lead soldiers on a model of the battlefield, sweeps them into a dustpan and throws them over his shoulder.

H. G. Wells' war-gaming pal Robert Louis Stevenson appeared in a Ladybird book of bedtime rhymes that I turned to surprisingly frequently in the confusing cusp between childhood and adolescence, when I craved holding on to the former, innocent state. A memory of one particular double page remains clear – Robert Louis Stevenson's poem 'The Land of Counterpane', accompanied by James Hodgson's illustration of a boy sitting up in bed, looking down at a duvet that has become a fantasy land, scattered with his toy building blocks and ships. In his smiling, fevered state, through his eyes it all becomes real: 'I watched my leaden soldiers go, with different uniforms and drills / Among the bed-clothes, through the hills.'

Like the kid in the book, I spent occasional happy sick days away from the boisterousness of school, drawing maps of fantasy lands and coastal promontories topped by castles, the 'pleasant land of counterpane' occupied by militarism. But unlike H. G. Wells and Robert Louis Stevenson, my generation didn't just have military forces made up largely of men with the occasional cannon; we had war machines too, of seemingly endless variety in shape, camouflage and firepower. I still have a file of drawings I made on one day sick home from school of an imaginary fleet of new aircraft for the Royal Air Force (bombers, fighters, weapons systems) and ships for the navy (aircraft carriers, destroyers, cruisers, each class with their own HMS names). The army, sadly, never got an updated force of artillery, infantry or armour. This was partly because I found them so hard to draw – the difficulties of making perfectly round circles for wheels and the complexities of the tank tracks – but also simply because I didn't find them to be as aesthetically satisfying as fighters, bombers and ships. I had zero interest in stories of the infantry in the First World War, but the escapades of W. E. Johns' character Biggles, and his hair-raising patrols over the Western Front, were always under my pillow. It was the glamour of flight that so appealed.

In the 1970s, young adult fiction occasionally had the Second World War as subject matter. I devoured Jan Mark's *Thunder and Lightnings*, published in 1976, a reflection of my own obsession with warplanes from the beginning of flight to the present day. It was set in the same part of Norfolk where I'd stare up looking for the Jaguar attack aircraft based at RAF Coltishall, though the boys in the book were fanatics for their predecessors, the English Electric Lightning. *Thunder and Lightnings* told the story of a new Norfolk arrival called Andrew and his pal Victor. Like me, Victor had model aircraft hanging from the ceiling that he imagined on night raids over Germany. He had a huge stash of war comics, the artists of which could draw a perfect aeroplane but not the human form. Together, the boys watched Lightning and Phantom fighters on their manoeuvres overhead. Just as I had, they traced the outlines of aircraft from books borrowed from the library. The boys loved to watch the Spitfire of the Battle of Britain Memorial Flight, then stationed at RAF Coltishall alongside the modern aircraft. A passing motorist tells them, 'If it wasn't for those, you wouldn't be here . . . never forget that.' Victor is unimpressed. Every time he sees a Spitfire some adult seems to tell him this. 'I don't want to be told. I don't need to be told. That makes you feel you should go round kissing their wheels or something.' At an ancient church nearby, the boys find British war graves, and others for '*Ein Deutscher Soldat*', identity unknown. Andrew remarks that you never see the dead in comics, that it's 'just the Hun and serve him right'. Victor's reply is that of so many of us of the post-war generations: 'Perhaps they don't want people to think what really happened . . . War's supposed to be fun.'

Unlike the fictional Andrew, I didn't have a Victor to share my love of the most physically beautiful of all the weapons of war. While other boys had birthday outings to the zoo or to Wimpy for burgers on plates, all I wanted was to drag my pals to see aeroplanes. On train trips down to London from our home in a Hertfordshire commuter town, I knew exactly when to look out of the right-hand side of the carriage to glimpse the flash of red, white and blue that was the RAF roundel painted on the roof of the RAF Museum, on the site of a wartime airfield at Hendon, just north of the capital.

My enthusiasm was just the latest incarnation of a British tradition. During the 1920s and 30s, as many as 100,000 people would arrive at Hendon for the annual RAF air pageant. Newsreels from the time promised 'thrills in plenty at World's Greatest Flying Spectacle'. Crowds dressed up to the nines watched RAF aircraft perform stunts – elaborate formation manoeuvres, dropping parachutists, shooting down balloons in flames and making graceful dives to bomb a mock village. Houses, barns and a church disappeared in choreographed explosions and fire. It was war as live-action entertainment, the thrill of the latest technology that might even be both metaphysical and erotic – there's a newsreel scene from the 1935 pageant in which a pilot helps a woman into the cockpit of a biplane, the narrator's clipped RP announcing 'the air force equivalent to a Tommy is in his element, of course, fitting wings to a couple of angels'. By the 1980s, London's suburbia had sprawled out over the former aerodrome; the museum's exhibits did not arrive by the grace of flight but dismembered on the backs of lorries. That idea of the romance of the airman hadn't died, however. If anything, the Second World War had made it even stronger, and I had fallen head over heels in love.

The Battle of Britain, which lasted for sixteen weeks between July and October 1940, is the prism of conflict through which our country sees itself today. While more recent studies have discounted the idea that a German invasion of Britain was ever particularly likely, that wasn't seen as the case at the time. Hitler's seemingly unstoppable forces had conquered the Low Countries and France in a matter of weeks. The British were reeling from the evacuation from Dunkirk and barges to carry invading troops and materiel started to appear along the Channel coast as the Luftwaffe began their campaign to destroy the RAF. The Battle of Britain was tangible to those on the ground, looking up into blue British skies to see the looping contrails of fighters, the dark plumes of smoke trailing from falling aircraft, floating parachutes, the distant crump of bombs. Fifty years later, I'd look up to the heavens and wish that by some magic I could still see them.

At primary school firework displays on 5 November (an older ritual celebrating national salvation), I'd excitedly imagine the rockets as RAF Spitfires and Hurricanes pursuing German Stuka dive bombers or Messerschmitt fighters, the spiralling whizz and explosions the destruction of friend and foe alike, the bonfire on the ground the mess of burning London. It was the Battle of Britain aircraft that I was first obsessed with modelling and hanging from the bedroom ceiling, pilots like Douglas Bader and Richard Hillary who I idolised, films like the 1969 flop *The Battle of Britain* that I recorded from the telly and endlessly rewatched. The battle seemed a glorious thing as it was usually depicted in fiction and documentaries, with the beautiful Spitfire and doughty Hurricane, piloted by suave young men sitting in the warm summer sun on deckchairs around dispersal huts, reading, smoking, waiting for the bell that would send them to their aircraft to roar into battle, returning at night for pints in the local pub. They were colloquially known as 'Brylcreem boys' for the slicked, side-parted hair that went with their sharp attire. Elite pilots flying aircraft at the forefront of technological innovation, they were the ideal of well-groomed Englishness. There was a class element, too, with the idea that this bunch of (at the start of the war) largely posh and private school-educated flying officers were in some way superior to ordinary me; unattainable, like martial film stars.

It was all very aspirational, to want to be like one of these brave fellows who, as Richard Hillary wrote, were flying 'for aesthetic reasons'. As he explained in *The Last Enemy*, being a fighter pilot promised 'a concentration of amusement, fear, and exultation, which it would be impossible to experience in any other form of existence'. If I felt uncomfortable putting the men in the cockpits of my Battle of Britain kits, it was also in part because I wanted to be like them. This allure was used during the war years to pull at the emotions of boys. A 1940 book called *Taking Off!* by Noel Monks glamourised the training of RAF aircrew, linking young masculinity and the joy of aerial combat – 'Flying in wartime belongs to Youth, and the youth of the British Empire have found a new heritage in the air.' In a second 1940 book, about Hurricane pilots in France, Monks wrote of how the intensity of the desperate war against the Luftwaffe gave the opportunity for these bold chaps to prove their masculinity. 'Boys of twenty became old men in four days [. . .] But even with their swollen red eyes, the fighter boys were always seconds ahead of the Nazis in seeing danger – and meeting it. Their hearts and their brains and their sinews remained young.' This was very much the view of the RAF's Fighter Command that had persisted long after the war, and into my childhood.

The Battle of Britain was a mass media combat, as seen in the famous news report of 14 July 1940, in which BBC correspondent Charles Gardner narrated a Luftwaffe attack on a Channel convoy as if it were a sporting event. The battle was the genesis of what have become the clichés of Britain carrying on – 'London can take it', damage to Buckingham Palace meaning that the king and queen could 'look the East End in the eye', the brave bombed-out Cockney – that have come down through the years to shape how Britain sees itself now.

As a child, like my country, I absorbed all this with relish. When, on 20 August 1940, Churchill gave his famous speech to Parliament in praise of the Battle of Britain pilots that 'Never in the field of human conflict was so much owed by so many to so few', it instantly created a minority of heroes who would go on to dominate our cultural memory of that part of the war. The myths of 1940, frequently summoned by the tabloids, conveniently ignore inconvenient facts, such as the most successful RAF squadron during the battle – no. 303, responsible for shooting down dozens of German aircraft in just forty-two days – was a Polish one.

On my birthday trips in the late-1980s and early 90s, I wandered around the RAF museum in a kind of trance, intoxicated by the smell of paint, metal and especially the oil that dripped from engines into trays beneath the aircraft. It was as if they were dormant but alive, the oil their blood and sweat. The Spitfires, Hurricanes and German aircraft of the Battle of Britain might have thrilled me at first, but they were merely the gateway to what ended up being my main love – the bombers and above all, the museum's Avro Lancaster S-Sugar, one of the few aircraft to have finished over a hundred raids. I peered up at the terrible looming bulk of the aircraft in awe, staring at the bomb symbols painted on the fuselage that marked each completed operation. A mocking transcription of Luftwaffe chief Herman Goering's empty boast that 'No enemy plane will fly over the Reich Territory' had been painted over the original nose art of a female nude kneeling in front of a bomb. It was enchanting to feel that I was in such close prox- imity to something that *had actually been there* so many years before, when the ice-cold slipstream chilled the aircraft's aluminium skin, its huge bomb-doors swinging open over Dortmund, Hamburg, Bremen. I loved this particular family of bombers so much that I even wrote to Jimmy Savile to ask if he could fix it for me to fly in the Battle of Britain Memorial Flight's Avro Lancaster. It's an aircraft that still does a turn at air shows and events of national significance. For the queen's platinum jubilee in 2022, I travelled to a vantage point on the platform of Bethnal Green station to listen out for its four Merlin engines amid the jets and helicopters of the modern RAF. I still wished I could have been on board, in the bomb aimer's position at the front, watching the streets of London zip past beneath me.

It's not that I was ignorant of what these aircraft had done to civilian populations; I knew how bombers killed children just like me – and had nearly meant I was never born. One night, a church hall in Loughton, Essex, was hit by a German bomb, the blast sending part of its roof arcing through the air, crashing into my grandparents' terraced house, through their bed and into the living room below, stopping just inches above the table under which my granny was sheltering with my uncle, then an infant. Granny never told me this story herself and I only found out the details recently, from my cousin. No doubt the memory was not one that she could or would want to articulate, though she did tell me about the night of 19 April 1944, when, during a German raid that was part of the late-war Little Blitz, the Bedden family who lived opposite heard the air raid sirens and went into their garden's Anderson shelter. It took a direct hit from a bomb. They were killed, though their house still stands today.

Perhaps then it was cognitive dissonance that allowed me to be seduced by the power and menace of the Avro Lancaster, just as so many boys had before me. The artist and writer Colin Spencer told me that at school during the early years of the war, his fellow pupils were consumed by the aircraft overhead. 'There were always the RAF aficionados who adored all that and rushed out to see what planes were bombing them and that kind of thing, that was the only thing that got the boys' attention,' he said. 'It was glamorous and there were constantly popular films and stories praising them. It was the new thing because there were hardly any in existence as war engines in the First World War, so they came into their own in the Second.'

Mass Observation File Report 87 of April 1940, entitled 'What Children Think of the War', found a strong martial instinct. Where children had previously wanted to be cowboys or engine drivers, now the dream was to be a soldier, airman or especially a commando. Twelve-year-old Leslie knew all the aircraft and built models of them from balsa wood. Gerald, aged ten, said, 'I'm mad on the Air Force. I want to be a pilot. I know all the different type of aeroplanes. I'd like to bring lots of Nazi planes down, and I will when I'm big.' Other boys marched up and down in mock battles, chanting 'silly old Churchill'. Another said prisoners should be shot to stop them going home to Germany and one group even played a game of 'concentration camp' outside a church, where the railings did for barbed wire.

Yet the report was unconcerned, saying that this was a 'natural reaction' of children to what they saw going on around them and that parents need not be worried 'by this tendency of the young to delight in the drama of war. It is probably better for children to externalise their doubts and fears and set them out.' What had been far more difficult, the investigators believed, was the uncertainty of the years leading up to the war. Eight-year-old Julian had been sent into 'hysterics of terror' in 1938 by the sight of a tank. In April 1940, he was calling tracer bullets in the skies 'pretties', wore a tin hat and 'says stoutly that he is going to kill Germans. All this does not mean that Julian, and others like him, will grow up into aggressives, avid for conquest. Children, like nations, have to pass through a barbarian stage, and the only cause for alarm is when, in nations as in children, this stage is unduly prolonged. Unlike little Germans and Italians, our children do not have glorification of war as an end in itself drilled into them at home and at school.'

After 1945, our parents and (in my experience) education system might not have glorified war, but capitalism did. The silence of the wartime generation was exploited by a huge industry devoted to recreating the recent history of a great British victory for the nation's children. In the cinemas were the war films I was still consuming decades later. Soldiers could now be made of cheap plastic rather than lead, vastly expanding their accessibility. Airfix, founded by Hungarian refugee Nicholas Kove in 1939, launched their first military kit in 1953 – it was, unsurprisingly, a Battle of Britain Mk 1 Spitfire. Comics like *Commando*, *The Victor* and *Warlord* boomed during the 1960s and 70s, with larger-than-life characters like Union Jack Jackson conducting missions of extraordinary derring-do, excitingly illustrated with accurate weaponry, explosions and Germans who screamed 'ACHTUNG SPITFIRE!' and died with a satisfying 'AIEEEE!!!'. There was glorification of war here, all right.

I certainly felt a strong platonic and martial romance over the heroes of the war films I watched, like Douglas Bader struggling on despite the loss of both of his legs in an air crash in *Reach for the Sky*, or the clipped bravery of the destroyer crew of *In Which We Serve*. Did this have a nationalistic element? I rather enjoyed the boshing of the French and Spanish in novels of the Napoleonic Wars and eagerly awaited the live broadcast of Trooping the Colour on the queen's birthday, though I was more excited by the salutes fired from field guns than the interminable pomp and marching. I felt a thrill at the pageant of the Royal Tournament at Earl's Court and for a while was even into the patriotic spectacle of the Last Night of the Proms, an enthusiasm that stemmed from the programme of music rooted in military history. Perhaps it all kindled within me a surprising small-c conservatism that became a large-C Conservatism when, in the 1992 school mock general election, I ran the Tory election campaign, though it was more of an act of rebellion than any true ideological conversion. It was a short-lived political allegiance.

During the 1980s, anti-war activists of the Left and beyond made explicit the link between boys' play and adult violence. A song called 'Take the Toys from the Boys' was sung at CND marches and the all-female Greenham Common peace camp. It became a slogan featured on activists' badges and a giant banner hung across the perimeter fence of the American base. But I'm not so sure that we should see this childhood fascination with guns as an example of nascent toxic masculinity, something that ought to be stamped out at all costs. Children and teenagers are often drawn to death and violence as part of the process of understanding the workings of the world. The Second World War was the prism through which I unconsciously investigated this elemental aspect of my own existence – it enabled me to get a sense of who I was. Looking back at the evolution of my interests from ships to warships, from sticks as pistols to militarised Lego and model kits, there was something instinctual about it all.

But where does this lead? In *A History of Toys*, Antonia Fraser wrote that she 'feels that children are better off provided with safe guns, to drain off their natural aggressiveness, than sheltered from things which will soon be apparent to them in the world around'. Footage from more recent conflicts showing young victims drawing pictures of tanks, soldiers and aircraft has been striking. I've wondered if the Mass Observation analysis of the wartime years wasn't quite right, that instead of going through a 'phase', the children who played commando and marched up and down their local streets were instead doing so to process their trauma. Was the Second World War enthusiasm of the Cold War generations a way of exploring a simpler ideal of combat to distract us from the knowledge that we were just minutes away from nuclear incineration? I certainly found release in my war culture, one that only became more intense as adolescence loomed.

Every Monday night, I would get dropped off at Dad's church hall for a few hours of wholesome activity with the Boys' Brigade. We'd start with a military-style inspection, lined up for the leaders to check the polish on our shoes, the gleam of our brass belt buckles, the angle of our caps. This would be followed by prayers, then military drill, marching up and down the hall. Then we'd 'fall out' for activities (model making, listening to weirdos on CB radio) before the bit of the evening that everyone else had been looking forward to but I hated – sports, usually football. I found it rather disrespectful when the ball ricocheted off the wall-mounted memorial plaque listing the men of the church who'd died in the world wars. More than anything else, I didn't understand why everyone wanted to do sport when we surely ought to have been learning about military tactics or going out for battle exercises in the local woods. We were a brigade, after all.

Instead, this longing to have a go at being a soldier was satisfied in my cousins' huge, semi-wild garden. We'd spend hours building fortifications in the bushes, cooking food on fires designed according to specifications in the *SAS Survival Handbook* and smearing burnt cork on our faces to carry out skirmishing patrols in the neighbouring field, where attempts at stealth were given away by our movement through the tall waving sweetcorn plants. It was thrilling, hiding in our stockade, fire crackling away, the night stealing in across the Essex countryside, for these grandchildren of a conscientious objector, planning or awaiting attack from my cousins' camp just down the hill. Our warfare had historical breadth – my uncle was quite the craftsman and armament varied from wooden swords and shields to guns, though the prize weapon was a full-size cap gun replica of a Luger, a pistol issued to German officers during the war and popular with Allied soldiers hunting for souvenirs. I can still feel the cool of the metal in my palm, the sense of power that came through it. There was a transgressive thrill to holding the Luger that came in part I am sure from it being doubly taboo – not just a gun, but a German one.

# COME AND SEE

The German Panzer III tank came rattling around the dirt road, grouchy and mean and belching exhaust. It lurched as it turned, scattering dust and pebbles, the turret slowly traversing, the sinister finger of the gun swinging around until it was pointing directly at me, its muzzle a tiny black dot. While ships and aircraft usually have an elegance necessitated by the laws of hydro- or aerodynamics, the tank is squat, brutish and graceless, designed purely to carry a powerful weapon onto the battlefield without being destroyed. I'd been afraid of tanks as a child, unnerved by their functional embodiment of an awful aspect of warfare away from my dreams of glory in sleek aircraft. Years after I'd last played at soldiers, I wanted to see how these steel incarnations of brute force made me feel as an adult and how the young male fascination with war machines had evolved since my youth.

Tankfest takes place every year at the Tank Museum at Bovington, located in one of the most militarised landscapes in the British Isles. I'd driven to the Glastonbury of armoured warfare across Salisbury Plain, where the A338 meanders through fields of barley, past thatched barns, golden stone cottages and Salisbury cathedral, its spire spiking the emerging blue of a perfect late summer morning. A timeless picture postcard landscape, what the historian Patrick Wright describes as 'Deep England', it is also martial terrain. On Salisbury Plain, you're as likely to see an Apache helicopter gunship hovering over the fields as you are a kestrel, and there are as many red-rimmed triangles warning of tanks crossing as there are brown heritage signs pointing you to nearby Stonehenge. The view out of the car window also featured symbolic and monumental nods to our military history: war memorial monoliths, a pub called The Churchill Arms, advertisements for paintball wargames, bronze sculptures of archers and, next to a rugby club, a full-size Spitfire lofted above the road.

In the Tankfest car-parking field, the decidedly unmilitary wheels of my Honda Jazz jolted over bumps and dips. From behind a hedge starting to glow with the first hint of autumn there came the sound of rattling machine-gun fire, a blaring tannoy and loud engines. A bang, then a puff of black smoke appeared above the dying leaves. I hurried through the crowd of lads and dads, exchanged my ticket for a wristband and made my way to the 'orange zone' viewing area. The focus of Tankfest is the Kuwait Arena, a messy amphitheatre of rough dirt roads, corrugated iron emplacements, large tyres and earth mounds. This is where, over the course of the day, the museum's exhibits are put through their paces in a programme bracketed by two battle re-enactments, the first of which, an early Second World War German victory, I had just missed. The tannoy screeched as the battle commentators gave their final remark about the German troops: 'What struck me about the people re-enacting is that they're so in character!' said one. 'A little too in character, sometimes,' the other replied with a chuckle.

I settled down on the grass, shading my eyes from the sun to look around at the Tankfest crowd. It wasn't that dissimilar to what you might find at a music festival, though one with an overwhelmingly male audience. There were two bald and bearded bikers, arms covered in tattoos, sitting in cheap deckchairs with slots in the arms to hold pints of beer. In front of me was one of the few women I saw during the day, in a hoodie with Liberation Society Disciple on the back, the initial letters aligned to spell LSD. There were quite a few people in official Tankfest T-shirts, featuring the names of popular tanks – Matilda II, Panzer III, Centurion – on the back in the sort of gothic font often used by the loudest rock bands and designed to look like merch you'd buy at a festival devoted to a different kind of heavy metal. The branding made sense based on the number of band T-shirts worn by festival attendees – Mötörhead, Black Sabbath and, more obscure, Norwich's finest crust-punk troupe, Deviated Instinct. The band most represented was Iron Maiden, which was fitting, given the group's long-standing use of Second World War imagery in their lyrics and aesthetic.

Roasting in the sun, I wandered off in search of shade inside the museum buildings. Tankfest was sponsored by online armoured warfare game World of Tanks, the website of which refers to the hardware in the main arena as 'the Tankfest offline event'. Players were encouraged to tune in to watch Tankfest on the Twitch gaming channel, where they'd be rewarded for spending more time online with boosts for their virtual armour. Inspired by what they'd seen outside, lads queued for the Gaming Zone, where they could have a crack at World of Tanks on high-spec machines. While comics and war films might have declined in popularity since their heyday in the 1960s and 70s, their visual allure and excitement had been replaced by the rise in hyper-realistic war games played online or on consoles. I'd spent a few years fairly hooked on Steel Panthers, a PC tank game bought for a quid in a charity shop. It involved taking charge of tanks and infantry in recreations of actual Second World War battles or long campaigns, leaving towns and pixelated hulls of armoured vehicles burning in my wake.

A stall selling jewellery was incongruous among all the war machines and didn't seem to be doing much business. More popular was the stand run by Models for Heroes, a charity which raises money for veterans. I noticed that the majority of the armour they'd modelled was German. On book and memorabilia stalls, the most fingered objects seemed to relate to our erstwhile enemies. I picked up a genuine wartime photo album belonging to a German soldier called Erich Ebel and flicked through the black-and-white images. It would have looked like a lads-on-tour holiday diary were it not for the uniforms featuring Nazi eagles, as Ebel and his comrades posed around the sites of Occupied Europe, larked about and leapt naked into the sea. The entries dried up in 1944. Likewise, it was the German tanks, and especially the huge Tiger, that got the most attention. Tiger 131 at the Tank Museum, captured in Tunisia in April 1943, is the only working example of its type in the world. Boys and men circled it, pointing out aspects of its design, the huge gun, the boxy turret, recounting tales of its exploits that they'd read in books or seen in documentaries and war films. There was an orderly queue to take selfies in front of it.

The Tiger, developed by the German war industry during the 1940s, was heavily armed with a powerful 88mm gun and its armour was able to withstand nearly anything that most British, American and Soviet weapons could throw at it. It might have been prone to breakdown and a terrible guzzler of fuel – a disaster given the impact Allied bombers like S-Sugar were having on the German petroleum industry – but it remains one of the most famous war machines ever produced. During the war years, it had a particular hold over Allied troops in Europe. In the semi-autobiographical novel *Flesh Wounds*, David Holbrook wrote that British Sherman tank crews newly arrived in Normandy after D-Day, suffered from a 'hysterical fear' of the Tiger, and 'the legend of their invulnerability was paralysing'. This mythos extended beyond the war to the present day. If the Spitfire has become the icon of the Battle of Britain, then the brutish Tiger is the projection of Nazi power and ideology.

I felt a sudden queasiness at the Tankfest punters' desire to be photographed up-close and personal to a machine that must have killed thousands of our forebears, and which would have spread terror among the civilian populations of Occupied Europe. In the museum shop, you could buy Tiger 131 lager for £5.99 (commemorative glass included), a Tiger watch, a Tiger glass decanter, a Tiger tank top and a Tiger 131 mug – 'Make a brew and see the iconic Tiger 131 in action with this heat sensitive mug – just add hot water!' Given British soldiers used to refer to tanks suddenly bursting into flame when hit by shells from Tigers and the rest of the German Panzer pantheon as 'brewing up', this seemed in questionable taste.

Outside the Kuwait Arena, various re-enactment groups who participated in the mock battles had their camps, men in the uniforms of Britain, America and Germany hanging around their neatly erected tents. These practitioners of 'living history', as they like it to be called, spend their weekends at events like this showing people *how it was*. I had mixed feelings about it. I could see the appeal – it was like the war games I played with my cousins but on a different scale, with proper uniforms and bigger bangs – yet some of it seemed like Second World War cosplay. I remembered an interview I'd done with Stephen Morris, drummer of Joy Division and New Order, and a military history enthusiast who has armoured vehicles in a barn outside his home in the Lancashire Pennines. He told me of trips to the War and Peace Show, a major military festival, where it seemed that the men who dressed up as the SS were always policemen.

At Tankfest, the various units hung around in their tidy camps, demonstrating weapons and equipment to the passers-by. 'You think I dress like this all the time?' I overheard one 'German' soldier say. 'I was an American last week.' He went on to explain to a kid how the bayonet works, with the groove down the flat of the blade to let the blood run out. 'It's not very nice, is it?' he said, cheerily. The different nationalities had their signifiers – a gruff Devonian of the British infantry demonstrated a Bren gun with pipe clamped between his teeth in a camp stocked with authentic-looking tins of sausage and bacon in lard. The Americans had cases of Coke and lounged around, their helmet straps undone just like in war films. The Germans had fizzy drinks with swastika logos and their most senior officer spent most of the day sat in the back of a staff car, embodying the sinister Nazi baddie.

The living history men seemed to be an open bunch. I spoke to a chef who had started out as a German Panzergrenadier before joining a British unit. I asked him why there seem to be so many people who like dressing as the Germans. He told me that the popularity of the Germans (and Americans) was purely a matter of tailoring. 'Who wants to be British? All that woolly, khaki crap.'

These men clearly get a sense of belonging from dressing up in the uniforms of years ago, a homeopathic flavour – as H. G. Wells might have put it – of the comradeship that kept their forebears alive. The gruff Devonian, a lovely bloke, was very much into the 'woolly, khaki crap'. He'd wanted to go into the military but a work injury put him out of contention. When he joined his living history unit he walked to their first event in uniform; it took him a week. Spending his free time taking part in uncomfortable field exercises was a way of connecting with the lives of those who have gone before. He told me, 'To have a mate who you've gone through training with and just see him disappear, I can't imagine what that would have been like.'

There seemed to be solidarity in geekiness, a camaraderie between the 'military' and 'civilians' – excitable young lads with bumfluff faces, blokes clutching pints of real ale who looked like they might well have had a lecture from their girlfriends, as I had the night before, on how male obsession with guns was purely a manifestation of phallic identity. (As *if* we've not heard that one before.) The lads at Tankfest do not come across as your confident boys, strutting in front of groups of girls or boisterously play fighting on the streets after school. They seem timeless, in a way, in their unfashionable, ill-fitting clothes, with a nervous energy that becomes utterly unselfconscious in their delight in seeing a favourite vehicle, or when they excitedly ask a living history soldier which mark of Sten gun he's holding. They're the ones for whom all this matters – not because of some toxic obsession with violence and killing, but because it gives them the means to imagine themselves away from the cultural expectations of their day. I know this because I was one of them. I well remember the time when, aged thirteen or fourteen, I looked up from the aeroplane magazine I was reading in WHSmith to see a group of girls my own age pointing at me and laughing. The humiliation was intense. In the 1990s, an obsession with the Second World War gave me, paradoxically, an escape from the boorish masculinity of the lad culture of the time. It didn't matter that I didn't have the latest trainers, wasn't into the music that everyone else liked, was terrible at sport and physically underdeveloped, because I had this history to disappear into. I imagine it's even harder to be an awkward young man now in the age of ubiquitous por-nography, the toned bodies of reality TV, peer pressure of social media, impossible ideals of physical strength and physique. Who needs any of that if you can imagine yourself sitting inside a tank, spitting fire at the world around you? Charging around a military festival, alone or with your only pal who shares those interests, must be wonderful as a teenager today, a vital connection with something honourable beyond the masculinity you are constantly being told is nihilistically broken, irredeemable, toxic.

However, I am not naïve about this. Obsessions and passions are carried this way and that by the hormonal tides of self-discovery and confusion. Young men seeking a purpose in life are easily manipulated through their teenage years and into their twenties. This has happened again and again, from the Hitler Youth to modern online grooming by Islamist terrorist groups, the far right and misogynist incel movements alike. Military equipment, uniforms and the possibility of proving one's manhood in combat are often deadly tools of seduction.

Michael Burn, known throughout his life as Micky, was born on 11 December 1912 to an upper middle-class family. He attended Winchester private school, where he had homosexual experiences and won a debate with the motion that the present age was superior to the Victorian, much to the consternation of one of his teachers who, weeping, held out a painting of the late queen like an icon for him to kiss. He dutifully went to Oxford, where, despite his relatively high social standing, he was blackballed by the now-notorious Bullingdon Club for being the wrong sort. He became an indifferent student but did manage to begin a career as a writer with a book about motor racing and spent the 1930s in a haze of bohemian privilege, floating around London and Europe, having affairs with both women and men, including Guy Burgess, future Soviet spy and traitor.

He first visited Germany in 1933, the year of Hitler's ascent to power. In a letter to his father on 19 July from a youth hostel in Freiburg, he wrote, 'The Germans are probably very nice; all the young men who seem to be all that matter wear shorts only, except for Hitler badges, and walk about magnificently, singing rather despondently but with determination what I suppose are National songs.'

Burn visited the country again in August 1935, using his connections to aristocratic Hitler nut Unity Mitford. In Munich, Burn met Hitler in a restaurant, telling the dictator – in German – that he was very popular with young people in Britain. At their second meeting, Hitler signed Burn's copy of *Mein Kampf*. He was invited to the September  rally in Nuremberg, where he was photographed looking suited and serious on the stand behind the leadership delegation.

Burn was fascinated by the rituals of the Hitler Youth: the ceremonies, torchlit processions, sports, the indoctrination using the feats of dead heroes. He praised camps populated by the new generation of Germans, with their 'apparently joyous youth' hard at work on public schemes that had 'abolished class warfare'. Hitler's policies had, he believed, ushered in a new era of social mobility. He also visited a very different kind of Nazi residential project – the concentration camp at Dachau. Here, Burn's writing is disturbing. He plays down the Nazi use of torture and on viewing the men imprisoned for psychiatric criminality, remarks 'their faces remain with me like a nightmare. I had not thought that such features existed outside medical journals . . . another race of beings . . . who when one spoke to them were not even able to answer normally.' He goes on to compare these men with the highly drilled physicality of the SS guards rehearsing for their appearance at the Nuremberg rally: 'They would not have made good Nazis. As criminals they were adequate.' Letters home were full of enthusiasm. 'I cannot really think coherently after this week,' he wrote excitedly to 'mummy' that September, 'It has been so wonderful to see what Hitler has brought his country back to and taught to look forward to.'

In his memoir *Turned Towards the Sun*, he reflects that he had sometimes felt it might have been sensible to burn the letters he sent back to his family in England. He bravely decided not to, believing that in doing so, 'I would have been destroying some of the guts and heart of truth not only about myself, not only about a period of history, but about an ever-renascent flaw in human nature.' Burn wrote that he had suffered from a 'mix of ignorance, blindness, and semi-criminal benevolence', which had made him a 'dupe' to the Nazi's 'intensely organised falsehood'. The Nuremberg rally, where the self-confessed dupe 'heil-Hitlered my way on to a cliff-top dais', was a day of hypnosis, where Burn's critical faculties were undone by the visual power of the parading Nazi uniformed groups, the mass saluting, Luftwaffe air displays, the thundering boots of the revitalised army 'and the insane euphoria of a nation considered to have "found itself"'. Germany had been made great again, had taken back control. It was at the 1935 rally that the Nazi party passed the Nuremburg Laws that defined German citizens as those 'of German or related blood' alone, stripping Jews of their rights. Marriages and sexual relations between Germans and Jews were banned. In his honesty about 'my long day's journey into night in Nazi Germany', Burn gets to the heart of the twisted appeal of the power of Nazi imagery and aesthetics, the seductive pull of an ideology that projects a cleanliness and strength that offers the slightly dissolute male, as Burn undoubtedly was, a tough purpose. Nazism was a danger-ous parasite that might infect a vulnerable masculinity and turn it toxic. Can we condemn him for being swept away in the steely euphoria of Nuremberg? None of us is as far from being seduced by these totalitarian aesthetics as we might like to think.

Once, on a visit to the Channel Islands, I drove with a friend to the high ground on the west coast of Jersey, where during their Second World War occupation, the Germans used slave labour to build vast fortifications to repel an Allied invasion that never came. A storm was blowing in, cold beams of sunlight stabbing the ground to make yellow gorse and purple heather glow with a lurid intensity. We were listening to the second side of David Bowie's *Low* on the car stereo, that quartet of tracks recorded in Berlin and inspired by the atmosphere of a city that was still haunted by the recent memory of the Second World War. We fell silent as the brutalist concrete of German gun positions, artillery ranging towers and bunkers loomed out of the drizzle and Brian Eno and Bowie's melancholy synthesiser filled the air. It was a troubling moment, like holding that replica Luger pistol, against my instincts loaded with a sinister beauty and sumptuous dread.

The lads taking selfies by the Tiger at Tankfest, the enduring popularity of model kits of German military equipment, even the Imperial forces in *Star Wars*, their weapons and uniforms inspired by the Axis of the Second World War – all are products of the appeal of this taboo aesthetic. In the 1930s, Micky Burn adopted some of that into his own appearance. When he returned from his sojourn in the belly of the beast, Guy Burgess asked for a photograph. Burn gave him one that was 'pioneerish-looking' and open-shirted, standing in front of a pylon. Burgess replied, 'I shall have to say it's one of my Hitlerjugend boyfriends.' Back in England, exposure to journalism superior to his own helped Burn realise the extent of his delusion or, as he piquantly put it, that 'what Hitler's Germany was offering men as soul-saving was shit'. Burn lost his signed copy of *Mein Kampf* when it fell out onto the road through a hole in his car.

There was a book that I encountered during my years of pubescent militarism that grappled with this tricky subject in a voice that seemed specifically intended as a warning to suggestible young male minds. You can keep your Holden Caufields and your Harry Potters. If there was a character I related to most in the canon of young adult literature, it was Conrad Pike. *Conrad's War*, published in 1978, was written by Andrew Davies, also responsible for the chilling BBC adaptation of Charles Dickens's *The Signalman*, the 1995 Colin Firth-starring version of *Pride and Prejudice* and the original, brilliantly mendacious British political drama *House of Cards*. *Conrad's War* might be a work of fiction aimed at teenagers but it articulates better than nearly anything else I've found just how strong an influence the Second World War exerted over British masculinity. If *Thunder and Lightnings* is a gentle tale about friendship and mutual male enthusiasm for flight, *Conrad's War* has an edge to it. The novel is a warning, of sorts, to all men thinking of violence that they should be careful what they wish for.

Conrad is a shouty, put-upon lad, always on at his parents to be allowed to indulge his passions, namely, 'Wars, Army, Killing, Guns.' He begs to stay up to watch war films and asks his hapless dad for help building a tank. His bedroom ceiling is hung with Airfix kits on string. At school, he complains, everyone would rather play football than war.

I read *Conrad's War* and felt that his life was my life: a soup of frustration, pompous hormonal ego and rage at not being understood; getting lost in obsessing over violence and Airfix kits and wishing that it was all real. I often fantasised about sticks of bombs from Avro Lancasters falling across the PE field so I would not have to do rugby.

For Conrad Pike, the fantasy becomes reality, as time slips and he ends up piloting his model Avro Lancaster on the RAF's disastrous Nuremberg raid of 30 March 1944, with his dad flying rear gunner, a grey, plastic, legless Airfix figure for a navigator, propellers gammy from polystyrene cement, the bomb doors jammed in. When they finally manage to drop their load on the German city, Conrad has to face an uncomfortable truth and starts imagining German bombs falling through his grandmother's roof in Leeds. 'Stop thinking, he said to himself, but he couldn't help it. There had to be grandmothers in Nuremburg too [. . .] It was a bad thought, and it wouldn't go away.' The discomforting reverie only ends when the Lancaster is shot down and Conrad is taken prisoner.

The timeslip starts to lead the young military enthusiast down a perverted path. He is more than comfortable in the German uniform in which he escapes from Colditz POW camp. The jackboots fit perfectly. The material tightens on his teenage body. He loses his fear and gains a sensation of power and strength. He stamps his feet on the ground, the German 'links recht links recht' and thoughts of the Fatherland, familiar from any dozen war films, coming to mind. Conrad becomes Kolonel Konrad Von Pikehofen, commanding a Tiger tank on a take-no-prisoners mission to kill partisans. 'He felt strong in his German uniform, strong and strange and fierce. In a way it was something he had always wanted, war and violence [. . .] He was the boss of everything now [. . . ] Together in their great Tiger monster-tank they could roll over the whole world, crush it out of existence beneath its tracks; win the war.'

Conrad has visions of Konrad's youth, in a military academy, a tough gymnasium, singing in uniforms, fencing. He feels himself disappearing into malevolence, seduced by the hulking beauty of the tank to commit a terrible crime not just in the name of the Führer, but violence itself. Much as *Conrad's War* was a favourite book as a teenager, I remember being startled by this plot twist. It had never occurred to me how this fascination with death machines, with the strange alluring power of holding a Luger, might be the gateway to something more sinister.

There were millions of Conrads in Germany in the early spring of 1945, teenage boys who had grown up never knowing anything other than the Nazi ideology that told them they were superior beings, that Jews, gypsies, homosexuals, communists and Slavs from the east were to be despised and seen as subhuman *unter-mensch*. As the German armies collapsed under the Soviet advance, ad-hoc defence units called Volkssturm (People's Storm) were formed by recruiting the leftover scraps of the nation's masculinity, from young boys of the Hitler Youth to old men, and instructing them to fight to the death with antiquated rifles and Panzerfausts, a single-use anti-tank rocket. Micky Burn describes a unit marching around the walls of his fictionalised Colditz Castle in his novel *Yes, Farewell*, the younger members seeming to have a 'terrible herd delight in destruction and self-destruction'.

Those units included in their number Alfred Zech, a twelve-year-old boy who became the unwitting star of the final film ever shot of Adolf Hitler when, just days before he was to commit suicide, he emerged above ground to award the Iron Cross to a group of his young fighters. It is some of the most sinister and unsettling footage of the man who groomed generations to murder and die for his demented ideology. A grim smile on his face, Hitler shuffles along the line of proud yet nervous children and adolescents, handsome and upright in their uniforms. We see Zech, one of the youngest of the lot, from behind, wearing a smart military cap. Hitler pats his cheek, puts a hand on his shoulder, playfully tugs his ear. Hitler asks Zech if he wants to go home or go back to the front. He replies that of course he would go back to fight. Zech was later shot in the lung and became a prisoner of war.

At Tankfest, you could buy a toy Panzerfaust. Made of soft grey material, stitched into an awkward sausage with arrows and German text indicating the direction of fire, it was a snip for your wannabe doomed youth at £14.99. The memory of that strange, floppy grey soft plaything would stick with me in the months after. Much as I was tempted by the kit of a Churchill tank in the museum shop, the kiddy Panzerfaust seemed a merchandising opportunity too far. What age was it even aimed at? Was it intended to sit among the soft-eared rabbits and teddy bears of the very young? *Conrad's War* captured that slipperiness through childhood and adolescence perfectly, as did Robert Westall's 1975 novel *The Machine Gunners*, another teenage favourite about a group of kids in a fictional north-eastern industrial city who find a machine gun in a crashed German bomber and use it to arm their own fort. It was their exploits that I'd had in mind as my cousins and I played at soldiers in the rambling back garden, wishing that we had the real thing.

For British children of the Second World War, the enemy was still remote, seen only in aircraft droning overhead, newspaper photographs, newsreels or propaganda. German boys, immersed from a tender age in Nazi ideology, were thrown at Red Army tanks. Boys of the Soviet republics witnessed the appalling savagery of the Eastern Front first hand. It was Soviet cinema that created the most uncompromising account of the impact of violence on young male minds.

The 1985 film *Come and See* is one of those rare works of art that is so powerful it can leave you physically and psychically disturbed for days. You would not expect to encounter it in the cosy Sunday afternoon war film slot I'd grown up with and I only saw it for the first time a few years ago. I wonder what impact it might have had if I'd encountered it as a teenager. It begins, like *The Machine Gunners*, with teenagers who find a weapon and use it to try to enter the adult world of war. Flyora (played by Aleksei Kravchenko, an untrained actor) digs up a rifle from the sandy soil of a Belarussian battlefield. A weapon is the passport he needs to join the partisans engaged in a fight against Nazi occupation, their actions met with horrendous reprisals.

It took years for director Elem Klimov to persuade Soviet authorities to allow him to make *Come and See*, an interpretation of

1977 book *I Am from the Fiery Village*, an account of the destruction of Khatyn in 1943 by brutal troops of the SS Dirlewanger Brigade, made up of convicted criminals and Soviet collaborators. About 150 people, half of whom were under sixteen, were shot or burned alive. The hallucinatory film-making is as beautiful as it is disturbing. The landscape is one of stunted trees, bogs, dense forest, bleak open steppe, bright lichen and moss that contrasts with the burned skin and flesh of a peasant covered in petrol and set alight by the Germans. The boy crushes a bird's nest, broken shells and yolk glistening on the embryos of chicks. Beavers scream. A stork, the bird symbol of Belarus, wanders into shot. The inhabitants wear clothes that seem from a different century and the frequent presence of a German Focke-Wulf 189 aircraft overhead, futuristic with its twin fuselage booms, is an oppressive intervention of the modern world. The violence, though, is medieval, barbaric and sickening. The naked bodies of villagers murdered in reprisals are piled up at the back of a house. The skull of a German soldier is covered with clay to make a hideous mannequin of Hitler, carried on a pointless raid. This horror is matched by a realism in the combat scenes. When shellfire hits the partisan camp, it's as if the film-maker called in the Red Army for the special effects, so real is the shattering of trees and gouging great clumps of earth from the ground. Live ammunition was used in a scene in which the young Flyora is sheltering from German machine-gun tracer fire, the bullets passing just inches over the actor's head, in order to get a genuine reaction out of him.

Come and See is an account of war with no honour and no glory, no prospect of a redeeming return to civilian life, just grinding and senseless murder, retribution and hate. Much has been made of the opening D-Day scenes of *Saving Private Ryan*, the bullets zipping through water and bodies, legs blowing off. Yet this is still only a technological and special effects advance on the ketchup splats appearing across the faces of Luftwaffe pilots in *The Battle of Britain*. After the initial scenes depicting the violence on Omaha Beach, *Saving Private Ryan* is just another narrative of heroes and anti-heroes, a tale of redemption and glory, the schlocky special effects eventually only heightening the Hollywood sentimentality. It is nothing like *Come and See*, with its mass rape and murder, with the metal objects found by excitable boys the passport to brutalisation and trauma. There was tragedy in *The Dam Busters*, *The Battle of Britain*, *A Bridge Too Far* and so on, but there was never the cauterising horror of that realist depiction of the Eastern Front.

Our war films generally contain doses of humour and acts of heroism that reflect the way that we like to see ourselves as a nation. It's hard not to fall for it. One of my favourite scenes in British war cinema occurs in *A Bridge Too Far* when a German soldier crosses the bridge at Arnhem waving a white flag to offer the men of the Parachute Regiment the chance to surrender. 'Sorry,' replies the crisply voiced British officer (he is brandishing an umbrella), 'we haven't the proper facilities to take you all prisoner.' The German, bemused, retreats. The killing continues. It might be a film about a defeat but in that moment is the ideal vision of Britain retaining wit as its troops struggle on against the inhuman, and humourless, Nazi tyranny. And, of course, the awareness that, in the long run, the right side will win. *Come and See*, by contrast, is nihilistic and grotesque but never gratuitous because its reality is in the horrific statistics of death and murder in the ideological war between Communists and Nazis, and the race war between the Aryan and those who happened to live in the twisted fantasy of their Lebensraum.

Yet *Come and See* isn't a film about the Eastern Front as much as it is an account of the brutalising impact of war on a young boy. I imagine its narrative is one that has been played out hundreds of thousands, perhaps millions of tragic times, in the grooming and recruitment of teenage soldiers throughout history. The title also perhaps reflects the idea that the war film as a genre is a form of cinematic ideal – it offers narrative structure in violent jeopardy and resolution, the possibility of a sumptuous and compelling stage set and, for the industry, the opportunity to experiment with new technologies and effects. At the same time, *Come and See* transcends this in a human face. That process of violent degradation is written upon Flyora as the film goes on: his severely cropped hair turning the colour of the burned ashen village, his lips parsed back, dried and swollen, his face sliced with lines, eyes broken in horror. If war is a ritualised act that for thousands of years has been seen as the means for boys to become true men, *Come and See* captures the process as a debasement, the crossing of the threshold into the inhuman realm of violent conflict, where men with wives and lovers and children at home, who grew up with the tender caresses of their parents, would willingly herd families into a barn and set it on fire. Come and see war, it asks, come and see and lose – your life, your youth, your mind.

# HEAVY METAL

Perturbed by the soft toy Panzerfaust and war tat in the gift shop, I wandered back outside to the Tankfest arena. Water was being sprayed on the ground to keep the dust down before the start of the next event, a parade of Second World War military vehicles. As a knowledgeable man with a microphone gave technical details, tank after tank came grinding into the arena to do a show pony circuit before the sun-baked crowd: a Japanese Ha-Go, British Valentine DD 'swimming' tank, German Panzer III, Russian T-34 and three Shermans, including the one used in the Brad Pitt war film *Fury*. Every tank made a unique cacophony – deep thrums, grunts, farting throbs of engines with a top note of squeaking and squealing tracks. Circuits done, they lined up in the centre of the arena, former foes in line astern, a snake of brooding power and malevolence.

Yet when they manoeuvred around the arena, the tanks looked vulnerable and clumsy; they moved slowly around obstacles, jerking as the left then the right tracks were used to turn. I was hit by a powerful wave of emotion at the extreme contrast between the might of machine and the figures of the crew, with their bodies half out of their turrets or heads protruding from the front of the hulls. Their skin and flesh looked so vulnerable, like meat against the metal. During the First World War, in a moment of macabre humour, the crew of one British Mark IV tank named it Fray Bentos, after the then-popular brand of tinned corned beef, now best known for its meat pies. Sherman tanks of the Second World War were called 'Tommy cookers' by the Germans due to their propensity to burn when hit.

It all reminded me of a film clip I'd seen on YouTube two summers before. I'd spent a hot afternoon exploring the Roman amphitheatre at Nîmes, flitting between shaded arch and shaded arch, the sunstroke queasiness increased by the enthusiasm the historical information panels had for the activities that used to go on there – the murder of Christians, slaughter of animals and the gladiatorial combat that provided mass entertainment to the people of the Roman Empire. How many centuries must pass before barbarism becomes something described with relish by the writers of these informative boards?

A day later, I was waiting for my partner and passing the time by watching a YouTube video of a performance by German industrial rock group Rammstein. Due to the vagaries of Google's algorithms, the sidebar of suggestion threw up a film called 'Battle for Cologne – tank duel'. I clicked play. Sweaty Rammstein disappeared from my phone screen to be replaced with black-and-white footage of a column of American Sherman tanks advancing along a bombed and blasted street towards the twin spires of Cologne cathedral.

Without warning, the shot changes to a close-up of one of the Shermans shortly after it has been hit. One of the crew starts to pull himself out of the turret, twitching with panic, and collapses off the side of his tank, barely able to move. His left leg has been blown away, horrifically shortened, smoke coming off a baggy mess of flesh, bone and uniform fabric below the thigh.

A flash of text informs that he died shortly later and two others of his crew were also killed. The film goes on, soundtracked by gently rolling stock piano music, which the credits tell me is called 'Dreamscape (Endless Fields and A Gift to Be Simple)'. The German Panther tank that destroyed the Sherman is attacked by an American Pershing, shells zipping across the field of vision in streaks of light, impacting in a flurry of sparks. The crew leap out as the Panther starts to burn, the steel body containing the blazing fuel and ammunition so that the flame thunders out of the open escape hatches in an angry torch. It reminded me of the teenage pyromania of our old war games, putting firelighters under cans of Lynx deodorant, waiting for the top to flip and bluey orange fire to roar out. Even in this blurry footage, shot at a distance, you can sense the panic and desperation in how the German crew sprint from the slowly exploding vehicle and race for shelter around the corner of the street. Yet that wasn't enough for the uploader of the video. The piano tinkles on as the clip is repeated in slow motion, stabilised, annotated in misspelled English and finally zoomed in, the ripped agony of the dismembered leg repulsive even in this grainy reproduction.

'Battle for Cologne – tank duel' was edited from film shot by US cameraman Jim Bates on 6 March 1945 from a window overlooking the combat area. It now appears in numerous YouTube documentaries. The version I watched had been seen 3.4 million times since it was uploaded eleven years ago. It has attracted over 5,000 comments, some in tribute to the combatants, others arguing over tactics and a few degenerating, as these things tend to, into accusations of another commenter being a 'fucking Nazi' or calling the American tank crew 'assholes' for continuing to fire into the doomed German tank (it was considered wise to keep firing at an enemy tank until it was seen to be entirely destroyed in case the shell had just burst on the exterior armour leaving the crew able to retaliate). That cloud of often irritable discourse and the sheer everyday ubiquity of the footage detracts from the narrative we see playing out, interspersed with adverts. The trite comments about the waste of life and so on and the geeky delving into the tactics of the engagement are the veneer that we use to justify the macabre entertainment value of such an extreme act of violence, part of the eternal desire for realism in voyeuristically consumed combat that, for the majority of Western men, is lacking in our daily lives.

I worry that this violence, largely shorn of context, has an insidious and desensitising effect. As a child and a teenager, I'd craved footage of the Second World War, hard to find in those days of four terrestrial channels and no YouTube. It was this hunger for seeing tanks and aircraft, battleships and explosions, that was the start of a new understanding of what the war was really all about, when it led me to TV series *The World at War*.

The title sequence still gives me the chills. Carl Davis's doomy clarinet and string eddies are the accompaniment to orange flames – colours wan as they were on all telly from the 1970s that you watched in the 90s – that consume photographs of people and, in the final frame, a young boy. Running to almost twenty-three hours, *The World at War* was commissioned in 1969 and took years of research before the first episode was broadcast on 31 October 1973. The series was one of the most expensive television programmes that ITV had ever produced, costing £900,000. Its strength lay in the breadth of interviewees, taken from all sides in the conflict, including Albert Speer (it is impossible not to feel rage as he simpers his excuses, claiming to have known nothing about what was going on, while also boasting he had the ear of Hitler), the German leader's last secretary, Traudl Junge, Vera Lynn, Sir Anthony Eden, Michael Foot, Bomber Command Chief Arthur Harris and Luftwaffe fighter ace Adolf Galland, among dozens of ordinary soldiers and civilians. The programme is devastatingly simple, brutally and poignantly effective. I'd tuned in for the footage of diving planes, crouching soldiers, torpedoed ships see-sawing up out of the water, fountains of mud and disintegrating buildings, real wartime action. I came for glory but what I saw changed my perspective forever.

Laurence Olivier, who I knew from favourite films *Battle of Britain* and *A Bridge Too Far*, gave the programme gravitas in his narration. 'On a summer day in 1944, the soldiers came . . .' the first episode opens, before telling the story of the village of Oradour-sur-Glane, where the SS committed a massacre of French civilians shortly after D-Day, locking the women and children of the community in the church and setting it on fire while they shot the men in nearby barns. For an adolescent obsessing over Airfix kits in the early 1990s, *The World at War* suddenly afforded the moulded pieces a whole new meaning. Here were those men I'd not wanted to paint into their cockpits. Here were the women and children they were dropping bombs on. Here were the things that were never recreated in handily craftable form – bodies. Burned bodies on the streets of Hamburg after the RAF and American air raids of July 1943 created a firestorm that killed nearly 40,000 civilians. Here were British airmen in flying boots lying broken alongside the wreckage of their bombers. Here were bodies on sleds in frozen and besieged Leningrad, wounded men gaunt, the broken eyes of the shell-shocked, rags from which hands reached like claws, a German soldier pulling out his pistol to fire into the head of a last living human in a mass grave. And then, the horrors reversed, German civilians lined up dead during the Russian winter offensive of 1945. Among the heady footage of Allied victories were German troops on fire falling from a truck in Paris and a soldier crawling through a French square, bullets kicking up dust around him until enough had found their mark to kill. Two civilians rushed over, grinning, to take his rifle.

I'd seen the juddering ketchup deaths of war films but this was the real thing. This was what guns, aircraft, bombs really did. *The World at War* is powerful even today because it bridges the gap between the seductive power of machinery and the human stories of conflict in a way that action films and decontextualised YouTube footage never can. It is a way of seeing the men behind the metal, that material that defines so much of the history of the Second World War.

Over the centuries, warfare has advanced through the development of metal technology, from spearheads to swords and modern weaponry. Although tanks had been introduced during the First World War, it was in the Second that they assumed a dominant role, forming the core of Hitler's Blitzkrieg tactics and later, the overwhelming might of the Soviet counter-attacks. The ability to carry infantry soldiers in vehicles allowed armies to travel far greater distances more quickly than ever before. Aircraft largely made of aluminium rather than the wood and stretched and doped fabric of the First World War biplanes were able to fly faster, higher and could carry more bombs. Steel hulls made submarine warfare a potent force that, in the Battle of the Atlantic, was sinking enough shipping to risk losing Britain the war. Sonar and radar sent invisible waves through air and water, hunting these objects so that they might be destroyed. Metal allowed the V-2 rocket to travel into near-space and return, at unstoppable speeds, to impact southern England with a thousand kilograms of high explosive. The war would end with metal in the deadliest weaponised form ever deployed by humans: 64kg of enriched uranium in the Little Boy atomic bomb that destroyed Hiroshima on 6 August 1945 and 6.19kg of plutonium dropped on Nagasaki three days later. All of these, and the steel in reinforced concrete, were the materials set in violent opposition to Churchill's blood, toil, tears and sweat.

We tend to associate archaeology with historical periods beyond recent memory: the ancient standing stones onto which we place modern meanings; evidence of Roman occupation, Norman conquest, Tudor religious strife. Not all things that are buried will remain underground. In times of heavy weather, objects churn their way through the soil and appear once again in the open air, ready to be rediscovered. Out on a forest walk one Sunday afternoon in January, a small metal object winked at me from the mess of twigs and rotting leaves. It's uncanny how things catch the eye, innocuous objects that will somehow make their presence known in the peripheral vision. I bent down to have a closer look, excitement rising as I guessed that this was probably the remains of one of the anti-aircraft artillery shells that were fired against German bombers attacking London during the Second World War. I'd been hoping to find one of these for years! I picked it up. It was encrusted with dirt and about the size of a satsuma, but surprisingly heavy in my hand, dense and dead. Look, I shouted to my partner and her pal, walking a little further ahead, look what I've found! They were less than impressed that I'd picked up a bit of a lethal weapon. What if it explodes?! It won't explode, I said, and threw it at a tree to prove the point. WHAT ARE YOU DOING?! WHAT IF IT GOES OFF? It won't go off, I insisted, my confidence based on little more than an assumption that the main shell stuffed with high explosive had been blasted into smithereens some grim night eight decades ago. I was relieved when it didn't go off. I retrieved my treasure and scraped at the mud with my keys, years of dirt crumbling away to reveal brass, a screw thread on the top and a few letters etched into the metal. Despite the protestations that I was bringing live ammunition of unknown provenance into our home, I slipped it into my rucksack and we carried on through the trees.

As a kid, I was fascinated by the stumps of metal in front of houses, around parks and other civic buildings, the remains of railings removed in the early years of the war to be recycled into aircraft, ships and tanks. These scars connected the world around me with the conflict, especially in my town which had seen little in the way of bombing (though I would always linger on the staircase at a friend's house, looking at a slightly dented stained-glass window, the metal framework supposedly pushed in by a wartime blast). The absent gates and railings were just as much a war memorial as the stone crucifix on a plinth in the town centre.

Recycling was one of the ways British people were told they could do their bit, their sacrifice putting up a metal barrier of aircraft, guns and so on around the British Isles. On 10 July 1940, the first day of the Battle of Britain, Lord Beaverbrook made an appeal 'to the women of Britain' for them to hand over their spare aluminium kitchen equipment, saying, 'We will turn your pots and pans into Spitfires and Hurricanes, Blenheims and Wellingtons,' and boys marched through the land fetching old saucepans, teapots, cups and other metal items (broken tools, stoves, knackered bikes) on trolleys and wheelbarrows. The Ministry of Information created posters for the Ministry of Supply, one featuring an illustration of a tin-hatted, metal-bodied soldier with a broken fork for his right leg, spanner hand and guttering arm with the slogan 'Private Scrap Builds a Bomber'. Broken-down vehicles and captured relics from previous wars all joined the railings in the melting pot. According to Harold Macmillan speaking in Parliament on 1 August 1940, this included 802 old cannons, Crimean War-era weapons and German field guns sited as part of First World War memorials in many towns and villages. Whether or not the scrap metal campaigns contributed to the war effort beyond a boost to morale in everyone 'doing their bit' is debatable. The modern suspicion that recycling is pointless is not a new one and rumours abounded of barges sailing from London's docks to dump railings in the Thames Estuary in such quantities that the amount of metal affected ships compasses. Yet wartime recycling drives make metal seem an elusive, slippery substance in an endless cycle of reconstruction – the biblical swords into ploughshares, and back into swords again.

I first saw Paul Nash's painting *Totes Meer* – German for 'dead sea' – in one of the many war books I took out of the local library. Though, like Victor and Andrew in *Thunder and Lightnings*, I craved the realism of line drawings of aircraft, ships and tanks I found elsewhere in those pages, *Totes Meer* had an eerie quality. In the lower two thirds of the painting is a mess of green and blue camouflage and black Luftwaffe crosses, the struts, spars and wheels of aircraft all piled in an undulating confusion. The geometric purity and aesthetic beauty of aviation are ruptured and distended, the wreckage taking on an organic presence. Although there isn't a single corpse in the picture, the painting reeks of violent death, absence and loss, much as Nash's paintings of the battlefields of the Western Front in the First World War rarely depicted men, but instead landscapes of defiled nature, shattered trees and mud.

*Totes Meer* was based on photographs that Nash took at the No. 1 Metal Produce Recovery Depot, known colloquially as the Cowley dump, situated just outside Oxford. In use throughout the war, it was where crashed and shot down aircraft were taken to be carved up, melted down and their aluminium recycled, to become new weapons. Nash's research photographs from Cowley are now in the Tate archive and are no less affecting than *Totes Meer* itself, thanks to the directness with which elements of the black-and-white images are echoed in paint. An aircraft wheel, for instance, is immediately recognisable in both the artwork and source material, as is the letter B and black Luftwaffe cross from a torn-off wing. Most of all, there's a feeling of movement in the metal that Nash transferred into his painting. He said that the mass of wrecked aircraft 'looked to me, suddenly, like a great inundating sea'. Under the glow of Nash's moon, this latent, impotent metal has an almost occult power.

In fact, the Cowley dump wasn't just for cutting up German aircraft; over the course of the war, far more wrecked RAF and American aircraft were recycled there. Nash ignored the remains of British aircraft in his composition, focusing purely on the enemy with the propaganda potential of the image in mind. Originally, it was called the *Iron Sea*. The painting was only given its German name later, with the idea that perhaps it might be reproduced and dropped by the RAF over Germany to undermine morale – Nash even added a cut-out of Hitler's head to one postcard-sized image.

On aerial photos of the Cowley dump taken in April 1944, the site stretches across open fields alongside a railway line, the stacks of wrecked aircraft in neat squares with narrow passageways between them, connected by wider roads, like an American city seen from above. If you search Google Maps now, the same site is a vast complex of automobile factories, including Serck, who, during the war, made over 65,000 aircraft radiators and 110,000 aircraft oil coolers for the Allied forces. Where there were once broken aircraft, you can now see row after row of brand-new cars – for example, the Mini, produced by German company BMW, who during the war used slave labour to build engines for the Luftwaffe.

In 1945, a Pathé film crew visited the dump to shoot a news-reel called 'A Gift from the Skies'. 'Hundreds of wrecked planes, once the pride of Goering's Luftwaffe, are playing their part in the reconstruction of the country to which they brought so much havoc,' the narration goes, over footage of swastika insignia being cut by blowtorches. The metal, we're informed, is being used in the construction of new homes. A dot appears in the sky, grows larger, becomes an aircraft that banks overhead. 'Over the remains of an enemy it helped to destroy, a Spitfire swoops triumphantly. Little could the Luftwaffe pilots had dreamed that one day their machines would be used for the tasks of peace by the people they hoped to bring low.' Orchestral music plays in the background as molten metal is poured into ingots, to be stacked in giant piles – 'There should be enough aluminium alloy here to make life bright for plenty of home-seekers,' the voiceover continues, before the clip ends with footage of new British suburbia. Shattered aircraft in which male bodies were crushed are now the homes in which surviving veterans might build a new life.

I didn't know about all this as a child fascinated with the idea that the vanished railings of my local area might have become war machines, but I think now about the afterlife of the aluminium and steel of the war years. It feels like alchemy to me – the same thought I have when rain falls to be flicked by windscreen wipers and I wonder from which ocean it evaporated, along which rivers its molecules travelled, whom it might have sustained and who pissed it out. I imagine atoms of a German Heinkel or Junkers from the Cowley dump melted down to become an Avro Lancaster only for that aircraft to be shot down over Germany, collected as scrap metal there, the process beginning again. I've always had an affection for the large aluminium teapots you find in church and village halls, light in weight, tarnished, stained a dark brown inside, witnesses to so many every day conversations. How many of these most ordinary of objects were made not long after 1945 out of melted down war machines? Might some of these same atoms even be present today when I open a tin of soup or a can of beer, metal ghosts living on in everyday items?

\*

Back at home, despite my girlfriend's protestations, I carried on scraping away at the heavy lump of metal, scrubbing it under the kitchen tap with the vegetable brush. The tough, encrusted dirt gradually wore away, exposing more of the dull brass beneath it. I spent hours using Peek polish and an old pair of pants to try to bring it to life. A join became visible, separating the remnants of the cone into two. The letters and numbers emerged, clear enough to be legible – No199IVRL4/37 and, on the other side, RL7/37. The brass started to shine.

The hobbyists of the internet confirmed my suspicions that this was part of an anti-aircraft shell, dating back to the Second World War – military admin and record-keeping made the code easy to decipher. No199IV stood for a 199 Mk IV fuse, used on British 3.7-inch anti-aircraft guns in the early years of the war. RL4/37 indicated that the fuse was made at the Royal Arsenal in Greenwich in April 1937, RL7/37 that the explosive charge was added in July of the same year. As European tensions increased, the little brass object, topped with an aerodynamic nose probably made of Bakelite, would have remained in storage full of its terrible potential until war was declared. Then, it was transported to an anti-aircraft gun site and, one day or night, blasted into the sky towards the incoming enemy.

There must be hundreds of thousands of these functional yet sculptural devices scattered around the British countryside. They're frequently turned up by metal detectorists – on one forum I read, someone posted they'd found so many of the things over the years that they generally just chuck them in the bin, to which a user called RRPG replied, 'Binned . . . Binned? I've come over all faint . . . Please don't bin any more! I'll gladly pay postage for them! Hate to see WW2 history lost forever.' A pristine version of the 199 fuse complete with its cone, unfired but deactivated, was recently offered for sale on the gunstar.co.uk weapons sale website for a princely £145.

While the word 'fetish' now conjures sexual arousal related to feet, voyeurism, latex and so on, there's certainly something fetishistic about the allure objects from the Second World War have over so many men, an adult development of the child's fascination with toy guns. In 1837, the Oxford English Dictionary defined a 'fetish' object as 'something irrationally reverenced'. During the war itself, this had a strange and tragic manifestation. In a typewritten memoir held at the Imperial War Museum, Flight Lieutenant T.W. Fox wrote about how the women who ran the church canteen in the village of Full Sutton would give bomber aircrew jewellery, watches and other trinkets to take on operations over Germany, to be returned at a later date. As Fox noted, many were never reunited with their owners. It was that need to feel connected to objects that had been with the men who fought that we now see in a potent cultural reverence for the machines of the Second World War, from the troubling allure of the brute force of Nazi tanks to the way in which aircraft like the Spitfire and Avro Lancaster have become icons of British national struggle.

I had been desperate to fly in the Battle of Britain Memorial Flight's Avro Lancaster as a means of connecting with the unnerving thrill of its years of combat, yet I now know that the aircraft didn't leave the factory until 31 May 1945, after the European war had ended. It never saw combat. Similarly, if in my dreams I thought of Lancaster S-Sugar at Hendon's RAF Museum flying operation after operation across Occupied Europe, I now know that Lancasters were composite aircraft that, when damaged, could be disassembled and the major constituent parts replaced. The S-Sugar in the museum today is technically not the same aircraft that flew its first mission on 8 July 1942, much like the Ship of Theseus, or more prosaically, the famous *Only Fools And Horses* sketch about Trigger's 'old' broom that has had both head and handle replaced many times. Even metal objects can become ghosts, or reanimations, of themselves.

In London's Imperial War Museum, not all the curated objects are perfect specimens to be glorified and admired. Visitors can look up at the beauty of a Spitfire suspended from the museum's roof, but the aesthetic admiration is tempered and made more acute by the imperfect metal and broken objects frozen in a moment of violence elsewhere in the building – a crashed Japanese aircraft, a mangled British midget submarine, the remains of a car blown up in Iraq. Like Paul Nash's *Totes Meer* or my fuse, these broken objects help to tell a story away from the glorification of machines towards which I and so many others tend to slip. Instead of the romance of the fighter aircraft, the thrilling menace of the bomber or the brute might of the tank, they force us to consider the absent human body. I think of a passage in Nicholas Monsarrat's novel *The Cruel Sea* in which Lieutenant Lockhart muses on how, 'The emphasis was now on the tireless machine of war; men were parts of this machine, and so they must remain, till they fulfilled their function or wore out [. . .] the cancellation of humanity was an essential element in the total price.'

The 199 fuse now sits on my desk, like a metal mushroom or a miniature model of some weird extraterrestrial settlement. I can hold it in my hand, feeling the smooth chill of the brass and the weight on my fingers and in the muscles of my forearm. I realise, sometimes, that I'm almost caressing it. For a moment, it occurs to me that there might be something more sexual about this fetish object for me too, but I dismiss this thought with a chuckle. It doesn't take long for the fuse to become warm in my hand, taking on my body temperature as I imbue it with meaning. It's the metal that gets me, the lifecycle of this inanimate *thing*.

The small brass object of the fuse has power as a symbol of the conflict but also as a key, opening a way in to the unimaginable vastness of the war. I can never know its complete biography, the date and time it was fired, at what height it detonated, whether the fragments of shell casing or even the fuse itself ripped through the fuselage of a Luftwaffe aircraft, or even aircrew – unlikely, given that in September 1940 alone, a quarter of a million rounds were fired into the skies above London, a tiny fraction hitting their targets. Nevertheless, it still led me off on hours of research. I discovered there were anti-aircraft batteries on the edge of Epping Forest. I thought of them firing into the sky, trying to kill young German men in order to protect, in a way, my granny and uncle in their Loughton terraced home a mile or so away. It was a terrible conversation in metal that made me think of Dan Billany's account of an air raid on Falmouth in his semi-autobiographical novel *The Trap*. 'You could see no injury and hear no cries [. . .] The guns were angry, the bombs were angry. They were arrogant, they shouted each other down. It was a mere side issue in their debate, that men and women and children were being briefly shouldered out of life.'

I spent hours researching the history of the north-east London and Essex anti-aircraft emplacements, reading government reports and official histories and looking at propaganda photographs of gun crews holding shells at jaunty (and admittedly rather phallic) angles. I discovered that although the targets were often tracked and the guns aimed by the women of the Auxiliary Territorial Service, only men were allowed to actually fire them. There had been two anti-aircraft batteries that could have fired my fuse into the sky. One afternoon, I walked between them, from the golf course on the edge of Chingford where one had been located to the other side of Epping Forest, where former gun emplacements are now part of a complex belonging to the police.

At the end of the war, the site had been used as a camp for German prisoners. Nestling just beyond its gates is the curious sculpted figure of a man made of grey concrete, unweathered by the years. The head is good-looking, cheekbones above slightly pursed lips, big eyes and hair in a side-parting. He's naked, with broad shoulders and pectoral muscles carved so they almost look like a line drawing of the bowing wings of a bird in flight. A towel snakes around the statue's body, as if to protect his modesty. A plaque on the base of the statue informs that 'THIS FIGURE WAS CUT OUT OF SOLID CONCRETE BY RUDI WEBER 540177 WHILST A PRISONER OF WAR AT THIS CAMP OCTOBER 1946'. The sculpture is Grade II listed, praised for its 'social realism' and how 'it provides an insight into the more domestic and humanistic presence adding a sense of warmth and creativity in the aftermath of conflict'. I can discover nothing about Rudi Weber beyond what is contained on that heritage listing; nothing about his war service and how he ended up imprisoned on this tree-covered ridge that stands guard over the capital of his nation's former enemy. He has left no record online and the International Committee Red Cross service that can provide information on German prisoners is currently closed to all but immediate relatives.

Who was in Weber's mind's eye as he chipped away and the figure of a man began to emerge from the hard, unyielding material? It could have been a fallen comrade, a dear friend – or perhaps to acquire the concrete, tools and permission to begin work, he suggested he model the figure on one of his guards. I'll never know. I hope that Weber's concrete ghost endures, a strange object that, like the twisted steel in the Imperial War Museum, or the fragments of wrecked aircraft dragged up by North Sea fishermen that sit amidst the grass of the Norfolk and Suffolk Aviation Museum, or even my 199 shell, are by their broken menace a means of breaching the iconography of war machines and touching the bodies and minds that fought within them, in all their glorious, fleshy sensuality.

# THE GENERATION GAME

I went to visit Colin Spencer in his bungalow at the top of a small hill in Seaford on the south coast. Spencer sat in a chair in a conservatory, and the smell of cooking filled the house as a bottle of white from the Wine Society had its cork popped. Spencer's old friend Johnny Worthy, an actor and activist, was round for lunch. They called one another 'bruv' and 'my dear' and 'darling'. There were spatters of paint on the floor, and various bits and pieces of artistic equipment around the place, though Spencer, now eighty-eight and a dominating presence in the sea-bright spring sunshine, hasn't dipped his brush for a while. Yet his paintings filled the otherwise ordinary bungalow with bright colour and eroticism – including a nude of a good-looking man with a large cock, who looked the spitting image of a younger fellow who had popped in to give a cheery hello. All around was the legacy of decades of creative work, encompassing art, novels, memoir, theatre, cookery books, a gay Karma Sutra, and a history of homosexuality.

Spencer's early life in the 1930s was overshadowed by the injuries, both physical and psychological, that his father had suffered during the First World War. Thanks to a wounded right arm, he was unable to carve the Sunday joint – a frailty symbolic of the broken masculinity of this man's man, a fisherman, huntsman and golfer, who showed his son how to skin rabbits, got him drunk at the age of eleven and regaled him with lurid stories of his sex life. In his memoir, *Backing into Light: My Father's Son*, Spencer writes that he believes his father's wartime experiences were at the root of his bleakly humorous sex obsession: 'Men like my father feel led by their penis which is a thought often expressed by them in defence of their behaviour. I think that this attitude was emphasised by the trenches, when soldiers communed in the depths of their despair. The acts of coition must have seemed the only reason for continuing to live, in the face of continuing death, and giving new life must have appeared more and more significant.'

If the First World War triggered his father's sex obsession and led to affairs that created a toxic environment for the young Spencer in the mid to late 1930s, he believes that the psychological trauma of the conflict was something shared across society. 'We were all wounded by it,' he told me. 'When you think of those trenches, no war since then has been quite so ghastly. It wasn't talked about because you didn't talk about things like that. You were meant to just grin and bear it and get on with it all. My father was an ebullient kind of man and used to crack jokes about it, which was his way of surviving. I don't know that succeeding generations have given enough credit to the fact that those who survived did so with a lot of mental guts to get them through it and carried the trauma through their lives with them after that.'

Those of us who absorbed the war culture of the late twentieth century had a very different experience of the legacy of conflict to the young boys who grew up after the First World War. It was part of the very identities of some wartime babies who were named after battles: Tom Ypres Roach and Robert Salonica Woodman, for instance, took part in the daring 1942 Commando raid on the dock at St Nazaire. Others would carry more than this macabre ink on their birth certificates.

One of the most famous recruitment posters of the First World War was published in 1915. It depicted a man sitting comfortably in his chair with his children gathered around. The son is playing with toy soldiers on the carpet, while his daughter, sitting on his knee, asks, 'Daddy, what did you do in the Great War?' The man stares out of the poster, a pensive and guilty expression on his face. I've always been wary of that shaming implication that to not fight for your country was also a dereliction of your duty as a father, but the image has a secondary, troubling aspect – the little boy playing with his toy soldiers, aged maybe eight or nine, would have been just about the right age to fight in the war that followed the one his father appears to have swerved. He too would have to undergo the transmogrification from a civilian to one prepared not just to kill, but to witness death in all its infinite and macabre possibilities, to be willing to bring into his psyche the traumas that that might provoke, and then perhaps to pass them on to his children.

Increasingly, psychologists are exploring the idea of transgenerational trauma. First discovered in studies of the families of Holocaust survivors, research examined how complex post-traumatic stress disorder (PTSD) might be replicated in the descendants of refugees, military veterans and other victims of terrible events. Sometimes this can manifest in severe emotional and psychological problems. In others, it had milder though no less insidious consequences, as boys were brought up by the war as much as by their fathers who had fought in it. First World War poet Wilfred Owen touched on the sinister truth to inherited glory in *Dulce et Decorum Est* and *Wild With All Regrets*. Colin Spencer was too young to fight in the Second World War but the First cast a lifelong shadow over his sense of self. When, as the Cold War fell across Europe, the time came for him to do his National Service, he would find himself clearing up some of the unexpected collateral damage of the conflict that had dominated his teenage years. It can often feel that the dates on our war memorials are too precise, that the twentieth century's conflicts extended beyond the confines of the history books. Even in the first decades of our own century, it has been possible to speak to men whose lives are still shaped by the 1914–1918 war.

Henry Danton peered out from my laptop screen. At 101, his aquiline features and gorgeously high cheekbones seemed to have been made only more handsome by the effects of time and ageing. His voice quavered a little over the FaceTime connection in an accent that sat somewhere in the middle of the Atlantic, thanks to his years living in Mississippi, where he continued to teach ballet after his one hundredth birthday in 2019. I'd discovered Danton via an article I'd read earlier that year about how wartime metal rationing meant he'd only just received his medal for participating in ballet's Genée competition in 1942.

Born Henry Down on 30 March 1919, he never knew his father, who had served in the Royal Artillery but was killed right at the end of the First World War. The tragedy of his father's death was to push the young boy into an early life playing at soldiers. As a King's Cadet, his entire education from prep school onwards was funded by the military. Danton's scholarship was served at Wellington College, a grand private school opened in 1859 as an educational monument to the Duke of Wellington, British prime minister and triumphant general of the campaign against Napoleon that culminated in the Battle of Waterloo in 1815. Its focus was on the education of boys who, like Danton, were the sons of army officers who'd died in the line of duty.

From the off, the young Danton struggled to fit in. He found even his preparatory school, Crowthorne Towers, to be ridiculous in its imposition of routine and discipline, which was strict and harsh and snidely designed with an element of arbitrary violence. If pupils were caught doing something wrong, they were sent to stand in front of a grandfather clock in the hall outside the headmaster's study for half an hour. If during that time the headmaster saw an unfortunate miscreant there, he'd be taken into the office, bent over and given six whacks with the cane. The clock's regular tick-tock, tick-tock was loaded with menace. Life became even tougher when, not long after Danton arrived at Wellington College, his elder brother died. During a gymnastics class, the master called out Danton's birth name, Down. The teenager responded only for the teacher to cruelly reply, 'Oh, I thought you were dead.' Danton didn't flinch as he continued to tell me the devastating story. 'This was a thirteen-year-old kid, everything crushed me.'

There was nowhere for the young Danton, now without his father and brother, to turn, though he had had a tantalising glimpse of what would eventually become his liberation. 'When I was a child, we had an old wind-up gramophone and I would dance around without knowing what I was doing. I just wanted to move to music. In the preparatory school, we had one teacher, he was Jewish and we called him Mo, and he understood about boys.' Mo had a gramophone that he would bring to a common room to play music for his pupils. 'He was a kind man. That was the only music we ever had. In the college, we had none.' Crowthorne Towers and Wellington College were not designed to help boys express themselves, but to make them into little British soldiers who, like their fathers before them, might one day give up their bodies in the service of their country. Many did – 707 former pupils of Wellington College were killed in the First World War; 526 lost their lives in the Second. Henry Danton would not be one them.

Henry Danton was too young to have remembered his dead

dad but, as was the case with Colin Spencer and for many others, the First World War was imprinted on their infant consciousness, often in connection to a sense of who their fathers were as men. The writer Julian Maclaren-Ross described his earliest memory as being dragged from his cot and taken outside of his house in Ramsgate 'just in time to see a German Zeppelin cast its shadow on the rooftop from the vast moonlit menace of the sky'. His family later told him that he 'crowed with glee' as he reached out his arms to this huge silver shape that seemed like a giant toy. Maclaren-Ross recalled that his father, a pacifist who had been wounded in the Boer War, forbade him from drawing the Kaiser on his boiled eggshell and smashing it like the other boys did.

Dudley Cave, born in Golders Green on 19 February 1921, was the only child of a local government official in Hampstead and a mother who had fallen in love with a Canadian soldier during the First World War, only for the relationship to end when he returned home. The romantic turmoil of war and the lack of freedom ordinary men and women had over whom they might love and learn to live with were not new problems in the 1939–45 conflict. His parents separated and Cave ended up living with his father, a man who he recalled was haunted by the guilt that his brother, married with a child, had been killed on the Somme while he'd survived. Cave recalled many years later that his parents had never liked the idea of his playing war but eventually gave in to his constant nagging and allowed him to have a toy fort and soldiers in armour.

Micky Burn wrote in his memoirs that he had no recollection of his life while his father Clive was at war, 'till suddenly, whoosh! up goes the curtain, in I go and on he comes, Soldier from the War Returning, limping, in khaki, wearing a moustache I never saw on him again.' Burn's father had volunteered for the Sussex Yeomanry, served at Gallipoli and was wounded at the

Second Battle of the Marne right at the end of the war, in 1918. Burn senior was a lawyer who rose to the heights of Secretary to the Duchy of Lancaster, the vast holdings of the Prince of Wales. He was a reserved, distant man who feared intimate proximity to others and even felt uncomfortable holding hands with his grandchildren.

Burn reflected in his memoir, *Turned Toward the Sun*, that he inherited a male chauvinism from his father. Not long before Clive Burn died, he asked his son to read out the names inscribed in the family Bible, but bluntly stopped him when he reached his daughters, saying, 'You can leave them out. The women don't count'. He was typical of middle-class men of the era, existing largely in the homosocial worlds of schooling, university, work and the military unit. Micky Burn reflected that the cause of his father's chauvinism might go back to the First World War, 'to legions of fathers in all the warring countries who, coming home to a son last seen as an infant and brought up by women for the duration, resolved as a priority to take them out of the women's hands and "make a man of them"'.

This anxiety over the masculinity of the children of the First World War who had suffered absent fathers and were too young to prove themselves in combat can feel like a driving neurosis of the interwar years. In his essay 'My Country Right or Left', published in 1940, George Orwell (born in 1903) wrote of how he 'grew up in an atmosphere tinged with militarism', with war news read over the breakfast table. The physicality of the soldiers left an impression on the young boy: 'I remember chiefly the square shoulders, bulging calves and jingling spurs of the artillerymen, whose uniform I much preferred to that of the infantry.' From wide-eyed admiration, the view shifted to shame. 'As the war fell back into the past, my particular generation, those who had been "just too young", became conscious of the vastness of the experience they had missed,' Orwell wrote. 'You felt yourself a little less than a man, because you had missed it.'

As Elizabeth Bowen wrote in her 1949 war novel *The Heat of the Day*, the post-First World War generation 'was to come to be made to feel it had muffed the catch'. This view was reflected in the wider culture and was picked up on by Robert Graves and Alan Hodge in *The Long Weekend*. Published in 1940, the book is a cultural survey of the years following the signing of the Armistice and the outbreak of hostilities in 1939, a period they refer to as 'the Peace', as if it was some sacred time of Arcadia. The generation too young to fight in the First World War 'felt misunderstood' as it 'was made to feel inferior simply because it had not fought for King and Country'.

The First World War had traumatised their fathers but left them feeling inadequate. It is a grim irony that, in 1939, the interwar generation were to get their baptism of fire after all. For post-1945 British children and youth, and especially those of us who saw the end of the Cold War in our adolescence, it often felt as if we had escaped being alive in an age where we might be conscripted into the military to fight. This marked a fundamental reset in the process of growing up, of acquiring manhood in the context of our wider society.

Nowadays, in conversations about what our grandparents did in the war, I tend to find there has been a shift from the temporal and geographical to their internal narratives and consequences of their service. Unlike Colin Spencer in the 1930s, or the Baby Boomer generation who were met with the silence of their fathers, we increasingly speak more deeply about the emotional front in war. If there is a positive reaction to the more jingoistic war saturation of our culture in recent years, it might be that some have started to think more about how those events of not-so-long ago have been felt in their own lives. I've had fascinating chats with, for instance, a man whose grandad was a Lancaster bomber pilot about how his post-war struggles with mental health and PTSD impacted the generations on. I've had conversations about how patterns in my own immediate family seem to reflect those of others who came back from the war forever changed. There is a growing acceptance that although the Second World War ended eighty years ago, the psychological echoes are with us today in intimate, personal ways as much as in our politics and culture.

This was never graphically shown in the war films I watched growing up, but the never-ending legacy of twentieth-century warfare was the subject of a film by Derek Jarman, the artist, writer and director whose work had changed my life. In my teenage years, when most of my peers were looking to America for a cultural and aesthetic lead, I found in Jarman's work a portrait of Britishness that was a safety net for someone trying to untangle ideas of patriotism and belonging. Jarman's films are not war films as we usually see them, but they're very much post-war films – comments on a country that was struggling to find a new identity in an era of supposed decline.

Born in New Zealand, Jarman's father, Lancelot Elworthy Jarman, served in a Bomber Command Pathfinder squadron during the Second World War, one of the most dangerous jobs in the branch of the services from which you were least likely to come home. There is a photograph of him in front of his Wellington bomber in the winter of 1940, right foot forward, hands in greatcoat pockets, moustache and deep-set eyes dark on his face, every inch the tough flier. Always demanding to be sent on the most dangerous operations, he had a reputation for never taking evasive action to avoid flak, was awarded the Distinguished Flying Cross and eventually rose to the rank of Air Commodore. The arrival of his son in 1942 was announced by the sending out of a drawing of the baby in a Spitfire and congratulations came by return from an air chief marshal. Derek Jarman grew up in a household suffering the consequences of his father's wartime experience. As he said in interview compendium *The Last of England*, 'returning from another raid [. . .] to a screaming baby, tempers frayed, the wartime aggression flared; and this carried on through the peace to the third generation, as the family became an extension of the war.' He had lost friends yet survived, something that Derek believed he resented. This trauma was manifested in crazed car journeys, a propensity to fits of rage and, eventually, kleptomania, the family frequently having to reclaim their possessions from odd places in which he'd hidden them.

The 'extreme patriotism' with which his father fought in the war was at the core of what destroyed the post-war suburban family's life. Derek Jarman called this 'a poisoned well and saw others celebrating the war, using it to bolster their dominant positions [. . .] All I saw was deceit and bankruptcy.' Yet Jarman described himself as a patriot. I have always been fascinated by and recognise the complexity of this identity: a love of country that tries to neutralise the poison of nationalism, rather than indulging in it. Jarman believed his search for origins in what we might see as an occult patriotism conveyed in his films stemmed from his homosexuality. Whether masculinity or nationhood, outsiders often refuse absolutism and can have the most acute and nuanced analysis of the dominant, mainstream culture. As Jarman himself put it: 'I don't believe in the gold at the end of the rainbow, but I do believe in the rainbow.'

The war and a complex relationship with Britain was often present in Derek Jarman's work. His father was himself a keen photographer and amateur filmmaker who shot footage of family and RAF life during the war that his son would eventually use in the film *The Last of England*. One of the hybrid painting/sculptures

Derek made at Prospect Cottage on the shingle of Dungeness, a place covered in the relics of military structures, is a 1:72 scale model Spitfire, entombed in black tar. The piece, finished in 1989, is called 'Battle of Britain'. He was unable to entirely reject his father's wartime service, to eschew a relationship with militarism. 'Is it fundamental? Is it our nature? Is it my narrative?' he says in *The Last of England*. 'Old RAF flying jackets, loaded pistols, medals and wartime souvenirs. They became my inheritance. I have never been anti-military in the way that some are, how could I be? My father fought a hard war. He fought Hitler, prosecuting the war with a violence that proved uncontainable. I don't know how to solve that, but without men like my father the war would not have been won!' To defeat a terrible enemy, you have to be tough and brutal yourself. Yet, as the elder Jarman's PTSD asks, at what cost?

Jarman's 1989 film *War Requiem* is his most explicit artistic comment on how these traumas are revisited on subsequent generations. The film takes its name from Benjamin Britten's opera *War Requiem*, which was first performed in 1962 at the consecration of Coventry Cathedral, rebuilt after the original church was destroyed by the Luftwaffe on the night of 14 November 1940. Wilfred Owen's poetry was brought into modern composition by Britten and into avant-garde filmmaking by Jarman, whose abstract set design and use of archive footage emphasises that this is a film not limited by the direct experiences of Wilfred Owen in the trenches, but about the enduring energy of war. Its use of violence moved me, just as *Come and See* and *The World at War* had done. In the 'Libera Me' section of Britten's opera, Jarman collages conflict footage from across the twentieth century: scenes of the triumphant German Blitzkrieg, flamethrowers in the Pacific fight against Japan during the Second World War, men carrying gruesomely wounded fighters in Vietnam, a man with his skull shot away in a post-colonial war, a blackened corpse crawling with flies. Bodies are dragged, dug up, buried; the order and ritual of death is replaced by violence and chaos. The horror is cut with the spectacular machines that I had spent my childhood seeking out – jet fighters, battleships and bombers, tanks and howitzers. It's a sobering thought that all this source material came from the mere seventy years of history in which war could be captured by the film camera.

In addition to the collaging of war's horrors, there's a scene in *War Requiem* in which two boys and a girl, all under the age of ten, conduct a cremation. One of the boys is in an outsized scarlet British military jacket, the other in khaki pith helmet, the girl dressed as a nurse. They scatter wildflowers on a small fire, carefully wrap a teddy bear in a red cloth, put it in a coffin and place it on the flames. Is this a memory of the soldier of Wilfred Owen's poem that Britten used as the material for *War Requiem*, the uniforms suggesting the writer's own childhood marred by grief in Britain's late nineteenth- and early twentieth-century colonial wars? Or could they be the children of the soldiers of the First World War? I like the temporal ambiguity in the scene, a tender moment that might represent the lost innocence of all children bereaved or traumatised by war. When I played soldiers with my cousins as a child we conducted no funerals but grunted and collapsed theatrically to the floor. After appropriate time down, we'd leap up, our toy guns in hand, ready to be killed again.

With age comes a different perspective on the passing of time and emotional development across it. Now that I'm in my early forties, two decades doesn't seem long at all. I look back into history and ask myself if the years between 1918 and 1939 would have passed in the blink of an eye. I wonder how some servicemen felt when they saw their children and grandchildren playing with toys modelled on the machines that killed their friends. It's only now that I understand how, for those of us growing up in the peaceful West during the later years of the twentieth century, we played at soldiers and slid into a fascination with war machines in a different way to our forebears, all of whom would have been aware that their games could one day become real. We can only imagine what it was like to be a teenager in the 1930s, to have had just a few short years between putting down the toys of childhood and engaging with weapons to fight for real.

If war was traditionally seen as a man-making exercise for society and state, what would happen to the psyche of the post-war generations, from the Baby Boomers to my own, who knew they were unlikely to be called upon to fight? Perhaps we, too, have felt the same sense of missing out as the children of the inter-war years did; at least, until their time came. Would it make us immature, perpetual manbabies? After all, our relationship with the Second World War was one of play and make-believe. The words of Roman military writer Vegetius, that 'the prospect of fighting is agreeable to those who are strangers to it,' were as relevant in the years after 1945 as they were when he wrote them in the fourth century AD. We didn't want to ask too much about what had really happened because then the veneer of our fascination would slip and leave us confronted with what war was actually about. I remember a constant moral anxiety over the danger that my plastic figures would become flesh. Of course, they already were.

# PRIVATE NORMAL

Taking part in the annual school play was a refuge for me, away from the sports and the fighting, the endless football chat and fibs about girls. Usually, we performed musical adaptations with huge casts to get as many bums on seats as possible, but in the fifth year there was a change of direction with a far smaller production, Willis Hall's *The Long and the Short and the Tall*. The play took its name from a sardonic military song recorded by the likes of George Formby, Vera Lynn and Gracie Fields during the Second World War (the original version had 'fuck' instead of 'bless' in its opening lines: 'Bless 'em all/Bless 'em all/The long and the short and the tall'). Set in the Malayan jungle in 1942, the play depicts the last afternoon of a British patrol, cut off behind the lines during the Japanese advance on Singapore.

When *The Long and the Short and the Tall* was first performed at the Edinburgh Festival in 1958, writer and critic Kenneth Tynan described it as 'the most moving production of the Festival'. The debut London performance took place in 1959, directed by Lindsay Anderson and starring Robert Shaw, Ronald Fraser and Peter O'Toole. Thirty-five years later, I played Welsh soldier Private

Evans, and would no doubt have horrified anyone from Cardiff to Conwy with my appallingly sing-song delivery of the line 'Friday, it's fish & chips!' Evans, always thinking of his stomach, is a slightly dim but thoughtful character, worrying about whether the nurse in the serial in a woman's magazine his mother sends him ought to give in to her boyfriend's lascivious demands before he goes off to war.

The play is one of eddying tensions in which archetypes – the Scot, the Welshman, the Tynesider, the Cockney, the coward, the know-it-all, the barrack-room lawyer, the cynic – wriggle in the situation in which they have been dumped by war. Despite this, as I read and reread the script to try to learn my lines, I felt that these were very different men to those I had encountered from most of my own reading and watching of books and films set during the Second World War. In the humidity of the jungle, the soldierly banter and grouching at army rules and routine constantly threatens to boil over into violence. Bamforth, a loudmouth Cockney, bullies Evans, teasing him that his girlfriend back home in Cardiff is 'away with her Yank', and the men come to blows. I (Evans) ended up lying on the floor, leg twisted by Bamforth, being forced to shout 'I'm an ignorant Welsh Taff!', playing out on stage the sort of toxic power dynamics all too familiar from the playground and corridors.

We wore army surplus uniforms and pomade in our hair, carried deactivated Lee Enfield .303 rifles and a Sten machine gun, and, in what I think was a deliberate bit of cheek on the behalf of the art teacher director to the headmaster, had to pretend to smoke on stage – cigarettes form a key part of the plot. I'm not entirely sure that schools would put on the play now, such is some of the language used to describe women and the Japanese, which seems a shame, given that it is honest in its depiction of British masculinity absorbed into the military and the hostile jungle, and exactly the sort of thing that, politically correct or not, would help adolescents understand men and war. I had a strong sensation that, finally, here was a way of sharing my war culture with the pupils around me who would normally think I was a geek for it, showing them what lads not much older than us had gone through. I can't remember anything during my school days into which I invested as much effort as inhabiting my role within that little squad of men in the jungle, represented in our school hall by green lights, cardboard trees and dry ice.

Looking back, those few weekday evenings I spent playing a soldier seem closer to the Second World War than they do now. Not in terms of time, but because some in the audience were old enough to remember the war years themselves. They included my granny. In my pocket, I had an old knife that my grandad had taken to war with him. When I walked onstage in my British army fatigues, hair slicked to the side in 1940s style, she started crying. It was, she told my dad afterwards, as if she had seen a ghost.

On Granny's sideboard in her terraced house in Loughton was a carved wooden head on a plinth with two right hands and the inscription 'KULU GOI', that my grandad had brought back from the war. I was always slightly afraid of its blank, staring eyes, but, like his pocketknife, it was one of the few physical objects that connected me with him. I never met Percy Leonard Turner. He died in 1965, when my dad was seventeen. I only know him from a handful of photographs – pelting around an Essex lane on his bike, with the members of his local cricket team, fishing on the banks of the Chelmer Navigation, and two from the war years: one a studio shot in his new uniform, familiar face in profile, the other in tropical issue shorts, shirt and cap.

Percy was the son of a family who had made their home in the Epping Forest area of London and then rural Gloucestershire, working as gardeners and farm labourers. He left home and moved back to east London to take a job as a clerk on the London and North Eastern Railway, renting the house in Loughton with my granny, Dorothy. In September 1939, this ordinary life was put on notice when Percy Turner, along with all British males between the ages of eighteen and forty-one, became eligible for call-up.

In his mid-thirties, Percy was a lot older than most of his peers summoned to do their bit for the country, many of whom were at the end of adolescence or just in their early twenties. Puberty is a trauma of coming to terms with a shift in understanding of the body in a sensory overload – the feel of it, the sight of it, the scent of it, in all its beauty, strangeness, potential, limitations and awkwardness. Only a few years after they had started to become used to themselves as adult men, the younger of the military recruits had to endure another ritual: the inquisitive, invasive medical inspection that formed their body's assessment by the military authorities. John Alcock, a gay soldier, recalled, 'It was perfectly straightforward, you took all your clothes off and you went from one doctor to another. One checked your eyes, another checked your ears and things like that until you went through the whole gamut. I was very nervous and very young and tender.'

From this moment on, the recruit would have been acutely aware of their form and its status as an object that now belonged to the state as much as it did to them, their family or their lover. After this, he would be classified, given a rating; his suitability for service decided his fate, the course of his life and possible death. The military was aware of the body in this threshold state, instructing in a 1937 training manual that 'it must be remembered that the youth of 18 is no longer so plastic as the boy. His physique will be injured rather than improved by too rapid and vigorous attempts to alter the shape and carriage of his body.'

As a democracy, Britain could not resort to brutalising its soldiers into fighting in the way that the Soviet Union or Nazi

Germany could, but it still exerted a power that's almost impossible for us to comprehend. Just as it had with their fathers, the state's strategic, operational and tactical decisions and needs decreed where the body would go, what it would eat and advised it what to do with other bodies. It decided what the body should wear. It had absolute control over who would be put at risk, where and why. The pouring of men into uniforms was expressed in the 17 January 1940 edition of *Punch* magazine, part of an acutely observed series called 'The Changing Face of Britain' by cartoonist Fougasse. Men in flat caps, bowlers and fedoras puffed on cigarettes and pipes in the top panel; in the panel below, their blank expressions have been replaced by stern-jawed determination, their civilian headgear by military caps and berets.

Born into a working-class family in 1913, Dan Billany had left school at fourteen to become an errand boy for a Hull grocer and then an electrician's apprentice. An intelligent lad, with sheer autodidact determination he enrolled in technical college, developed a love of reading, music and writing, eventually gaining a scholarship to study English Literature at Hull University. By the outbreak of war, he was a teacher and, given his socialist and pacifist views, many were surprised when he enlisted, becoming Private Billany of the Royal Army Service Corps in October 1940. The shift into military life was intolerable. He wrote to his sister, 'You're allowed to do exactly nothing unless you are told to do it. [. . .] I shan't see anybody belonging to my old life till next Spring or Summer. You can't imagine how this feels. And as for taking up any of the threads, that can't be done while the war lasts. One has to accept the fact that the slate has been wiped clean.' His civilian existence now felt like 'my dead life'.

In *The Trap*, a work of autofiction written during the war in which the lead character Lt Michael Carr's experiences mirror Billany's own, he wrote that the conformity of the Army left him feeling 'deadly afraid of being deprived of my own soul'. It was the uniform that particularly bothered him. The distinctiveness and choice of his own clothes (in a biography, there's a photograph of Billany wearing a preposterously voluminous pair of trousers) had been taken away. The army confined him physically and spiritually, so that Carr felt 'imprisoned on my own dumbed body, in its khaki that could only be removed for sleeping. Nothing, nothing of me was left.' When he looked in the mirror, he saw only a 'strange lost creature'. The young lieutenant tries to fit in by performing a kind of military masculinity, telling dirty stories, putting the effort in at PT, chanting 'dirty songs when I shaved at reveille'. But behind this facade, 'my soul crouched behind the barrage and hoped to get by'.

Uniforms give so little indication of a man, which is rather the whole point; join the military, disappear into the wider whole: the pool of comradeship, discipline and military efficiency that is the physical representation of the nation at war. Yet there was a tension between the idealised, useful military body and the unfortunate problem that men didn't always fit the forage caps, the moulds made for them. A couple of months after the Fougasse illustration, on 13 March 1940, *Punch* ran a cartoon depicting a burley, moustachioed PT instructor conducting a squad in their morning exercises – squat, arms up, bend forward – at which point, one recruit spots a flower, picks it and, with an innocent smile, offers it to the instructor, to be met by a splash of red-inked, chin-jutting rage.

British military doctrine of the interwar years was shaped by the determination that the casualties of the First World War could not happen again, as the academic David French explores in his book *Raising Churchill's Army*. In 1927, Sir George Milne, Chief of the Imperial General Staff, said that wars of the future could not depend on the levels of manpower thrown into the trenches of the Western Front, and that 'Civilisation itself would go to pieces if a war similar to the last one were fought.' After 1930 and the abolition of the military death penalty, men had to be encouraged – not threatened – to fight. As French points out, 'The General Staff's commitment to an autocratic command and control system clashed directly with the dominant liberal political culture in Britain that emphasised the importance of individuals exercising a wide degree of freedom of choice inside the boundaries of the institutions within which they existed.' French writes of how the men of the British army were not ideologically committed to the fight and had little understanding of the reasons why they were doing so. They saw surviving the combat to return to their families and civilian lives as fast as possible as their main priority. That legacy of the First World War was a significant factor in this reluctance to fight, as the Army, French writes, was likely to 'exploit them, ignore their needs, and possibly needlessly sacrifice them'.

Dan Billany used *The Trap* to convey the utter cynicism that some men felt about the organisation that had swallowed them up: 'An Army! Not an idea in it [. . .] just a dead, frozen, congealed mass of routine, restriction and prejudice [. . .] paltry, petty, incapable, craven, dead-brained: betraying the faith and courage of the soldier.' In 1942, Army recruits were surveyed as to their 'eagerness to enter combat'. Out of 710,000, only 5 per cent declared themselves 'markedly suited by disposition and personality to a combatant role'.

James Sims was a private in the 1st Airborne Division in the doomed Operation Market Garden in 1944, the one depicted in that most popular of war films, *A Bridge Too Far*. In his memoir, *Arnhem Spearhead*, Sims wrote, 'Getting the English worked up enough to defend democracy was an uphill task, as the average soldier appeared to have only three basic interests: football, beer and crumpet.' This sort of attitude worried commanders. 'We are nothing like as tough as we were in the last war [. . .] British and Australian troops will not at present stand up to the same punishment and casualties as they did,' wrote General Wavell to Chief of the Imperial General Staff Alan Brooke on 31 May 1942. 'It is softness in education and living and bad training, and can be overcome but it will take a big effort.' General Montgomery wrote to Alan Brooke on 27 November 1942 that 'the trouble with our British lads is that they are not killers by nature'. The director of military training, in a report called 'General Lessons of the Italian Campaign', dated 18 December 1943, also blamed the culture of the interwar years for men's weakness when they first came under fire. At fault were books, cinemas, plays, education and propaganda, for damaging the martial instincts of interwar manhood: 'The army can achieve nothing if the young soldier has been brought up from the cradle, and during the most impressionable period of his adolescence, to look upon wars and battle as beyond human endurance and something not to be even contemplated.' It was hardly a surprise, the report said, that men crumbled in the face of action when their culture had made them soft.

This sort of invective is curiously familiar from the angrily rattling keyboards of contemporary right-wing tabloid crusaders. Young people – the infamous 'snowflake' millennials and Gen Z – are often negatively compared with the supposedly heroic wartime generation. In February 2022, shortly before Russia launched its brutal assault on Ukraine, *Sun* columnist Jane Moore quoted the Conservative Party chairman's belief that young 'social justice warriors' were threatening Britain's 'freedoms' with 'painful woke psychodrama' in a risible article suggesting a new TV show called *Strife Shop*, in which members of Generation Z could be sent to the front lines in Ukraine to be taught a lesson in how much tougher than them the youth who had gone off to fight in the Second World

War had been. The army reports concerned about the fighting quality of the British male in the 1940s paint a very different picture to this simplistic tabloid view that the men of 1939–1945 were dutiful heroes determined to fight for our freedom, etc and so on, ad infinitum. The official documents are certainly backed up by one of the best writers on the British army during the Second World War, even if his fame, or rather infamy, was later owed to his reputation as a thirsty Soho dilettante.

Julian Maclaren-Ross was offered a salient piece of advice as he boarded the train to take him to the Infantry Training Camp at Blandford in Essex in July 1940, as he recalled in his posthumously published *Memoirs of the Forties*. 'They can do anything to you in the Army bar give you a baby,' a railway porter and army veteran told him, 'but keep your trap shut and your bowels open you can't come to no harm,' Maclaren-Ross had been called up into the Army as 6027033 Private Ross too late to play any part in the first battles of the war. Instead, he spent its early years in the kind of camps that would inspire his writing, during what he called the war's 'Brown Period': 'Browned-off was the phrase one heard most often in X company, the other recruits owing to difficulty in finding any skirt started jocosely to talk of having Bits of Brown (buggery), the RAF blokes next door called us Brown Jobs, it was autumn and the leaves were brown, and everything was uniquely brown.' His experience of a life and an army as gross as a five-day sock, rather than battle and manly heroics, oozes through his debut collection of short stories, *The Stuff to Give the Troops*, published in 1944. The title, loaded with barrel-chested vim, was a commonly used saying in morale-boosting wartime newspaper articles and advertising. I've seen 'stuff to give the troops' used to describe anything from beer, a rousing concert featuring a Mr F. Cavendish's *The Nit-Wits*, a recipe for a mock goose dish, intra-services football matches, gift ideas for sweethearts, George Formby films, Christmas hampers, light entertainment broadcasts and Bisto gravy. Maclaren-Ross's usage is ironic. The military world that his characters inhabit in these 'twenty-five tales of Army life' is an endless tyranny of waiting around and training, just as it would have been for millions of men during their time in the services. The tone is world-weary and cynical, yet ripe with a humour that combines a Kafkaesque frustration with bureaucracy and a very English sense of the absurd: a proto-*Catch 22* for those who'd say *left*enant rather than *lieu*. *The Stuff to Give the Troops* does for the ordinary soldiers of the British army in the Second World War what Tim O'Brien's *The Things They Carried* did for Vietnam. It has the same urgency, fiction powered by lived experience.

There's no glory in this military bubble of cold and leaking Nissen huts, beds with broken springs, inflexible bureaucracy that becomes cruel in its mundanity, the tensions of strangers confined, endless routine, drill before breakfast, menial tasks, bad food and worse smells (dead mice, cigs, farts). It is damp, too hot or cold enough to chilblain ears. The men who populate these grim barracks are frequently drunk, excused from duties with scabies, on charge for minor crimes, or being brought up and court-martialled for slackness. In the story 'They Put Me in Charge of a Squad', on the day before a route march an entire company goes sick. The soldiers who make up Maclaren-Ross's fictional units are no paragons of English masculinity – in the same story, the narrator is put in command of a group detailed with shifting some furniture: 'A squad of men shivered sullenly on the kerb outside. Their denim suits, buttonless, flapped open in the bitter wind. My heart sank when I saw them [. . .] All the worst janker wallahs were there, mixed with a few well-known malingerers and a man just back from detention barracks with no top teeth.' They're covered with pimples and blue with cold, unable to march on blistered feet, unable to march because they can't keep time, wiping snotty

noses, claiming broken legs and sprained ankles. Like the men of
the patrol in *The Long and the Short and the Tall*, they're a hapless,
ill-disciplined rabble that makes the Walmington-on-Sea Home
Guard platoon of *Dad's Army* seem like the SAS.

It is all a far cry from the crisp formality of *Infantry Training:
Training and War*, a regularly updated manual published by the
Army and intended to encourage the best in its fighting men. The
1937 edition is prefaced by adverts for products and services that
promise to ensure the reader is spruced up both on and off duty as
the best man he can be: Aquatite trench coats, the latest cars and
Bluebell liquid metal polish, so that the good soldier could always
keep his bugle buffed and gleaming. After these ads for the stuff
to give the troops, the manual gets on with the serious business
of war. As well as how to attack, defend and patrol, it provides
instruction on 'the development of moral qualities', physical
training and drill, all with the object of moulding the recruit the
Army's way – 'determined, inquisitive and self-dependent', he
must 'always remember that he is acting as one of a team' and
'above all, he must be highly disciplined, for by discipline alone
can morale be maintained'. An earlier edition, from 1932, focused
more heavily on routines for drill and the need for the recruit
to subsume himself into the unit, to take pride and develop an
*esprit de corps*. 'On and off parade the man should work and play
as a member of his section, platoon, or company, and not as an
individual,' it states, stressing the importance of tidy appearance
on the march, where a straggler might be shamed into feeling he
has disgraced himself and his unit.

The art in Maclaren-Ross's fiction is that for all their grouching,
malingering ineptitude, the men he conjures are not unheroic. In
fact, I sense something tender in their unconscious resistance to
the demands of training manuals, stuffy officers and barking regimental sergeant majors. From cat burglars to clerks and farmhands,

they're ordinary blokes forced by extraordinary times into a tedious situation. Like the narrator of the story 'Dodging the Column', they might volunteer for and deliberately flunk an afternoon exam to join the signals corps because it'll get them out of a hard day of battle drill, but in the tone of Maclaren-Ross's writing that is a noble act of the small man getting one over on the military system. 'Yes, battle drill was safely over now. I congratulated myself on taking the test. I thought of the others swimming canals, going through tank traps. I went to a canteen and ate ten cream buns to celebrate. Then I went to sleep in a chair. I was tired out. It had been a good day.'

I think of the men of *The Stuff to Give the Troops* in stark contrast to those of 1965 film *The Hill*, set late in the war in a military prison in North Africa, in which disruptors, malingerers, spivs and men who just could not cope are sent to be straightened out by screaming sergeant majors, the action a blur of endless drilling, prisoners marching quick time around a claustrophobic desert fort, their legs and arms jerking up and down, up and down as if under the control of a puppeteer. The sole aim is to break them as men, to make them 'clockwork soldiers' who will pick up orders 'like a dog picks a bone'. Here, cinema takes Churchill's idea of the required 'blood, toil, tears and sweat' to an extreme.

On 2 February 1942, my grandad Percy Turner resigned his membership of his local Home Guard unit. The next day, he travelled from Loughton to the Royal Engineers drill hall on London Road, Romford, to enlist. I'd sent off to the Army records office to get hold of his military documents, but Covid-19 and the sheer volume of people trying to find out about their ancestors' wartime service meant that it took a couple of years for the facsimiles of the forms that described his fate to arrive. It's funny how Percy's attestation form puts flesh (albeit not very much of it) onto the bones of this man I never physically knew – he was five foot nine, weighed 124lbs and his chest when expanded measured thirty-five inches. He had a 'fresh complexion', blue eyes, fair hair, scars on his right shin and knee, and was marked as medical grade 1, educational grade C. He was given army number 1953241, the rank of sapper/clerk and posted to the Royal Engineer's railway establishment at Longmoor in Hampshire. His expertise as a railway clerk meant that after a period of army training, on 30 July 1942, he was 'released from army service and relegated to Class "W" Res for an indefinite period', meaning he was in a reserved occupation. Using his professional skills was deemed more useful to the war effort than sending him to the front lines. Nevertheless, I find that use of 'relegated' interesting in terms of how we might understand it today, that to be in a reserved occupation was in some way lesser than joining a fighting unit. It's an uncomfortable memory that, when I talked to school friends about what our grandads did in the war, I sometimes felt it wasn't exciting to tell them about his work on the railways when theirs had been in the Army, Navy or the RAF.

I have a collection of letters home Percy Turner wrote during the war years, diary entries to give my granny and Uncle Barry an idea of what his strange new life was like. After spending the spring and early summer of 1942 at Longmoor, he was posted to Freetown to work on the Sierra Leone Government Railway, a line used to transport palm oil to the sea. His handwriting is terrifyingly neat and small, the lines of text ordered and straight on the thin paper. He wrote home from the Blue Star Line steamer the *Andalucia Star* on 2 August, anticipating the coming voyage to West Africa with 'a certain amount of dubious excitement', given the U-boat activity in Atlantic waters. He 'felt resigned to the acceptance of "come what may" . . . I a real greenhorn was really going into danger . . . I confess to very mixed thoughts just about then.'

Percy and some of the other rail workers were thrilled to find they'd been allocated first-class cabins that in peacetime they would never have been able to afford. The excitement is evident in the meticulous detailing of all the fixtures and fittings in his accommodation, just like you might video call pals to show the contents of the minibar if you've had a hotel room upgrade. He describes the chrome fittings, silk sheets on the beds, a dressing table with five drawers and two mirrors, an electric fan and 'a most elaborate gold-coloured reading lamp with pink silk side shades'.

Percy Turner had never intended to see the world. 'It may broaden the mind this thing called travel but it surely reduces the waistline – and I can't afford to lose any of mine,' he wrote, ruefully reflecting on his slight build. Percy had a mild patriotism and, as the ship set sail to the cheers of a small crowd of well-wishers on the quayside, he joined a group at the rail 'to get a last glimpse of the country that meant so much to us all'. The *Andalucia Star* was a fast ship and didn't need to travel in convoy for protection. As she headed out into the Atlantic, Percy's diary fills with a mixture of excitement, worry, routine and seasickness. The ambivalence he felt, the strangeness of it all, must have been shared by millions of men, from all the different nations involved. He wrote, 'This diary contains a summary of perhaps the strangest but certainly not the most happy nor least happy week of my life.' He bought Capstan Medium navy cut tobacco at 2/4 per quarter pound and drank 'bon voyage' with a bottle of lager, ate elaborate meals that must have been a joy after the stringent conditions of Army training and rationing back home, struggled to get out of bed in the morning (that still sits in this family) and worried about news reports of air raids in East London and Essex, family at home and the state of the war. Percy and his pals played deck tennis and watched flying fish launch themselves across the wave tops, attended film screenings (*Krazy Kat* cartoon; *Tom, Dick and Harry* starring Ginger Rogers) and weekly church services. Percy shared an intimacy with his railwaymen colleagues as they discussed 'promotions, ambitions, private lives' mixed with banter, as they ribbed him for bringing a brolly with him to Africa, something that turned out to be rather useful.

Percy also had a sense of duty. He volunteered to spend watches looking out over the Atlantic briny for U-boats. He describes the vivid metal colours of the sea and sky, the sense of being 'truly in the hands of a mighty power' to which the ship appeared to 'pay homage' as she rose and fell in the waves. He thought he spotted a U-boat periscope but it was only a whale – a creature that an early twentieth-century Essex man could never, in his ordinary life, have expected to see. On each watch, Percy was thrown together with a new companion. The sheer strangeness of being in the darkness of a blacked-out vessel steaming through the waters of the Atlantic sparked off conversations that I imagine he'd never have had in the works and offices of the LNER back in London. One old salt told him of a sinking earlier in the war and how, after he was torpedoed, the U-boat surfaced to ask if they had enough water. 'Such apparently is the spirit of the sea the whole world over!' Grandad reported home. 'It was somewhat comforting to know that one's enemies, even in a war such as the present one, do not in all cases disregard the human side of life.' Sometime later, he shared the watch with an Oxford mathematics graduate. 'We chatted on various topics – our own private lives, our differences in social position, our hopes, our prospects and how the war has destroyed class barriers that apparently nobody ever admired or really wanted. He was young – is 23 young? – and full of life. We had a great deal in common after all.'

On the last night on board, Percy and his mates decided to mark the event with five Worthington beers each. They got carried away and continued the boozing with some naval personnel. Trumpet and sax were produced and the motley ensemble carried on drinking, singing popular songs and nautical ditties they didn't know until 3 a.m. The next morning, Grandad lamented his hangover but reckoned that the voyage was 'entirely worthy of a binge. It is pretty difficult to say truthfully after one of these affairs that the after-effects are justified but in this instance we did so and suffered headaches and dry tongues cheerfully.'

When the ship finally docked in Freetown, Percy wrote of excitement and strangeness of customs and surroundings, getting used to new tastes, the sweetness of the food, the smallness of the eggs, the Muslim cook who won't make sausages (he seems to have loved sausages). It's the writing of a man overwhelmed by new experiences while still yearning for home. Take, for instance, a diary entry about the flora and fauna so different from the Epping Forest and Cotswold landscape he knew – vultures, the flowers 'very gay', the leopards in the hills 'quite timid really' and the five-inch cockroaches that scuttled across the floor at a terrific speed. And then, listening on the wireless to a church service from St Mary's Holborn, he heard an anthem 'the solo of which I had sung in Dowdeswell church. A link with home'. One evening, during a showing of newsreels about West Africa's contribution to the war effort, 'in the darkness at 9pm I felt a sudden urge to look at my watch and felt my agreed link with home was very real'. There's tenderness in how, every night at the same time, he does this, writing, 'Goodnight London Gloucester Chelmsford I think of you.'

I feel quite emotional reading his words, this curious diffidence and lack of confidence from the thirty-four-year-old married father of one who, until the war came along, had just been trying to get along as best he could in the world.

Percy's letter diary goes on until 1944, ending in January. On 4 May that year, he returned to the UK, arriving in Liverpool on the MV *Loriga*. We don't know why, exactly, he returned. There was a surprise on his army records – an ink stamp of 'DISCHARGED' with the explainer of 'medically unfit for further service' on 5 September 1945 – quite a decline from the grade 1, wiry, fit as a fiddle recruit just three years before. Perhaps this and the stopping of his diary was because of what we do know – that he'd refused to take a bribe to give a local a job, was beaten up and left for dead. He came around lying next to the coffin that was being prepared for his burial, a shock that was enough to make him cling on to life. Like the part of the church roof that crashed through my granny's ceiling during a German air raid, this is a curious reminder of how close my dad came to never being born and the arbitrary nature of life and death in time of war.

When I think of Percy Turner it's not as anyone special out of the multitude who served. Rather, I find him so fascinating because he was an everyman, doing his best to improve his lot in life and for his family, only for the inescapable vastness of the Second World War to scoop him up, plonk him in a ship and send him to the other side of the planet. There's one line he wrote during the voyage out in which I see an articulation of a thought that must have been so common: 'But for the war my life would have been infinitely easier and happier. No parting from my kin – but on the other hand, no chance to prove my worth – if any.' There must have been tens of millions of letters and diaries that expressed similar sentiments to my grandad's, sent by soldiers, sailors, airmen, British, German, Soviet, American, French, all sides and all nations, normal blokes writing their sadness at being parted from family and homeland for so long.

Yet the more I read on the masculinity of the mid-twentieth century, the more that 'normal' seemed to be a nasty, slippery word, cropping up in all sorts of places through the 1930s and 40s and again in the literature that emerged post-war on sexuality and mental health, or in the categorisation of men. It reminded me how, growing up, my own sexuality and desperate fear of not fitting in meant that I craved the feeling of normality, even if it seemed evermore elusive the older I got. For the white male who made up the core of British self-identity in the early twentieth century and who dominated the war culture I'd grown up with, 'normal' existed as the default position and therefore an exclusionary term, the place to which all ought to aspire to become good citizen soldiers. I wonder how I would have felt, so at odds with the expectations of the time.

In *Nationalism and Sexuality: Respectability and Abnormal Sexuality in Modern Europe*, the academic and Jewish refugee from Nazi persecution George L. Mosse wrote that 'the distinction between normality and abnormality was basic to modern respectability'. Writing in the mid-1980s, Mosse examined how the masculine ideals of Germany and Britain had a lot in common, setting themselves up in opposition to the Catholic nations of southern Europe, which were seen as sexually loose and disreputable. Under the influence of evangelical Protestantism, the British and Germans believed that 'controlling the passions' was at the core of the respectability that made for a strong nation. This was even more extreme when used to discuss men from further afield, often legitimising racism. Fighting forces from overseas nations, within the Empire and Dominions or outside their jurisdiction, were often seen as outside the common context of 'normal'. In the *Royal Air Force Manual of Army Cooperation*, published by the Air Ministry in 1940, the tribesmen of the Indian frontier are described as a 'semi-civilised enemy'. At the start of the war, the King's Regulations stated that anyone serving in the British military 'must be of pure European descent'. Non-white peoples were subject to assumptions as to their sexuality. In *The Long Weekend*, Graves and Hodge refer to popular interwar ethnographers who 'could not disguise their bawdy relish in the sexual habits of primitives, and their reports were published rather as refined erotic reading than as stern works of research'.

At home, those perceived as sexually deviant were put outside the realm of normality, even considered a threat to the state. The word 'decadence' has its roots in the Latin 'decadere' – to fall or sink – and was commonly attached to ideas of national decline. By describing homosexuals as 'decadent', the implication was that their existence was evidence for, or even the cause, of a nation's decrepitude. To be anything other than heterosexual was to be seen as so deviant it might undermine your identity as a true English-man, as reflected in this story Henry Danton told me. 'I heard that two men in London had been arrested for kissing each other and taken to court,' he said. 'And in the proceedings, the judge said, "Were they French?"'

In *The Long Weekend*, Graves and Hodge make a great survey of British mores, class, tradition and societal upheaval, in which the 'normal' male is tossed and turned and, eventually, spat out into the grim Monday morning of the war. Sexuality forms a key part of this concept of the 'normal' ideal: 'Homosexuality had been on the increase among the upper classes for a couple of generations, though almost unknown among working people.' The public school system is blamed and the authors claim that most of these men 'became normal' after leaving the temptation of lights-out dorms and the post-rugger bath. There's a self-denial, an abrogation from the 'normal' in this sentence, for Graves himself was bisexual. Quentin Crisp wrote in his memoir, *The Naked Civil Servant*, 'the idea that between a man and a woman the sex act can be natural, unnamed, inevitable and lead to total oneness gives normality the radiance of the Holy Grail.'

Crisp was, of course, not the only homosexual who self-diagnosed as not being 'normal'. Perhaps leading among them, in terms of etymology at least, was the gay author of the 1927 book *The Invert and His Social Adjustment*. The anonymous male writer, aged forty and describing himself as 'Anomaly', writes that he hopes the book 'may be a source of comfort and encouragement'. Keen to escape the common clichés of homosexual identity, Anomaly writes that he's no bohemian, actor or artist, but 'an ordinary workaday man'. He argues against those who believe gay men 'cannot perhaps be expected to exhibit virtues and qualities which are assumed to be particularly masculine' and writes that he would not have addressed the issue were it not for his experiences in the First World War, when the bravery of other gay men on the front prompted him 'to challenge the suggestion that they are weaklings'. All of Anomaly's homosexual friends signed up, many were wounded in action and some were decorated for valour, receiving medals including the Victoria Cross, Military Cross, Distinguished Service Order and the French Croix De Guerre. According to Anomaly, the problems that faced gay men didn't interfere with their 'war-time efficiency, and may even have increased it'. Although the early twentieth century often feels alien in its conservatism today, the expectations of normality, and how those who didn't fit it might behave in military service, were starting to be challenged.

There is a broad swathe of masculinity between that idealised in the *Punch* cartoon of men abandoning their civilian garb for uniforms, in the wartime propaganda newsreels and photography or today in the dewy-eyed sentimentalism with which veterans are often perceived, and the dirty, bawdy, ill-disciplined types that Maclaren-Ross so vividly described in *The Stuff to Give the Troops*. I suppose my grandad must have had elements of all and though I never knew him, I love him for that. The addition of this further layer, the men whose sexual identity was so far from 'normal' that some thought it challenged the very selfhood of the state, makes the masculinity of the war years even more gloriously slippery. Even for the most superficially 'normal' white, heterosexual man in the British military of the Second World War, there was no one way of being. They had their private lives, their desires, their discomfort at their physical selves, the dread of shame, worry at not doing their best, a potential for cowardice and bravery, moments of abject self-loathing and, surely, some of transcendence too. There was a richness in the mind of every man on board the SS *Andalucia Star* with my grandad that, if by some future alchemy it might be extracted and turned into radiant film, would outdo any of the simple tales of heroism on which so many of us grew up.

All these men did what they could to retain some kernel of themselves among the expectations of comradeship within the military structures in which they were forced to live and the extremes to which they, ultimately, might be asked to reach. The 'normal' man must be persuaded to perform the most 'abnormal' duty – not the feats of heroism and derring-do that characterise the myths that spring forth afterwards, but the act of killing another human being. When the patrol of *The Long and the Short and the Tall* capture a Japanese soldier and realise they're surrounded by the advancing enemy, their banter dissolves in the face of the serious question of whether or not they can kill this man. They dismiss and other him as 'a bloody nip', but he has photos of a wife and children in his wallet, and Bamforth, who had taunted him using pidgin Japanese, ends up, at the despairing conclusion, wanting to save him.

The soldier's civilian skin had to be shed. As hard-bitten platoon Sergeant Mitchem says, once overseas and in a uniform, the soldier was a different man to the one who had left his home and family. And what of killing, asks Lance Corporal Macleish, unsure if he has what it takes to do it. 'It's inside all of us,' Mitchem replies, 'that's the trouble.'

The Second World War challenged 'normal' men, just as it proved that they didn't really exist. Yet when I was a child, this was a hidden truth and it felt impossible to get a rounded picture of who these men were. After 1945, they had disappeared into our culture's misty-eyed nostalgia for the war years and had been consumed by the uniforms and machines that they'd once operated.

The first time that VE Day was commemorated in a large-scale, national event was in 1995, on the fiftieth anniversary. With many of the men who had participated in the action now in their seventies, time was running out to celebrate them. On 8 May, the focus was on London's Hyde Park and along the Mall. Our teacher had somehow wangled a slot for us to perform part of *The Long and the Short and the Tall*, a day of respite from preparing for our GCSEs. We were hidden away in a small tent, far from the main event, where tens of thousands crammed in front of Buckingham Palace to see Vera Lynn singing 'The White Cliffs of Dover' and the Queen Mother, Queen Elizabeth and Princess Margaret appear on the palace balcony, as they had done for crowds of Londoners half a century before.

I was disappointed that we'd acted out a couple of scenes from the play to disinterested spectators who came and went at random, but it wasn't just unsatisfied ego that made me feel ajar. As I wandered around in the sunlight dappled by soaring London plane trees, eyes itching from their bombardment of pollen, I was frustrated by what felt like the tasteless accoutrements of British mass entertainment – the wacky hats and fast food concessions, a giddiness in the air. Around and about were veterans sitting in groups in deckchairs, seemingly ancient to my teenage self but I realise today many were only in their seventies, the same age as my dad is now, a quarter of a century later. I yearned to go and speak to them, to hear their stories, probably to blub something out about gratitude, but felt as if I shouldn't impose, as if my awkward teenagerhood wasn't worthy of these normal men who had done and seen so much.

# FIGHT OR/AND/OR FLIGHT

I had tried, in my naive, teenage way, to put everything I had read and learned about the war into becoming Private Evans in that play. I tried, but I failed. I couldn't access the truth of the men who served, or answer the fundamental question of whether or not I could have faced the extremes they had.

Behind the models, the books, the films and the dread and fear at the prospect of a Third World War that persisted through most of my pre-adolescent childhood was one simple question: would I have gone willingly when the call-up papers came? I had turned it into a mental photocopy of that recruiting poster with one word changed – 'what *would* you do in the war, Daddy?' – forever pinned up in my psyche. But what would I have fought for? It was a question I used to ask myself as I put the latest war novel away and looked up at the fighters and bombers silhouetted against my bedroom ceiling.

My average comprehensive school was a former grammar founded in 1938 that had held onto many pre-war traditions – a smart uniform of blazer and tie, a bewildering obsession with rugby and an extremely formal daily assembly. The rows of boys in the grand wood-panelled hall had to stand as the headmaster and senior teachers walked in wearing gowns. We'd have Bible readings, poorly sung hymns, admonishments that we were representing the school when in uniform, and that wandering the local streets carrying 'pizza boxes' (the headteacher pronounced it 'pittsa') was deeply shaming to our collective reputation. Never much of a rebel, I sort of agreed.

Every now and then, a different teacher would give a pep talk on some school or wider subject. All have slipped from memory but one, which sticks with me now as it moved me then. Mr Meier was a French teacher and a bit of a pioneer. He was the first to connect a computer to the internet and made our class gather round as a new thing called a 'website' slowly appeared on the screen, bemusing us all – it just looked like telly info service Ceefax, but with grainy pictures. Mr Meier stood behind the lectern (a short man, he almost disappeared) and began to speak. He described the town we lived in, the school, the streets around, the cathedral, the park full of Roman remains. It was a familiar picture that gradually shifted as he continued, describing the rise of a government that was full of hate and a population that aggressively supported it, quietly acquiesced or said nothing. Mr Meier continued to outline events that were ominous in their slight subversion of the familiar – a school assembly just like ours, after which some boys were told to stay behind, never to be seen again; of shouts and pleading screams in the night-time streets, followed in the morning with the sight of windows smashed, neighbours vanished, a terror of speaking out becoming an acceptance of what had gone on. When he finished, the assembly hall, usually murmuring with sniggering, fake coughs, bored shuffles and comedy farts, was silent. More than any history lesson, Mr Meier had managed to make what until then had been the abstract horror of the rise of Nazism and the Holocaust feel real. Not long ago, an old friend reminded me that the racist bullies at our school didn't just target fellow pupils – a bunch of kids liked to taunt Mr Meier, a Jew, to 'watch out, the Germans are coming'.

I'd seen the Holocaust episodes of *The World at War* and read about it in books, but it was such a vast subject that it was hard to grasp the horrendous reality. This was before films like *Schindler's List* and *The Pianist* hit the mainstream. The Holocaust was always present in the background of history, but it was so grotesque that it got in the way of the simpler war pleasures (for want of a better phrase) of admiring the machines, glorying in explosions and fire. Mr Meier's assembly shook me precisely because it forced me to see the Second World War in the context of my present day, to understand that it might happen again, and shook my complacency. As adolescence loomed, I had become more conscious of global events, with the fall of the Berlin Wall and collapse of the Soviet Union. The Cold War that seemed to have been a continuation of the Second but with our former allies as enemies was over. I wasn't aware of Francis Fukuyama's theories of the end of history, but there was a strong sense that, while there might be far away wars over oil and territory in the Middle East or Balkans, these were not conflicts that should worry us, secure in the beige safety of early 1990s Britain. The narrative that Britain was involved in – and won – an existential battle with the pure abjections of Nazism is a comfort blanket that allowed us to see the Second World War through cosy nostalgia as a simpler time of moral absolutes. This is of course nonsense when discussing something as complicated as global war, or the frailties in human nature that, as Mr Meier's assembly had so eloquently explained, lead supposedly civilised societies to genocide. There is an irritating phase that I've increasingly noticed being used by those on both the right and left of the political spectrum in recent years, about wanting to be, or judging others not to have been, on 'the right side of history'. It is usually deployed by people who are possessed of a kind of moral absolutism and conviction that they are already on that 'right' side. How can they be so sure?

I'm cynical about that perspective now because I used to hold it myself. While Percy Turner was off running the railway in Sierra Leone, my maternal grandpa, Edwin Bazlinton, was a conscientious objector on religious grounds. As a child, I had understood that war and killing were sinful and that this was why I wasn't allowed toy guns, but was confused that there was a lot of it in the Bible – God seemed to approve of a bit of smiting if it was carried out in a good cause. One of my favourite Bible passages has always been Ecclesiastes 3, verses 1 to 8, that glorious affirmation of human agency within God's creation, in which there is 'a time to kill, and a time to heal; a time to break down and a time to build up [. . .] A time to love, and a time to hate; a time of war, and a time of peace.' The more I learned in my early teenage years about the Holocaust and life in Nazi-occupied Europe, the more I struggled to understand why Grandpa had not seen it as his moral duty to get involved. He was a strict but kindly old man with his bald head and white beard; I remember in his house the exotic treat of Sodastream fizzy pop, the old-fashioned smell of orange coal tar soap in the bathroom and prayers of grace full of 'thees' and 'thous' before we sat down for lunch. I'd long to ask him why he had decided not to fight. In truth, I sometimes felt uncomfortable about it. I was jealous of friends whose grandads had driven tanks or flown aircraft, who even had their medals on shelves at home. If Hitler and Nazi Germany were the epitome of evil, then surely it was a Christian duty to fight them?

My grandpa wasn't alone. There had been 16,000 conscientious objectors in the First World War. After the conflict ended, 'conchies', as they were often derisively known, were discriminated against. In 1918, the Representation of the People Act gave the vote to civilian men at twenty-one, servicemen at nineteen, but disenfranchised conscientious objectors and prevented them from voting for five years, whatever their age. The power of 'what did you do in the war, Daddy?' came in its threat of shaming.

At the start of the Second World War, twenty-two in a thousand men claimed conscience. By the summer of 1940, with France defeated and Britain under bombardment from the Luftwaffe, this had fallen to six in a thousand. By the end of the war, 59,192 had applied. There were 3,577 unconditional exemptions; 28,720 had to take up approved work; 14,691 took non-combatant roles in the military and 12,204 had been turned down. Around 5,500 were jailed but none were executed, compared to the unknown number, but thought to be at least 15,000, shot by their own side in Germany.

The memory of the First World War allowed some sympathy for those who had decided not to fight. On 10 January 1940, the Coventry *Evening Telegraph* reported on the story of Sidney Thomas Turvey, a brewer's drayman of Aston who came up in front of a conscientious objection tribunal in Birmingham, accompanied by his father. Turvey the younger 'appeared to be nervous and had some difficulty in answering questions', at which his father interrupted and, holding up two medals he had won in the Great War, said, 'I am a sufferer as a result of the last war. These are all I got from it.' He added that he was the one responsible for Sidney's attempt to avoid conscription: 'I have taught him it is immoral.'

Yet in other quarters, to not wish to fight was a dereliction of one's duty as a British male. Popular illustrated newspaper *The Sphere* declared on 8 April 1939 that those who had volunteered for territorial forces in the year running up to the war 'are of the finest type of British manhood'. A year later, in the Lincolnshire *Echo* on 28 May 1940, 'The Gossiper' of the City & County column noted a decrease in the number of men registering as objectors in the labour exchange and wondered if maturity was a factor in making men less likely to do so: 'It would be satisfactory to think that refusal to serve one's country was a state of mind which men grow out of as they grow out of measles, chicken-pox and whooping cough.' However, far more preferable, according to The Gossiper, would be 'to find evidence that the authenticated reports of women and children being bombed and machine-gunned had removed the last vestiges of objection. Does the sincere objector take no heed of these things and always pass by on the other side of the road?'

Collective anxiety and dread of civilians being killed in their thousands during a major European war had haunted society in the interwar years and led to the rise of pacifist sentiment. In 1935, the Peace Ballot on British attitudes towards the League of Nations and pacifism received 11.6 million votes, an overwhelming major-ity of which were for arms reduction, especially of military aircraft. Three years before, on 10 November 1932, Stanley Baldwin had delivered the famous parliamentary speech in which he announced that 'the bomber will always get through'. The pre-war assump-tion was that Germany would seek to deliver a 'knock out blow' against urban centres. This insecurity was reflected in fiction – in 1913, H. G. Wells might have dreamed of a world where war could be solved with toy soldiers, but such naivety was gone by the time of his 1933 novel *The Shape of Things to Come*, a prediction of a long world war in which cities would suffer from heavy bombing.

On 28 November 1934, Winston Churchill gave a speech to Parliament in which he warned of the dangers of German re-armament and predicted that, 'no one can doubt that a week or ten days' intensive bombing attack upon London would be a very serious matter indeed. One could hardly expect that less than 30,000 or 40,000 people would be killed or maimed.' He went on to envision three or four million Londoners taking shelter in the countryside around the capital and predicted that an air assault might 'expose us not only to hideous suffering, but even to mortal peril, by which I mean peril of actual conquest and subjugation'. Churchill's speech came at the time of what historians call the 'air panic', a widespread fear of German rearmament and the potential for the destruction of British cities. Then came the Spanish Civil War, and the Republican use of German bombers to attack Guernica in 1937 seemed to add credence to these apocalyptic views. This prospect of mass destruction is what, in part, haunts the pre-war atmosphere of Patrick Hamilton's novel *Hangover Square*, when the weather is 'fine for Mr Chamberlain, who believed it was peace in our time – his umbrella a parasol!' and, 'You couldn't believe it would ever break, that the bombs had to fall' – the bombs *had to fall*, in an inevitability of destruction.

On 25 May 1940, the chiefs of staff reported to the war cabinet on the likelihood of Britain being able to continue resisting Germany in the event of a French capitulation. The paper, with the gloriously understated, evasive and euphemistic title 'British Strategy in a Certain Eventuality', had as a core concern 'whether the morale of our people will withstand the strain of air bombardment'. When bombers did arrive over the cities of Britain, the doomiest predictions of the 'air panic' never quite came true, but the damage wrought created a spiral of reciprocal destruction as air power became a means for Britain to take the war to Germany.

In the spring of 1942, the new leader of the RAF's Bomber Command, Air Chief Marshall Sir Arthur Harris, recorded a speech in which he gravely intoned that, 'The Nazis entered this war under the rather childish delusion that they were going to bomb everybody else and nobody was going to bomb them. At Rotterdam, London, Warsaw, and half a hundred other places, they put that rather naïve theory into operation. They sowed the wind and now they are going to reap the whirlwind.' Harris's paraphrasing of a line from the Book of Hosea reflects a very Old Testament way of looking at war. The Germans had pioneered the tactics of area bombing, after all. They were the aggressors, the builders of the camps. Remember that scene in the 'Germans' episode of *Fawlty Towers* where Basil becomes apoplectic about who was to blame for the row in the hotel? 'They started it!' he shrieks, eyes popping, to denials. 'Yes, they did! They invaded Poland!' This adversarial and even vengeful attitude of 'an eye for an eye' was the total opposite of the motivation of my grandpa and so many others not to fight, to follow the New Testament Gospels and Christ's teaching to turn the other cheek, that to kill another human was a mortal sin.

All of Air Chief Marshall Sir Arthur Harris' Bomber Command aircrews were volunteers. Their aircraft might have been at the forefront of aeronautical technology, but they were uncomfortable, relatively slow, poorly armed and, when it came to the job for which they were intended, far from accurate in terms of delivering explosives onto a target. The 1941 Butt Report found that less than one third of aircraft that claimed to have attacked their targets had actually dropped their bombs within five miles of them. The shock of this abject failure led to the tactic of area bombing of German cities, euphemistically called 'de-housing'. If bombers were unable to precisely hit German factories, then they would attack the homes of civilian workers, disrupting routine and crushing their morale. This was the whirlwind that 'Bomber' Harris had promised.

For the next three years, ever more numerous and powerful aircraft guided by sophisticated electronic devices like Gee and Oboe dropped 955,044 bombs on Germany and Occupied Europe. A recent study suggested that the bombing had so much destructive power it even disturbed the ionosphere, 1,000km above the earth. During Operation Gomorrah, an eight-day, seven-night raid on Hamburg in July 1943 and the infamous April 1945 attack on Dresden, bombs dropped by British and American aircraft started fires on the ground that reached temperatures of over 1,000 degrees centigrade. These sucked oxygen towards the flames, creating an infernally hot wind called a firestorm that uprooted trees, suffocated civilians in their shelters and melted the fat in human bodies. Tens of thousands of civilians were killed in single raids. Over the course of the war, 3.5 million homes were destroyed and as many as 353,000 German civilians killed, along with many more in Occupied Europe. As W. G. Sebald points out in *On the Natural History of Destruction*, his peerless analysis of what the bombing did to the German psyche, there were 31.1 cubic metres of rubble for every resident of Cologne and 42.8 for Dresden.

Some claim that the Bomber Command campaign against Germany was a modern-day atrocity, the Allies' own Guernica that calls into question the idea that the Second World War was a just one. The traditional yet mythical conception of the male as protector of 'innocent' women and children at home is disrupted by modern warfare that deliberately targets civilians, such as in the 'de-housing' tactics of Bomber Command's nightly operations over Europe. The pastel-coloured *What did you do in the war, Daddy?* posters take on a grimmer tone when the answer is, 'I killed children who looked just like you.' It is possible to assess the Second World War as merely a reflection of a more base and primitive form of combat seen in periods of ancient and medieval history, where an army might conquer a town, city or region and butcher its inhabitants. No babies were slashed with swords, but why does twenty or twenty-five thousand feet of German or Japanese sky and air make a moral difference? Death is still death. Men remain the killers. A culture seeking to remember war needs heroes to boost the image of itself, so we remember the maverick engineering and pluck of the crews of 617 Squadron on the Dambusters raid as it supports the national myth, whereas the consequences of 'de-housing' remain contentious.

Yet heroism is something bestowed afterwards, by those who were not there. Bravery is the act of surviving from day to day against impossible odds. Just because Bomber Command's war was fought thousands of feet above the enemy in their flak positions, or against fighter pilots invisible in the dark, didn't make it impersonal. The bomber was alone within the vastness of the sky. Inside the fuselage, the crew were likewise isolated at their posts, deafened by the roaring engines, howling slipstream, flak bursts and defensive machine-gun fire. Each man would have been as acutely aware of his vulnerability as a soldier in a foxhole facing an advancing infantry troop or tank. Bomber aircrew had a surreally bipolar existence of spending days in the tranquil countryside of eastern England, taking leave in local towns or perhaps a trip to London, then when the moon and weather permitted, climbing aboard their Halifax, Wellington, Stirling, Manchester, Mosquito and Lancaster bombers to unleash destruction on Hamburg, Nuremberg, Cologne and Berlin. They were vulnerable to Germany's anti-aircraft guns and, later in the war, fighter aircraft armed with a powerful vertically firing cannon called Schräge Musik. The German pilots hunted the British bombers using radar and moonlight, positioning themselves beneath their victims before pouring explosive cannon shells into the bomb bays and fuel tanks, causing the aircraft to explode. British aircrew mistakenly assumed that the hideous sight of a descending garland of fire was a new form of anti-aircraft shell that they called a 'scarecrow' rather than the blazing remains of yet another bomber and its crew.

In the First World War, pilots in the nascent Royal Flying Corps, predecessor to the RAF, weren't issued with parachutes in the belief that, overcome by terror, they might simply bail out of their aircraft. Even though they were provided in the Second, they offered no guarantee of escape from an aircraft or a simple descent after. A bomber hurtling to earth, sometimes in a crazed spin, shattered by cannon fire or flak, exerted such strong g-forces that crew were often unable to move towards an escape hatch and were pinned in place against the sides, floor or roof of the fuselage. If they did manage to parachute down, or survive a crash landing, airmen had to face the wrath of civilians whose towns and cities they had been bombing. Some were lynched.

The men who flew these operations over Germany and Occupied Europe night after night were among the bravest who fought in the Second World War. Bomber Command was the most dangerous part of the British armed forces. Of the 384,000 British, Empire and Dominions servicemen killed during the Second World War, 55,573 were from Bomber Command. Given that there were only 125,000 aircrew in Bomber Command during the war, this is a staggering proportion. Every nation that made up this multi-national force suffered. Two per cent of Australia's men in uniform were in Bomber Command, yet they made up 23 per cent of that nation's casualties. Fifty-eight per cent of Canadian volunteers were killed, along with 977 Poles. Of the 495 volunteer aircrew from the Caribbean, a third died. Nearly 20,000 further aircrew were either wounded or taken prisoner. As each Bomber Command volunteer had to fly a tour of thirty operations, the chances of him surviving were incredibly low. Only 24 per cent made it to 1945 entirely unscathed – physically, at least. The average age of the dead was just twenty-two.

Bomber Command aircrew seemed to be the polar opposite to conscientious objectors like my grandpa, who, while they were facing a strong probability of being blown out of the sky, was safe at home with his Bible and his prayers. I wanted to know what made them take to the sky to follow the ultra-modern romantic dream of flight, but to use it to rain steel and high explosive destruction down onto people they had never met. I went looking for answers on the map.

# STRENGTH IN UNITY

The scars left on our cities by the Luftwaffe have been gentrified out of existence; those few bombsites and gaps in the houses that I knew when I first moved to London have mostly been filled. The Second World War largely left rural Britain alone in terms of violence, but paradoxically, its topography holds traces that endure to this day. As Dan Billany put it in *The Trap*, when writing about how one day his army base in Cornwall will be empty of men but never quite vanish into the landscape, 'Nature has a long memory.'

Take a satellite view trip up the eastern counties of England on your phone or computer and, among the rich browns, greens and yellows, you'll find the occasional geometric anomaly in the landscape, like a giant Viking rune. Sometimes these are three lines that meet to form a triangle and might be made of wide concrete strips, narrow paths or perhaps just an unusual arrangement in hedges and field boundaries. Often, they appear as crop marks, where a building, paved area or structure has been removed but disturbance in the soil has affected the growth of vegetation. These are the ghosts of the hundreds of airfields built in Great Britain during the Second World War, when millions of tonnes of concrete and tarmac gobbled up requisitioned agricultural land to provide stations for the RAF first to defend the country, and then, as the war went on, to take the fight to Germany. For the obvious reasons of flat terrain and the proximity to the continent across the North Sea, most of these airfields were up the east coast, in a thick stripe from Suffolk and Norfolk up through Cambridgeshire and Lincolnshire to East Yorkshire. Many of the airfields in East Anglia were given over to the United States Army Air Forces, while the Lincolnshire and East Yorkshire stations became best known for being home to the RAF's Bomber Command.

I wish I'd known just how many of these airfields were still extant during the height of my RAF fever. A few minutes before it whizzed past Hendon Air Museum, I would peer out of the train to London at the old runways of Radlett Aerodrome, where Handley Page built Halifax bombers, but a factory wasn't as exciting as an active military base. On holidays in the north and east of England we must have passed many of them, sitting cold and unused in the flat landscape, but hidden from the car windows by low hedges. I remember staying in some dilapidated huts on the edge of an old airfield on a church away weekend in Suffolk. I drove go-karts on a track that used part of a former runway and sneaked off to explore some old bunkers. As my eyes adjusted to the gloom, I realised that it was filled with the carcasses and skulls of hundreds of rabbits. The stench of death filled my nose and I ran out gagging.

Neil Thomson, known to his friends as Tommo, is my main aviation enthusiast pal. He lives around the corner from me in north-east London and over the lockdowns of 2020 we'd go for walks around the local area, talking about aeroplanes and weathering tips for the model kits that were just about keeping us sane in our confinement. He invented the brilliant term 'Garden Centre Nationalism' that seems to sum up so much of Britain's relationship with the

Second World War – those displays near the tills in horticultural retail establishments with books about *BRITISH* tractors and *BRIT-ISH* cars and *BRITISH* sheds where you might also be able to buy a cheaply produced DVD series about Nazi tanks or the Holocaust, a Keep Calm & Carry On Weeding mug or a Live Laugh Love wall-hanging.

Even when society started to open up, for various reasons Tommo and I both had to be more cautious than most, and the kit-building and walks continued. Tommo grew up in East Yorkshire in the 1980s, in a time where there were still derelict wartime airfields all over the local area. He learned to drive on the expanses of old concrete and would wander round the ruins taking drugs and pot shots at rabbits. It led to a lifelong fascination with aeroplanes that eventually fed into his photography, documenting the lives and work of air-sea rescue and anti-submarine aircrew in the Sea Kings and Nimrods of the modern RAF, but also a more personal project. A few years ago, when his dad was a patient in a hospital in Hull, Tommo would make regular trips up and down the A1 (he called it 'Thunder Road'), stopping off to photograph what remained of these places from which many young men took off never to return, publishing the pictures under the title 'Phantom Fields and Ghost Squadrons'. He'd told me about a particular war memorial at RAF Lissett, one of the stations nearest to the North Sea and, in endless hours wandering Google Maps, I became obsessed with the place and the men who flew from it.

158 Squadron has one of the few remaining active squadron associations, originally set up by veterans of the unit but now run by their descendants. Its website revealed that a surprising number of the Squadron's pilots and aircrew had become writers. The conflict was a terrific enabler of creativity – penning memoirs, novels and scripts was a way of processing what they had been through, of placing meaning on their experiences. I spent months

during the Covid-19 confinement buying and reading as many of these books as I could. I downloaded 158 Squadron's war diaries from the National Archives, reading accounts of their raids, the names of German and French cities occurring and reappearing as if intoned, the laconic use of 'gardening' for operations laying mines ('vegetables') off the coast of Europe. Time was marked out by the fading and then blotting of type as the ink ribbon dried out and was replaced, recording formal debriefs about engine trouble and coolant leaks, flak damage, ice-frozen guns, thick cloud or fog. The destruction on the ground is both vividly precise – 'a church spire was noticed ablaze' – or vast 'fires still visible half way back across Channel'. There are reports of crash landings and the occasional burst of aircrew lingo – one raid is described as a 'jolly good show'. More poignant are the endless lists of names of airmen – Fletcher, Jeffrey, Reid, Lomas, Mann, Goodwill, Skidmore, Skinner, Sangren, Crawford, Warr – appearing for operation after operation until, one day, some of them didn't, their fate recorded long ago in the crack of a typewriter's key. From that moment on, they were no longer a matter of military record but, somewhere, personal grief. I downloaded the photographs taken from bombers above their targets during raids, images of intricately patterned and jagged grayscale light that looked more like abstract art than anything martial, yet each bright line representing fire, high explosives and unimaginable destruction. As I read, I zoomed in and out of Google Maps, travelling across the squadron airfields, now scars in the agricultural patchwork of East Yorkshire, looking for traces of hangers, bomb dumps, accommodation blocks. It was this terrain that the thousands of men of 158 Squadron would call their home – for some, their final home – for three years of the Second World War.

158 Squadron was formed at Driffield on St Valentine's Day 1942. They flew Wellington bombers on their first operation from

RAF Pocklington on the same day, attacking Mannheim. In June 1942, the squadron switched to four engine Halifax bombers, an aircraft you won't see loaded with the soubriquet 'iconic' like the Avro Lancaster, star of the Dambusters raid. 158 Squadron then shifted to RAF East Moor, then RAF Rufforth in November 1942, before moving to the new airfield at Lissett in February 1943, where they remained until the end of the war. If you look on a map, the stations that 158 Squadron flew from sit in a line, from just west of the City of York out east towards the seaside resort of Bridlington.

The sites of airfields are the closest thing that Britain has to twentieth-century battlefields. By walking them, I reasoned, perhaps I could connect them to the words written by these young men, to try to understand how, night after night, they could leave this unremarkable and sleepy part of the English countryside to risk their lives in the thundering, flashing void over Occupied Europe. That peaceful existence by day might sometimes have seemed more unreal than the hours of danger in the dark.

As soon as Covid-19 restrictions eased in the summer of 2021, I drove up the A1, through Bomber Country, to find them. This is a largely flat terrain made up of huge fields of wheat, barley and potatoes, more reminiscent of America than the English pastoral, especially in the summer when puffs of clouds drift across the horizon like piped icing. The roads wind around, cars slow behind tractors and lorries with oversized loads of static caravans, built at factories on the outskirts of Hull. They reminded me of photographs from the 1940s of low loaders growling through the landscape with dismembered sections of bomber aircraft riding on their backs.

Leaving my B&B, where two retired couples who'd been strangers to one another until that morning's cornflakes droned on about traffic, Boris Johnson and the state of their eggs, I drove out of York towards the site of RAF Rufforth, the most westerly of 158 Squadron's airfields. Here, one of the wartime runways is still in use by light aircraft. I set out along the public footpath that runs along its edge. The towers of York Minster were thick blocks in the distance above a line of trees, a symbol that must have seemed impossibly ancient and secure against the moving silhouettes of bombers taking off on an operation. Where the runways once met was a scatter of feathers and a farm truck bounced along what was the perimeter track. The old control tower sat squat but battered in front of dull green agricultural sheds, with signs warning sightseers to keep away. The tarmac laid over wartime concrete was a patchwork of greys encroached by tall weeds, dandelions rising from the fissures, forget-me-nots, thistles, fool's parsley and a few ears of barley from a previous crop. Scattered gently through them was the crimson of poppies.

From the end of the runway, a thin whine joined the sounds of gulls, mewing buzzard and a church bell somewhere nearby as it rang out for a quarter to ten. An aeroplane, a light trainer or glider tug, taxied slowly past. I stopped and sat on the grass to watch as it reached the runway's end and turned around. The engine increased in volume as the pilot opened the throttle and the little plane accelerated along the runway towards me, wings bouncing, propeller a blurred disc of light. Even this tiny civilian aeroplane set off a childlike tingle of excitement as the negotiation between gravity and forward motion was eventually won by lift and it unpeeled itself from the ground, crosswind making it sideslip as it climbed away. We can take the surreal thrill of flight a little lightly in the age of EasyJet, but up close the hairs on the back of my neck tingled as I thought of what a complex emotion it must have been for the men of Bomber Command, in their early twenties mostly, to lift off into the heavens. If it looked a struggle for this small aircraft, what must it have been to be inside a Wellington or Halifax fully loaded with fuel and bombs for an operation to a target as far away as Italy?

They might have been dressed in identical uniforms, but the typewritten legacy of the men who flew with 158 Squadron between Valentine's Day 1942 and New Year's Day 1946 reveals that their motivation and understanding of the time they were living through was varied and unique. James Campbell's wartime experiences as a bomb aimer inspired two novels, *Bomber Stream Broken* and *Maximum Effort*, which was described by the *Sunday Mail* as 'The *Cruel Sea* of the air'. As well as these racy thrillers that I would have lapped up had I found them as a kid, Campbell wrote a pacey factual account of the Nuremberg raid of the night of 30 March 1944, on which weather, moonlight and tactics combined to create a disastrous night for Bomber Command. Of the 779 aircraft sent out, 105 did not return, including four from 158 Squadron.

Like most Bomber Command squadrons, 158 was an international outfit. There were Canadians, Australians, New Zealanders, South Africans, Poles and, thanks to the RAF going back on its colour bar in October 1939 to allow non-white servicemen to fly in mixed crews, men from Jamaica, Trinidad and Ceylon, now Sri Lanka. Ekanayake Amerasekera was awarded the Distinguished Flying Cross for being a 'navigator of outstanding ability' who had 'displayed a high degree of courage and determination', including on one operation successfully getting his Halifax to the target and back despite the failure of his oxygen supply. By the end of the war, he had completed fifty-two operations. When peace came and he returned home, Amerasekera eventually became Air Vice Marshal in the then-Ceylon Air Force and a writer of religious tracts. He had volunteered for the RAF 'in search of adventure and I had an abundance of it.' He had fitted 'many lifetimes' into his service, and the strange duality of existence had a profound impact on him. 'I found myself in the midst of death and destruction, in the thick of fun and gaiety,' he wrote in one of his religious pamphlets, 'I understood joy and sorrow, as I saw them then, amidst life and death. I had friends today and they were gone tomorrow. I became callous and insensitive to finer feelings. I began to live for the day. Money, friends, everything was only for the day. At the end of so much death and destruction and the release of pent-up feelings and nervous tensions within me, I began to wonder what this was all about.' Reflecting on why he had survived and so many others perished, Amerasekera embarked on a lifelong search for meaning via reading, thinking and meditation to the point where, 'An understanding of Karma now points to me the true significance and purpose of life.'

In a similar vein, Kenneth Skidmore's *Follow the Man with the Pitcher* is as much a sermon as it is a military memoir – after the war, Skidmore became a Methodist preacher, like my dad. The conviction of this man of faith who did fight is as strong as that of my grandpa who did not. On 11 November 1943, Skidmore's Halifax H-Harry was hit by flak and shot down on an operation to bomb a railway junction near Cannes and to drop poppies on French towns on the way back. To leap out of a doomed aircraft and then evade capture while making the long march to Spain with your mind full of the glory of God and the vow to read a Psalm every day is not a narrative that tends to feature in war films or fiction, but that is the zeal that propels Skidmore's extraordinary book, and what became for him 'a personal spiritual revelation'. The emotions and struggles of survival and escape are often of simple, humanist energies of resilience, despair, fear, fortitude, a focus on the physical sensations of pain, hunger, cold. Skidmore's short book possesses the strength in Christianity that resonates with me from my own upbringing and throws open the question of how, in a more religious age, faith bent, strengthened or broke for men who endured these unimaginable privations. While for many, the carnage of the two world wars made for proof of the absence of God, I find the conviction of those for whom faith remained twice as fascinating, for there is no transcendence in nihilism. Skidmore's spiritual belief is a bond both metaphysical, between God and humanity, and fraternal. In the epilogue to *Follow the Man with the Pitcher*, Skidmore pays tribute to the pilot of H-Harry, Arthur Evans, who died to save him. 'I can still see him struggling to hold the plane in his control as I helped him on with his parachute while he urged me, the last of his crew, to "Go!".' He ends his book by quoting from the gospel of John, chapter 15, verse 13: 'greater love hath no man than this, that a man lay down his life for his friends'.

In the archives at the Imperial War Museum is a box of material from Geoffrey Dawson, who turned his life at war into art. I lingered on an etching of a Halifax bomber powering through flak and searchlights, the marks of his tools vividly scratching the kinetic energy of explosives and light into the deep black background. The etchings, drawings and paintings are accompanied by an unpublished memoir in which he wrote of his comfort growing up in 1930s Manchester, his security in the natural social order and a love of his country. It was when Dawson saw a student at his architectural school who had signed up with the RAF that he was overcome with 'wonder' at the sight of this 'paragon of smartness and unique attainments now before us'. To fly seemed 'incomparably more interesting and potentially romantic than one which condemned its units to creeping about the ground like frightened mice, hastening from cover to cover. Better by far to soar like eagles in the light and sunshine, playing hide and seek in the clouds or ride swiftly across the countryside hopping over hedges and trees with the multiplied swiftness of ten greyhounds.' Dawson trained as a bomb aimer, joining 158 Squadron at Lissett in 1943 and flying his first operation against a Dunlop rubber factory on 15 September. He wrote his memoir because he felt that 'most accounts I have ever seen appear to incline towards the bitterness of unfulfilled purpose, or supposed injustice, that youth should be killed before it had hardly tasted of manhood [. . .] But in general, that is not how it was. It was all much simpler and more innocent for all we always thought ourselves wise as serpents and never gave a thought to the gentleness of doves.'

In May 1945, Dawson flew over the ruins of some of the cities he and his comrades had bombed. His words capture the shock at what he saw: '[Mannheim] has gone. It just simply does not exist any more. I really mean it. A city as large as Manchester has gone, has been utterly and hopelessly wiped off the map. Without seeing it I could not have believed it.'

In 1995, Harry Lomas published *One Wing High*, one of the best Bomber Command memoirs I've read. Where Dawson wrote that he and his comrades did not hate the enemy, but rather pitied them, Lomas tells of a fellow RAF recruit called Michael, a gregarious, worldly man who joined the service due to his loathing of the Germans. 'I hate the bastards. All of them,' Michael told him. He had lost his home and family during the London Blitz, and ever since had been desperate for revenge. During German raids, Michael told Lomas, he'd stand in the street and shake his fists at the sky shouting, 'Your day will come, you murdering swine!' Lomas says, however, that this vengeful bitterness was rare among his comrades in Bomber Command. Like Dawson, his own motivation was simply a fascination with flying, and an article he read about a bomber crew in which they all seemed stylish, handsome and photogenic. He had no animosity towards the enemy – after all, his Aunt Elfreide was German. Her husband, a merchant navy officer, had been killed by a German U-Boat, her home had been destroyed in the Luftwaffe's blitz on Liverpool and in Hamburg, her parents were under attack by the very air force that her nephew was about to join.

Lomas has an eye for picking up on the rough edges of the men, a piquant ability to capture the mundane privations – fried Spam and a rubbery disc of powdered egg for breakfast, the atmosphere of the Nissen huts where thousands of men spent their days waiting to fly and die in 'an early morning miasma of stale smoke, cold ashes and damp blankets'. He writes of snogging WAAFS, of the boredom and the fear, the frustration at rules and regs and the censorship of letters – 'all I've got to write about is my bowel movements and my wet dream!' Lomas's writing is sensory and sensitive; he understands the rituals of masculinity that were part of staying alive and simply coping with the terrible likelihood that he wouldn't. Once he arrived at RAF Lissett on 3 December 1944, he found that the days seemed to drift. The aircrew were not required to carry out drill or attend church services, so the week was defined purely by the schedule of operations, the serviceability of aircraft and so on. Time itself had become subservient to the needs of war.

*One Wing High* is a tender and sometimes witty tribute to the men Lomas flew with in 158 Squadron – men he didn't always know. A bomber model kit comes with five, six, seven plastic men to paint and glue into place. Now and then, you'd get a figure designed without legs so he could easily fit into a gun turret (something that feels a little grotesque when I think of a passage in Len Deighton's intense novel *Bomber*, in which a mid-upper gunner is chopped in half by flak). Each was identical, lined up attached to their plastic sprue by legs and feet. By focusing on the narratives of comradely brotherhood, war films and fictions often ignore the anonymity of the military experience. Lomas, nearly better than anyone I've read, captures both.

Camaraderie was what would keep the men of Bomber Command alive. This was reflected in 158 Squadron's motto, 'Strength in Unity', and the crest of seven links of a chain, representing the seven members of a Halifax bomber's crew. A gunner's tired eyes might miss the shadow of an approaching night fighter. A pilot needed split-second reflexes to corkscrew the huge aircraft out of the beam of a searchlight or gun sights of the Luftwaffe. Dodgy calculations by the navigator or flight engineer could mean flying miles the wrong direction out into the North Sea or running out of fuel short of home. Lomas writes of how each crew, their fate so mutually dependent, had a relationship often fuelled by booze and banter – during training, six pints a night each. After an evening out with his newly forged crew, drinking with American troops, eating burgers, taking the piss out of his new captain for being Australian, Lomas lay in bed, unable to sleep, reflecting on the day. The ritual of finding a crew had felt lighthearted, but on reflection he realised that it had a deeper significance. The decisions made and groups formed in a spirit of banter and playfulness were 'quite literally matters of life and death', and fate would decide that unfortunate alliances meant some of these young men were doomed even before they flew their first operation. He dismisses this 'morbid thought', choosing instead to reflect that 'we were committed to live, work and play together as a bomber crew, the most integrated fighting unit of all.' This unique comradeship might form friendships that, so long as they survived the war, could endure for the rest of their lives.

This closeness within crews, their status as a hermetic unit, was vital because, in a large airfield like Lissett with accommodation dispersed around the base, it was impossible to know everyone. Lomas recalls going to the station intelligence library to look over photographs taken on operations. Also pinned to the walls were pictures of aircrew who had failed to return. As often the different crews didn't know one another, this was the only way of putting a name to a face no longer seen through the cigarette and pipe smoke of the mess.

It wasn't just combat that provided the full gamut of intense emotion and sensation that would stick with these young men through their lives. On a training exercise that, bedevilled by bad weather, nearly went terribly wrong, Lomas 'seemed to have gone through the full range of human feelings and emotions. Optimism, hope, doubt, discomfort, frustration, anger, pessimism, anxiety, nausea, fear, despair, terror, elation and thankfulness. In that order. Everything in fact, except religious mania or sexual gratification. Now I just wanted to forget it all.' He also understood the strange ways in which men tried to cope. Dark humour was one, the laconic use of 'getting the chop' or 'going for a Burton' for being killed in action.

Lomas recalled his first briefing for an operation with 158. At the end, a morose Canadian flying officer called Samuels, would perform his 'party piece' to jeering from the assembled navigators – an assessment of the likely losses on the operation. He pointed around the room, announcing that 'Sammy says tonight one crew meets the Grim Reaper. Just the one. But it might be you, or you, or you!' Encountering this macabre ritual for the first time during the briefing for his first bombing raid from RAF Lissett was perturbing enough. Lomas was then told that Flying Officer Samuels often got his predictions spot on.

These were men who never expected to be writers, but through the war found a voice. The one who always wanted to write, though, did not survive. Bertram James Warr was born 7 December 1917 in Toronto, Canada, the second son in a family of six. With university beyond his financial means, Warr took a job as a clerk, all the while studying an evening class in journalism. Frustrated by office life, he moved to Muskoka, a rural area of woodland and lakes, to spend a summer as a hotel porter. There, he made the decision to move to England to follow his dream of becoming a writer. Warr had a friend who wanted to cross the Atlantic to join the RAF as the likelihood of war loomed. The two young men travelled together to Halifax, Nova Scotia, where they worked in a restaurant (and were paid in meals) while Warr's pal earned some money as a photographer's assistant. Unable to find a berth and a job on a transatlantic cargo ship, the duo stowed away on a liner on Christmas Eve 1938, only to be caught the next day. Rather than setting them ashore, the captain employed the stowaways as stewards for the duration of the voyage to Liverpool, where they then hitched a ride to London with a truck driver. Warr washed dishes in a café before getting a job as a clerk to an oyster company at Billingsgate fish market, enabling him to enrol in writing classes at Birkbeck college.

When war was declared nine months after his arrival in London, Warr decided to remain in England. He considered himself a pacifist, writing that he was 'against the war as it is for capitalist profits only', and became a fire-watcher during the Blitz, scouring the rooftops for German incendiaries. In 'The Outcasts of Society', an essay eventually published many decades later, Warr wrestled with the position of pacifists, who, whether motivated by religion, intellect, science or left-wing politics, found themselves 'branded as shirkers, traitors, or simply madmen' by a society at war. The tormented man of peace, separated by his views from the rest of public opinion, had three options. One, die for his principles. Two, stick firmly to them, ready to accept 'the universal oppression that is his portion'. There was a third way, however, one that Warr believed was the most 'rational' – to realise that he had to 'compromise with the mass view' and amend his position. Warr thought that for the political and religious pacifist, like my grandpa, this would be 'a surrender of his most vital convictions' and therefore impossible. For the sociologist or anthropologist, the war might be an opportunity to remodel society in a radical, revolutionary way, yet, in the end, 'No participation in war is possible for him.

He has a higher duty.' It's a strange, convoluted essay that, I think, is an articulation of the young, idealistic Canadian's own internal wrangling over his moral beliefs as to his involvement in the war.

He tried and failed to join the Red Cross, often an option for men hoping to avoid combat for pacifist reasons, but when called up for military service in the summer of 1941, he made his own 'compromise with the mass view' and joined the Royal Air Force Volunteer Reserve. In his small blue diary, Warr scribbled names of girls, addresses, thoughts about metaphysics and class politics alongside mundane things to do – on Friday 13 June there is a now-haunting note, 'next of kin Father change address to be notified'.

Warr was described in the TLS by John Gawsworth, who served with him for a couple of months in the RAF, as 'frail in appearance, a very *"parfait gentil"* serious young man.' Shortly before he disappeared into the confinements and strictures of military life, Warr published a broadsheet of poems called *Yet a Little Onwards*. In his introductory essay, Warr railed against an 'age of renunciation' in which 'nothing much matters any more'. The Depression and war were 'successive shocks' that 'have proved too much for us'. Against this turmoil, Warr argued that, 'No wars, no universal upheavals must be allowed to drive out the fineness that is in men.' In this zeal, Warr's poetry and notebooks fizz with the youthful energy of a man trying to get to grips with who he was, the war and his intensity of feeling. His handwriting has an outré flare and flourish, just the sort of thing I remember attempting as a young man trying to conjure gravitas when putting down my thoughts, as if great inky loops would instil them with poetic wisdom. I sense a man overwhelmed by the world, his desire to set it down earnestly, and now. Warr's poetry is ambitious in its subject matter – an absent God, the mourning of dead children, class, corrupters of religion, the eternal existentialism of the young man writing who is 'as lonely as the universe'. A moral anguish with his latent Catholicism comes though on the pages of his notebooks too, with a two-line and somewhat pompous poem about sex – 'Loins of the man, thou inmost secret gives / Where lurks dark passion, votary of Sin' – contrasted with the word 'PHOOEY!' written in large letters after it, popping the pomposity. Warr's poetry in *Yet a Little Onwards* had a potential that started to reach the literary establishment. Robert Graves wrote to him, 'It was a great pleasure in times like these to know that there is another poet about. As you must be aware, it is always a small number.'

Around 24 October 1941, Bertram James Warr, poet, became Warr, 1391138, Royal Air Force Volunteer Reserve. His diary notes change in tone and content. In November, there are scrawls on the centre of gravity and the application of force in pale ink alongside one of his characteristic 'statements' in black: 'I disclose hypocrisy.' The trainee man of the air and the thinker become blurred together on thin blue paper. Where the other writers of 158 Squadron had the benefit of time passing, reflection and the desire to create their own narratives of what they'd endured, Warr's earnest immediacy is what makes the youthful energy in his notebooks, essays and poetry so powerful. There's an unguarded sincerity and a naivety to his writing that strikes me, in our more open, confessional, emotionally driven age, as surprisingly modern.

The war sits as a backdrop to his writing, in the direct address of the description of a blitzed and empty London street in 'Stepney 1941', and in a poem questioning the glorification of the war dead in monuments and poets in a time of war, written in memory of Wilfred Owen. It appears too in his work on sex and relationships. In 'Discord', he is surprised when for the first time he is told he is loved, a moment of beauty amid 'the familiar, monotonous beat / Of clash and retreat'. The strange duality of the airman's existence, who, unlike most servicemen, was able to see his partner around duties, shapes 'The Heart to Carry On'. Warr bids farewell to a lover with a kiss and a wish for her contented sleep, asking that she 'Pray tomorrow I may be / Close, my love, within these arms, / And not lie dead in Germany'.

Bertram Warr was posted to 158 Squadron at RAF East Moor on 24 September 1942, his role a bomb aimer in the crew of a Halifax II. He joined the unit at a terrible time. Between March and August 1942, the Halifax squadrons of No. 4 Group had been running at an unsustainable loss rate of 6.2 per cent on each operation. Of the 158 Squadron crews who had attacked Bremen on 25 June, half would be dead or missing within six weeks. Five aircraft and their crews had failed to return from an operation to Berlin on 23 August, and four more were lost on a trip to the same city on the last night of the month. Bertram Warr was one man among many who was dispatched to replace them. What must it have been like for this young man who so intensely disliked war, travelling to York, pulling into its grand station and then being driven out past the ancient city walls through the countryside to his new home, a place where he was just a new face fitting into the ghost of a man who had vanished over Germany? What must it have been like on his first mission to know that he had the fate of men and women on the ground in his hands? In his poetry, we have a glimpse of the internal wrestling that led to Bertram Warr becoming the human element in a machine of mass destruction. As a fire-watcher during the Blitz on London, he would have had no illusions about what these could do to cities.

Warr would have seen Occupied Europe unfold from his position lying prone in the front of his Halifax bomber, a perfectly clear oval of Triplex glass in the nose giving him a vivid view of exploding flak, probing searchlights and the flicker of deadly tracer bullets from German night fighters. Peering through the bomb sight, the nocturnal gloom would have been lit by flares as the aircraft approached its target, a city, with its houses, factories, churches, schools illuminated in fire. It was Warr's instructions – port, starboard, a little more, a little less – that would have guided the aircraft until it was time for him to release its payload of high explosives and incendiaries down onto the streets below.

His life through that autumn and winter into early 1943 does not appear in his own writing, but instead can be traced through the type in 158 Squadron's Operational Records Book. Warr's name appears as bomb aimer in various aircraft through entries reporting raids on Cologne, Genoa, Turin, Duisburg, Lorient. There are details of planting 'vegetables' on 'gardening' raids off the German coast, an aborted operation to Frankfurt after a delayed take-off due to a gunner's aircraft intercom becoming unserviceable – the crew decided to turn back ten miles after crossing the English coast at Dungeness. Too many aborted raids for faulty equipment could result in the suspicion of senior officers.

After the unit departed East Moor, Warr flew from the runway I had walked alongside at RAF Rufforth. On 6 December 1942, the night before his twenty-fifth birthday, he flew on a raid to Mannheim. At one point his bomber was followed by a German night fighter, which was shaken off, though the risk was not yet over – short of fuel, the crew were forced to land at Middle Wallop. In the early spring of 1943, after a spell away at a training unit, he arrived at Lissett to reunite with the rest of the squadron. After a horrendous four winter months during which nine crews had been lost on operations and a further two in crashes in the United Kingdom, the shift to the new airfield was welcome – one pilot, Sgt Sandgreen, recorded in his diary, 'This move had a wonderful effect on the squadron's morale [. . .] everyone was in a better state of mind.' Operations, though, were just as dangerous as ever. Heavily damaged by flak on the 29 March, Warr's Halifax returned to base early with holes in the port wing, fuselage, upper turret and an engine out of action.

At some point, Warr began writing a painful, heartbreaking essay with the opening line, 'This is to be the story of a death, my own.' He predicted that he had just six months to a year left before his 'desire to die' would be realised. Though he was consumed by this morbid state of mind, Warr wrote that he would not commit suicide 'like some unsophisticated savage, believing himself touched by a dread spell', but was convinced that he would be killed in the war. All that was left in an existence that seemed to him to have no meaning was to continue with 'this new purpose for life, to adjust itself to the business of dying'. He would not have long to wait.

# DEAD MEN'S BEDS

Saturday, 3 April 1943 had been a warm but cloudy day at RAF Lissett, the East Yorkshire countryside pushing its way into spring under a gloomy sky. In the afternoon, Sergeant Bertram Warr made his way across the airfield, perhaps on foot, maybe by bike, to the briefing for that night's raid on the city of Essen, location of the huge Krupp steel and munition works vital to the German war effort. So central was the company to the German masculine martial identity that in a speech to the Hitler Youth, the Führer said that the nation's boys must in the future be 'hard as Krupp steel'. Essen was part of the sprawl of industrial towns along the banks of the river Ruhr, defended by ranks of searchlights and flak guns, its skies patrolled by deadly German night fighters directed onto target by powerful radars and radio coordination. The Ruhr area was, with the bleak and ironic humour typical of Bomber Command, known as Happy Valley.

As the light faded to the west, Warr and the six other young men of his crew climbed into a truck to be driven across the expanse of the airfield to where their Halifax – call sign NP-F, F-Freddie – awaited them, heavily laden with aviation fuel, two

1,000lb bombs to shatter walls and windows and nearly 600 incendiaries to set the broken buildings ablaze. They clambered aboard, bulkily dressed to keep out the cold at high altitude, and laden down with parachutes, flasks of coffee or Bovril, sandwiches and chocolate. Perhaps some of the crew carried good luck charms – soft toys, St Christophers, four-leafed clovers, rabbit feet, trinkets from wives or lovers.

Their aircraft left the ground at 19:42, three minutes after sunset, the sound of their engines receding into the gloom over the North Sea as RAF Lissett fell silent. Halifax DT635 F-Freddie joined 347 aircraft – Lancasters, Halifaxes and a few Mosquitos – in the bomber stream heading to Germany. The beams from German Freya and Wurzburg radars probed the darkness over the water, invisible fingers that touched the metal of the bombers and sent signals back to concrete bunkers, blips and blotches appearing on the oscilloscopes of their Luftwaffe operators. They tracked the force as it crossed the Dutch coast at Egmond aan Zee and flew inland towards the German town of Dorsten, where it made the turn south to begin the final bomb run to Essen. 158 Squadron's records and Bomber Command Night Raid Reports give a fine level of detail of what happened on that raid, from the clouds en-route to maps of where bomb loads impacted the city. The 158 Squadron Halifaxes that had taken off at a similar time to F-Freddie arrived over Essen shortly before 22:00, finding visibility surprisingly good and the bombing accurate, with large fires on the ground. They dropped their loads, then turned back to the north towards Haltern am See and west again to recross the Dutch coast and head home to land at RAF Lissett in the cold early hours. F-Freddie was not among them. Luftwaffe records suggest that around 23:20 local time, the bulk of the four-engine bomber drifted into the sights of a Bf 110 night fighter piloted by Major Werner Streib.

There are enough powerful, moving, intense accounts by

aircrew who had lucky escapes from air-to-air combat to speculate on the final moments of the crew of F-Freddie. In Len Deighton's novel *Bomber*, he goes into such intricate, physiological detail of the process of death in an aircraft destroyed by cannon fire that it reads to me as gratuitous. I try to resist this macabre instinct to imagine violence and hold in my mind instead the names of those who died. Sergeant Bertram Warr, bomb aimer; Flight Lieutenant John Cole, pilot; Sergeant Ronald Gowing, flight engineer; Pilot Officer Ronald Stemp, navigator; Sergeant Albert Ward, wireless operator; Sergeant William Robinson, mid-upper gunner and Pilot Officer Clifford Dawson, tail gunner were all marked in the 158 Squadron Operational Records Book as 'Missing from air operations and posted to No.1 Depot, Uxbridge.' I find this sentence, repeated for so many unfortunate men, referring to their removal from the strength of the squadron and the transferring of the administration of their effects, incredibly haunting, imagining the Depot, in actuality the administrative hub of the Royal Air Force, as a netherworld, populated by the ghosts of dead airmen. The bodies of Warr and his comrades were eventually interred at the Rheinberg War Cemetery, their final resting place marked by white stones. Major Streib claimed F-Freddie as his forty-seventh victory, the third Halifax he had brought down within the space of just one hour out of a total of twenty-one RAF aircraft lost on the raid. After the war, in which he shot down nearly seventy aircraft, killing hundreds of men, Streib went on to train pilots in the new West German air force, Britain's NATO allies.

Many years later, a deeply heartfelt and tender poem written by Warr's friend Patricia Ledward appeared as a preface to *Acknowledgement to Life*, the sole posthumous anthology of the young airman's poetry, published in 1970, thanks to the efforts of his sister, Mary. Ledward wishes someone could write Warr's epitaph with the satire of Siegfried Sassoon and the feeling of

Wilfred Owen to do justice to this young man who hated war, who was kind in word and deed to those who suffered, who saw the irony in his own task when young German men just like him were attacking London. In a poignant exchange between the dead and a friend left bereaved, half of the poem is based on words that Warr had said to Ledward after a raid, telling her not to dread his passing, believing that the individual death was just a small moment in the wider tragedy of the war. He had told her that he found a comfort in the 158 Squadron motto, Strength in Unity, in becoming one of the seven links in the chain depicted on its crest.

> In a bomber one is not alone,
> Courage is met with quietness and all
> The members of the crew are strong,
> And all for one another,
> And that is how the end would come.

I drove east from RAF Rufforth, where Warr had flown his first combat operation, to the Yorkshire Air Museum, situated at another former Bomber Command station, RAF Elvington. The control tower was painted camouflage greens, the grass mown; old sheds and Nissen huts housed different displays and exhibits. In the chapel, flags crowded the pulpit and the prayer cushions all had the crests of bomber squadrons carefully embroidered by volunteers.

The exhibit I'd come to see was in the main hanger. After Bertram Warr's aircraft failed to return in the early hours of 4 April 1943, the order would have gone out to send a replacement to RAF Lissett. It too would have been given the code letters NP-F, assigned a crew and begun operations. It too was shot down, replaced and the grim cycle continued – in just a year, 158 Squadron lost seven Halifax bombers with the call sign F-Freddie. In his novel *Maximum Effort*, James Campbell, who joined 158 Squadron as a bomb aimer a year after the death of Bertram Warr, used as a key plot line a bomber code letter (in his case S-Sugar) that appeared so supernaturally doomed that it was undermining the unit's morale. His fiction was based on reality. In early 1944, Pilot Officer Cliff R. R. Smith decided that the growing superstition that this appalling rate of attrition had something uncanny about it was 'stuff and nonsense'. To break the supposed curse, he deliberately made the latest F-Freddie, Halifax LV907, as 'unlucky' as possible by renaming her Friday 13th. The new name was painted on the port side of the nose with an upside-down horseshoe, skull and crossbones and a bloodied Grim Reaper scythe added for good measure, along with the motto 'As ye sow so shall ye reap', echoing Bomber Harris's infamous words of vengeance against Germany.

The charm worked. Friday 13th returned from her first operation, the disastrous Nuremberg raid of 30 March 1944. She went on to survive the war, flying a total of 128 operations and bringing two crews safely through their tours. When the conflict ended, she was part of a victory display of aircraft located in the bombed out remains of the John Lewis department store in central London before being broken up at a site much like the one Nash had painted in *Totes Meer*. Many Halifaxes taken to pieces at the Handley Page repair depot at Clifton near York were used to build prefabricated bungalows to meet the housing needs of Britain's destroyed and damaged cities. Not a single intact Halifax bomber of the 6,178 built survived into the twenty-first century. In the 1980s, a project began to construct a 'new' Halifax, and scrap sites and wrecks provided the Yorkshire Air Museum with the parts from which they built their replica of 158 Squadron's Friday 13th. Engineers collected a section of fuselage from a crashed bomber used for decades as a hen coop on Stornoway, the wings of a Hastings (a transport aircraft fairly similar to the Halifax), brand-new tail and front fuselage sections, Bristol Hercules engines from France, broken gun turrets and propeller hub parts from a wartime crash excavated in Germany. The replica is a warlike reincarnation or Frankenstein's monster, an aircraft that even more than the endlessly repaired and rebuilt S-Sugar Lancaster at Hendon, was a fake of sorts. Occasionally, Friday 13th taxies out of the hanger, Hercules engines growling, but she cannot fly. This machine is there as a symbol now, like the Tiger tank that had been so popular with selfie hunters at Tankfest. For many, any meaning that the replica has comes with the legend, the myth of power, but not for me. I looked up at the recreation of the nose art, originally chosen in a moment of bravura to break a jinx, but didn't feel the same excitement I remembered from my encounters with Lancaster S-Sugar in a similar pose at Hendon all those years before. It wasn't the machines of war that had been there that I felt drawn to now, but the words that the men who flew had left behind, and these places that had shaped them.

The drive from York to RAF Lissett would have been a final one for some of the men of 158 Squadron, maybe returning from a night out at Betty's Bar, the most popular of the pubs that the airmen made rowdy with their presence during the war. Now, on this bright summer's day, I followed the slow roads out east, towards the North Sea. It was impossible to imagine their thoughts taking a similar journey, perhaps in the back of an RAF truck, bouncing on poor suspension, or in one of the more well-to-do airmen's private cars, whirling alongside the bright hedges, dark woodlands and fields of rural England, conscious that the air that lifted leaves and carved eddies in the crops might soon be carrying them to their deaths.

From my research, I'd managed to get a pretty good idea of the layout of RAF Lissett, though according to most sources there was very little of the base remaining. Tommo had come along on the trip and we drove down the knackered slabs that had been the main entrance road to the airfield. On the left was a long, low, single-storey building, grey concrete bruised with moss, windows shattered, grass growing from the roof. We parked outside and wandered in. The building, the airfield's former guardhouse, had the musty air of abandonment familiar from years of poking my nose into the remains of wartime bunkers and pillboxes. The light was green and low, illuminating a broken piano tipped onto its side, spilling keys and hammers across the drifts of litter and leaves.

As I wandered the semi-ruin, I thought back to Harry Lomas's memoir and his recollections of arriving in the very same building so many years before. The place was full of bustling energy as the fresh-faced crew came through the door, to be dispatched to a gloomy and dusty Nissen hut where wooden shelves for home comforts had been burned during a fuel crisis. Lomas recalled how the airman sent to show them their billet apologised that it was such a state because they'd barely had time to remove the kit of the former occupants. It dawned on the new arrivals that they would be sleeping in beds vacated by a crew who had not returned from an operation. Lomas writes of being taken from the Nissen hut to the thankfully warm and lively sergeants' mess. He looks for signs of nerves and fear in men's faces, but hears only 'shop talk', conversations about a WAAF who'd had three boyfriends all killed and a fragment about a woman who'd said that 'this doesn't mean I don't love my husband and I said of course not'. Lomas remarked that 'what a fascinating story, I thought, could be woven around every one of them'.

How right he was. The guardroom of RAF Lissett was a threshold, from training to the real thing, from time on leave and the tender caress of a lover to a return to duty and, for many, from life to imminent death. I felt a shiver as I noticed that alongside some graffiti abusing the men of distant Lancashire, someone had sprayed a swastika on the wall.

Tommo and I stepped out of the hut into bright sunlight and started walking deeper into the old airfield. A four-wheel drive slowed and the window came down. A face, not entirely friendly, appeared from behind the sliding glass to firmly ask us where we were going. As ever in these circumstances, I nearly started sputtering, 'Are you the farmer? I'm not from London!' but instead explained our interest in the airfield. It was, indeed, the farmer. James Tennant's family started working this land in the 1930s, only to lose it within a few years when the RAF requisitioned it to build the airfield. They didn't get the full extent of their farmland back until the 1970s. When they did, the concrete of the runways and dispersal areas was broken up to make hardcore. Just like the ghostly metal of war machines that I feel all around us, many of the runways from which thousands of men took off for the last flight of their lives now form the base of Britain's post-war motorway network. Farmer Tennant told us about the guardhouse, claiming that the broken piano had been in use during the war. I wasn't entirely convinced. He said we were fine to carry on into the airfield and to say to anyone who asked that he'd given us permission, especially if we encountered Dave, who breaks up used cars in one of the old RAF buildings. 'I have him here to keep the bad lads away,' Tennant said with a grin. 'I wouldn't want to meet him on a dark night. You've got to meet fire with fire.' The window hummed shut and he drove on.

By the end of the war, 158 Squadron had flown on 456 operations and, including training operations, 144 aircraft were lost. In the total of 5,366 sorties, 308 men became POWs, 61 evaded capture, 851 were killed of whom 78 have no known grave. The strain of flying, the likelihood of being killed, the knowledge of the destruction being wrought on the ground had a terrible psychological impact on the men of Bomber Command. Harry Lomas recalled a new ditty, popular in singsongs when aircrew were together boozing:

> They say there's a Halifax leaving the Ruhr,
> Bound for old Blighty's shore,
> Heavily laden with petrified men,
> Prostrate and prone on the floor. . .

The coping mechanisms of superstition, song and morbid humour did not work for all. The Royal Air Force had developed its own particularly harsh way of dealing with the problem of mental breakdown among its crews, branding those who refused to fly as Lacking Moral Fibre, known as LMF. Bomber pilot Peter Johnson succinctly described this as 'gobbledegook for cowardice'. Since the formation of the RAF in the First World War, the designation of aircrew struggling to cope with the demands of their operations had been 'flying stress'. The shift to Lack of Moral Fibre seems to put the blame onto the serviceman – he was no longer suffering from the stress of his difficult, dangerous work, but failing, deficient in the essence of what was required to be a member of an elite military force. An officer diagnosed with LMF would be dismissed from the RAF, losing rank and wings, while NCOs were reduced to the lowest rank, put on lesser non-flying duties or discharged to enter the Army or the mining industry.

If a flying officer was a high-status individual in the hierarchy of glamour, sex appeal and masculinity during the Second World War in Britain, then to be deemed LMF was an unwinding too of the fibre of his identity. It also went to the heart of a certain kind of martial British male selfhood as projected by propaganda, accepted in public opinion and subsequently cemented in myth

– the private-school educated, stylish flier, a pleasing scarf at his throat and bravura in the face of death. A familiar trope from the war films and literature of my childhood was the post-raid ham and eggs and cup of tea; the idea that the experience of surviving night after terrifying night over Occupied Europe, watching aircraft disappear from the sky in a blazing star of fire then landing to wait to see who had made it back, might be washed away with a fry-up in the wan light of an English dawn. In the most brutal months of losses during the bombing campaign, gallows humour had it that the only way to finish flying was 'coffins or crackers'.

The memoirs of 158 Squadron took a dim view of the cruelty of men who ended up 'crackers' being branded as lacking 'Moral Fibre'. In *Life Is a Great Adventure*, pilot Douglas Robinson described what happened when he was about to take off for his first raid to Berlin. The rear gunner came onto the intercom to say that his Browning .303s weren't serviceable. He then claimed that his eyes weren't right, before finally admitting that he didn't think he ought to go. The Halifax bomber pulled up on the perimeter track while a senior officer came to find out what was going on, took the gunner away and delivered a replacement to the aircraft. Robinson took off, now at the very back of the bomber stream – the most dangerous place to be, as by the time he arrived over the German capital, all the flak guns and searchlights were fully alerted, and lanes of flares had been set off in the sky, silhouetting his Halifax and making it easy prey for night fighters.

Robinson's aircraft was hit. The bomb doors jammed open. The intercom failed. Fuel tanks leaked. The fuselage filled with the smell of burning rubber. Communication with the outside world was impossible as the radio equipment had been damaged. Robinson was forced to make an emergency landing in southern England, damaged tires bursting on the runway. The aircraft was so badly shot up that the crew had to endure a long journey back

up to Lissett by train, in full flying gear and carrying their Mae
West lifejackets and parachutes. Despite the close shave that the
gunner's refusal to fly had caused, Robinson was forgiving. The
rear gunner had been court-martialled, reduced to the ranks and
sentenced to eighty-four days in prison, though the incarceration
was never enforced. Writing in his memoir, Robinson reflected
that, although the RAF had to discourage men from deciding that
they could no longer fly, the air gunner had already managed to
subdue his terror sufficiently to fly on five or six operations. This
was more, he noted, than those who had condemned him had
ever done.

I am sure that many wouldn't see it as fair that my grandpa
Edwin had been excused fighting and remained safely at home
while young men were humiliated when their resolve cracked from
night after night of seeing friends and comrades disappear into the
skies over Germany. I cannot make a binary judgement between
his pacifist convictions that endured through the conflict and
Bertram Warr's decision to forgo his to drop bombs on civilians.
Instead, I hold in my heart an intense admiration for Warr, Harry
Lomas, Douglas Robinson and all the other men of 158 Squadron
and Bomber Command, just as I now admire the bravery of my
grandpa's decision not to fight. I do not believe my grandpa was
a coward. I know that he received terrible abuse from soldiers
and civilians alike while carrying out his duties as a conscientious
objector. That his principles were resolute I know from how I see
it manifested in his children and grandchildren. I might disagree
with his interpretation of Christ's teaching on war and peace but I
respect the courage of those convictions. At the time, with Britain
under fire and the threat of invasion, with Europe under the power
of Nazism and unable to liberate itself, to not do one's bit would,
to most, have seemed unconscionable. With the benefit of eighty
years of hindsight, my inclination is to believe that the right to

conscientiously object to war is part of any humane society. If we are constantly told that the wartime generation fought for our freedom, today, in the twenty-first century, then that includes the acceptance of pacifism, to refuse to take up arms.

Most of the concrete buildings that had been part of RAF Lissett were padlocked, settling into banks of nettles and brambles. Dave, scourge of the bad lads, was busy underneath a car. To the right, the place where one of the giant hangers had stood was now the base for Farmer Tennant's grain driers. The perimeter track, once wide enough to carry a fully laden bomber, has been narrowed to maximise the farmland. Ahead of us, the blades of a group of wind turbines span in the determined air. As we approached, we could see that each one had a name painted on the base of the body of the turbine tower: Friday 13th, Lily Marlene, Jane, Xpress Delivery, Blondie, Goofy's Gift, The Menace, Zombi, Maori Chief, Minnie the Moocher and Git up dem Stairs. Wind farm operators Novera Energy had named eleven of the turbines after bombers that had taken off from Lissett during the war, with one in memory of the ground crew who died in an explosion at the airfield's bomb dump on 2 July 1943, near to where the huge machines now rise from the agricultural fields. There were fragments of the farm's military past in this eco-friendly landscape: a rectangle of remaining runway, the demolished remains of a wartime building, cylinders of straw stacked up like bombs. Above them all, the turbines spun where propeller blades once bit the air.

I checked my watch and looked at the PDFs I'd saved from 158 Squadron's war diaries on my phone. At this exact moment, on the afternoon of 9 August 1944, the Halifax bombers of 158 Squadron were coming in to land after carrying out two daylight raids, one on Bois de la Haie, the other on Landes-Vieilles-et-Neuves, from where V-1 flying bombs were being launched towards London.

Would anyone flying that day have remembered Bertram Warr, the Canadian writer who spent six months with 158 Squadron before he was shot down over Germany? I suspect not. Crews would have been transferred, finished tours, marked as missing just as he had been. Anyone still at RAF Lissett in the summer of 1944 whose time had overlapped with Warr would have seen a blur of hundreds of faces pass by since he died that April night nearly a year and a half before. There wouldn't have been time, or the desire, to dwell on the past. The need to survive trumps looking back over the shoulder.

F-Freddie's descendent, Halifax LV907, Friday 13th, flew on that operation to France in August 1944, taking off at 11:15 and landing back at Lissett at 14:57. I wondered what her crew thought as the Yorkshire fields had blurred into the end of the runway where I now stood and their wheels bumped back onto terra firma. Relief, certainly, but what of the future? A worry, perhaps, that the attempt to trick chance with magic painted onto the nose of 25-odd-thousand kilograms of fragile, vibrating metal, could not hold. Seventy-eight years later to the second, wind turbine Friday 13th stood unmoving, broken, in the warm summer wind.

# THEY DON'T LIKE IT UP 'EM

Bertram Warr had taken to the skies of a country far from his home in one of the most advanced machines of his age. He had directed his Halifax to drop bombs on German cities. Maps are still scarred by his actions. One night, a tick of fate decided that his aircraft would fall into the gunsight of a German fighter, to send this young man who had been so unsure of war to his death.

Until the advent of the German V-weapons and American atomic bomb, this was war at its most distant and technologically advanced. War is always the catalyst for innovation that, paradoxically, tries to protect men by removing them from the intimacy of violence while increasing their killing capability. Tank armour, speed, manoeuvrability and firepower were all improved by the lessons of combat. In 1939, biplane aircraft that looked as if they had more in common with the First World War and early days of flight were still in service, yet the war's end was the start of the jet age. Bomb loads had increased from a few thousand pounds to atomic weapons big enough to destroy cities. But men were still men, and those who joined the Army were trained for the most primitive form of killing humans have carried out since they discovered the art of making metal – beating one another with blunt objects, or the cutting and penetration of another with a blade to cause sufficient blood loss and internal trauma that the body can no longer function. This is the side of war that we veil with our love of machines.

Operation Chariot was a British Commando raid on the Normandy dry dock at St Nazaire, exactly the sort of audacious operation that was the staple of post-war comics and thrillers and the inspiration for 1952 war film *Gift Horse*, 1968's *Attack on the Iron Coast* and Jeremy Clarkson's 2007 documentary *Jeremy Clarkson: The Greatest Raid of All Time*. Intended to deny the Germans the use of the facility to repair their battlecruiser *Tirpitz*, the plan involved ramming an old destroyer called HMS *Campbeltown* into the dock gates and blowing her up with a delay fuse once the British Commandos had been withdrawn. There is a famous photograph taken by a German propaganda unit in the aftermath of the raid of a group of Commando prisoners being escorted through the St Nazaire port area, their hands raised in surrender. One of them is Captain Micky Burn of 2 Commando, the young man who, a decade before, had so nearly been seduced by Nazism, cheekily making the V for Victory sign to show that, although he had been captured, the raid had been a success. The explosives hidden in HMS *Campbeltown* blew up not long afterwards, destroying the dock gates.

The night before, Burn's motor launch had been hit by gunfire, throwing him into the water. He was dragged onto the harbour mole, to be confronted by the prone form of a German soldier, whereupon, 'I found myself – the phrase describes someone I had not met before and never wish to meet again – bashing and bashing away at his head with the butt of my Colt revolver.' Burn, later awarded the Military Cross for his part in the raid, was captured not long after this brutal and intimate assault. If he had not been, it is likely that this would not have been his only meeting with this shadow self. Not everyone could come back from the breaking of the taboo against personal, close-quarters wounding of another human being. Yet this violence of last resort, when machines had failed and it was left for men to fight men in hand-to-hand combat, was part of British army training.

Central to the narrative in *The Long and the Short and the Tall*, the play that had shifted how I felt about being so turned on by war, was the question of how the patrol would kill their Japanese POW. Our Lee Enfield rifles came with bayonets, blunted but still sinister, and it was discomforting to wonder if they, or the next weapon on the production line, had ever been used. My character Evans is about to shoot the cowering prisoner but, fearing the noise might alert any other Japanese troops in the vicinity, is commanded to stab him instead: 'Come on lad! Use your bayonet! In his guts! Come on! Come on! You want it in between his ribs.' Evans can't do it. Bamforth, the gobby Cockney, grabs the bayonet and says, 'It's only the same as carving up a pig.'

In 1983, Kenneth Williams appeared on the chat show *Look Who's Talking* with Derek Batey. As he often did, Williams started discussing his memories of bayonet practice during his army training, describing how he was ordered to charge down a field swearing at the dummy he was to 'kill'. Williams roars 'mmmmy-wooaahhh' and mimes a bayonet thrust, and then holds up limp wrists. 'This sergeant said, "You couldn't kill a German, you'd probably kiss him."' To which Williams replied, 'Yes, why not?! Love is a splendid thing.' The sergeant, Williams continued, told him to go and make the tea.

The bayonet was the simplest weapon in the armoury of the combative nations of the Second World War – just a long spike, sharp at the end. As such, the bayonet had a relationship with ancient weapons that also doubled up as tools – it was as useful for puncturing a tin of condensed milk for a brew as it was a German or Japanese soldier. George Orwell referred to the bayonet in 1941 essay 'The Lion and the Unicorn', as he decried a British military that he felt lacked capability due to the influence of an indolent ruling class, writing, 'Even at this moment hundreds of thousands of men in England are being trained with the bayonet, a weapon entirely useless except for opening tins.'

The standard bayonet drill is familiar from war films and, at the time, cinema newsreels – men charging at sacks of hay hanging from wooden frames, with flopping heads, arms and legs. A 1941 film hailing the realism of British army training featured footage of soldiers going one better, throwing one another to the ground and mocking a rifle thrust as the narrator crisply announces, 'It's all good training for that infinitely gratifying job of "pig-sticking".' One edition of the 1937 War Office *Infantry Training: Training and War* describes bayonet combat as a key part of infantry warfare, especially in unexpected close-quarter clashes when 'bold action is the most effective, and the patrol relying on surprise should attack with the butt or bayonet before the enemy has had time to collect his wits'. The bayonet is, then, a primitive and ancient terror weapon, to be used in attack and defence. Going forward, positions should be 'rushed in silence with the bayonet without hesitation'. If it came to a last desperate stand, 'all ranks should realise that it is a disgrace to lay down their arms in the field [. . .] If ammunition is exhausted, recourse should be had to a final effort with the bayonet.' Army Training Memorandum Number 35 issued in 1940 asserted the violent masculine energies of bayonet training in which 'what is aimed at in the instruction is "blood, hate, fire and brimstone". It is "guts and gristle" instruction, with nothing peacetime or "pansy" about it'.

This weapon encapsulated a British warrior tradition. At Waterloo in 1815, the British troops fixed their bayonets and formed up in squares, bristling with steel, to repel Napoleon's cavalry. The bayonet becomes a symbol of British violent imperialism in John Atkinson Hobson's 1901 critique of the Boer War, *The Psychology of Jingoism*. He describes otherwise sensible people becoming 'victims' of the war fever, in which 'death and destruction by firearms do not satisfy; it is the cold steel and the twist of the British bayonet in the body of the now defenceless foe that bring the keenest thrill of exultation.' This, Hobson writes, is not mere animalism, but has a violent patriotism at its core, as 'the essential brutality which underlies the glow of patriotic triumph in "another British victory" is discernible'. There's an echo of this grisly bloodlust in the years after the war in Boer War veteran Corporal Jones, star of the sitcom *Dad's Army*, and his obsession with the 'cold steel', expressed in his catchphrase 'They don't like it up 'em!' Humour is a way of processing this personal means of killing.

I think of that living history soldier dressed in a Wehrmacht uniform cheerfully explaining how bayonets work to a child at Tankfest. None of the training manuals touch on the gruesome reality of using a bayonet to try to kill a fellow human being and the potential psychological impact of doing so. What would it feel like to use all your strength to push a 'pigsticker' into another man's body, to hear the slicing of flesh and gurgling blood, to see the reaction across his face and eyes, to feel his body struggling through the steel and wood of your rifle?

In her Mass Observation contribution on 14 September 1939, Nella Last reflected on the departure of her son into the military. 'The last day of having a "little boy" – for so my Cliff has seemed, in spite of being twenty-one at Christmas,' she wrote. 'He has been so thoughtful and quiet these last few days, and so gentle. I watched his long sensitive fingers as he played with the dog's ears, and saw the look on his face when someone mentioned "bayonet charging". He has never hurt a thing in his life: even as a little boy, at the age when most children are unthinkingly cruel, he brought sick or hurt animals home for me to doctor [. . .] it's dreadful to think of him having to kill boys like himself – to hurt and be hurt. It breaks my heart to think of all the senseless, formless cruelty.'

It was the prospect of having to bayonet other men that pushed Henry Danton over the edge. Despite constantly running away from Wellington College, Danton eventually passed the exams to get into the Royal Military Academy in Woolwich, London. Confronted by army discipline, things soon got worse even than they had been at school: 'We had a commanding officer, who later became one of the war generals, I just wondered how we ever won the war, because he said some very stupid things,' Danton remembered. 'In one lesson he said to us, "If you're in a battalion and your commanding officer commands you to walk over the edge of a cliff, you do it." I thought, "Well, I'm not going to do that, it just does not make sense." So I was against everything. Their mindset is horrible. You just do what you're told and there's no other way about it. I couldn't accept that: it was not logical.'

But nothing was as bad as the training for combat, being taught where exactly on the body they should shoot to kill, and, most of all, the bayonet practice. 'We had to run, stick this bayonet into the sack, imagining it was a German,' he said. 'If I'm going to be faced with a young German guy, I'm not going to do that to him, and I'm sure he doesn't want to do that to me. So it was completely against what I felt.' Danton found the aggression unbearable. As if it were a symbol of his masculinity, his superiors tried to force him to grow a moustache. At the annual gymnastics display, attended by the parents, Danton had to vault over a horse, one of those infernal wooden boxes that I suspect still make life miserable for thousands of schoolchildren everywhere. A military band played an accompaniment and Danton, carried away by the music, jumped on the trampoline and flew elegantly over the horse, greatly displeasing the officer in charge, who gruffly shouted, 'What do you think you are, a bloody ballet dancer?' Little did he know how right he was.

Danton's military career came to an end when he was ordered to command a troop of men with four lorries towing four artillery pieces on an exercise on Salisbury Plain, not far from where Tankfest now takes place. 'It was completely barren: there wasn't a tree, there wasn't a stone, there was nothing on it. I was supposed to be reading my map to know where we were and, of course, I got lost. I said to the driver, "You have to go that way," and my corporal said, "Excuse me, Sir, I think you're going the wrong way." And he was right: I had to turn around. When I got back, I was completely upset, I had a little cry. I was driving home and I remember thinking, "I just cannot do this any longer."'

All the years of military education and indoctrination, the attempts to squeeze him into the mould of officer class, had failed. It was the beginning of the end of Henry Danton's Army service. He was repeatedly sent to face military tribunals, where, he remembered, 'I think they already began to realise that I had psychological problems around being a soldier; and finally, they caught on.' He recalls the tribunals as being like the Spanish Inquisition: 'The first time, I was sweating and so nervous I could hardly talk.' At the third board, he managed to speak about how it was bayonet practice that he simply could not face. 'They had to find out if I was genuinely sick. They did what they had to do, but it was psychologically very painful. I have to give it to them: they said I was temperamentally unfit. I didn't like it but I think they were fair. If you were not in the Army at that time, you were a conscientious objector, a white feather, and that was something awful. I was neither a conscientious objector nor a white feather: I had psychological reasons why I did not want to do it. I did not want to stick my bayonet in a German soldier's stomach. It was nothing to do with conscientious objecting.'

When I spoke to Henry Danton, his eyes closed and head tilted back, iPad now showing his face, now the ceiling, as these words came out as if in a reverie, I was struck by what might seem to be a paradoxical insistence that he was not a conscientious objector but someone who physiologically could not fight. The militarised society and memory of a just war conditions us to question men who do not fight, to ask why they could not share the risk of maiming or death, and why they would not be prepared to give the ultimate sacrifice. It's the question I'd spend much of my youth thinking about asking my grandpa and then, hypothetically, myself. Yet with Henry Danton it didn't feel like a moral question – I believed his insistence that he was not a conscientious objector to the war – but that there was a physiological aversion to the prospect of killing. The army tribunals that dismissed him from service had their reasons, after all.

It's all very well to tut at the likes of Danton, to point out that if everyone had found themselves unable to contemplate sticking bayonets into Germans, then Nazism would never have been defeated. But just as I believe the Second World War was fought for the right to pacifism, so it was also for someone like Henry Danton to escape the expectations of the masculine society that surrounded him. I recall how he was on that Zoom call and I look at a photo of him from back in the day, his kind yet sharp good looks, and I do not see a coward, but a rare and gentle man.

It was ballet that saved Henry Danton. 'I was completely inert, wondering what was going to happen to me because I didn't want to go back into the Army and I didn't know what to do,' he told me, 'until finally, this lady drew me into dancing.' The soldier who was deemed by the military to be too mentally sick to fight started taking ballet lessons at one of the few open dance studios in London, run by a Judith Spinosa. Living with his mother and sister in a house in the countryside outside the capital, Danton would cycle to the local station whatever the weather and take the train to his classes, pretending to his family that he was going to visit a friend who had been wounded in the war. They eventually found that he was hiding his dance clothes in his canvas gas mask case, provoking a scene. Danton recalled cries of, 'Oh, we're going to send you back to the Army!' and 'You were supposed to be a general!'

Nevertheless, the crisis merely spurred Danton on and he increased his classes to one a day. He had to unlearn the military rules that governed even the shape of his own body. At the Royal Military Academy in Woolwich, the kilt-wearing Scottish trainer had insisted that the men stand with 'Bellies in and bottoms out, which is the reverse of what dancers have to do, stomachs in and bottoms in!' Yet Danton seemed to be a natural. His skills soon caught the eye and, with many male ballet dancers away at war, he was able to progress, joining the short-lived Allied Ballet, then the International Ballet and Sadler's Wells. The military hadn't entirely been washed out of him. When rehearsing at Sadler's Wells with the choreographer Ninette de Valois, 'She called me boy, which I thought was an insult, because even in the Army, I'd been a captain in charge of a group of four guns with men on each gun, you know. I had experience and she was calling me boy. She called me boy for the entire time I was in the company. The entire time. She damn well knew my name.' Whether it was the military or ballet, Danton did not like being told what to do. I love his determination not to be thought of as being a certain way purely because of discharge from the Army. He contradicts everything that society expected of a 'normal' man of his time. His defiant rejection of the military private school education that was forced onto him by the trauma of losing his father in the First World War is a victory for a proud yet sensitive masculine identity. I also have no doubt that Henry Danton was brave. Each morning during periods of German bombing, the ballet company would conduct a roll call to ensure no one among their number had been killed. Danton himself had spent a night sheltering in the London Underground, but found it dirty, smelly and crowded, not for him. Instead, he carried on sleeping in a rented room, in a bed in front of two floor-to-ceiling glass windows that looked out onto a communal garden. 'I thought, if a bomb falls, I'll be cut to pieces by the glass: well, that's too bad,' Danton remembered, 'there's nothing I can do about it.'

The first flying bomb was launched from a ramp in Occupied Europe and hit London on 13 June 1944, just a week after the initial success of the D-Day landings. The V-1 (V for 'Vergeltungswaffen' or 'vengeance weapon') had a long and pointed cylindrical body containing an 850kg high explosive warhead, stabilised with stubby wings and powered by a jet motor in a second tube on the top. These engines made a distinctive, unpleasant ripping roar that would suddenly cease as they cut out and the missile began the silent dive that terminated in a huge detonation. My granny would tell me that everyone longed to hear it angrily buzz overhead, off to land elsewhere on someone else, for a sudden silence spelled trouble.

At the time of the V-1 assault on London, Henry Danton was appearing in a production of *Swan Lake*. During the second act, the prince and the swan queen dance together. Danton was playing a huntsman and, in the scene, he was to stand on stage with a swan on either side of him, a tableau backing for the lead movement. I imagine it must have been almost imperceptible at first, the dread 'whumwhumwhum' of what Danton called 'that goddamn bomb' bleeding in over the music of the orchestra. It got louder and louder, a wave of consternation passing through the audience and then, a sudden silence as the V-1 motor cut. The music ceased in the clatter of instruments, the rustle of coats and the thudding of seats as musicians and punters alike dived to the theatre floor. 'The audience and the orchestra had been told, "Get down under your seats." We had been told, "Don't move!" So we didn't move,' Danton remembered. 'The principal dancer, Margot Fonteyn, was absolutely fabulous: she finished her dance in silence, got up, took her bows in silence, and walked off the stage in silence. I mean, if you ever want to see discipline, that's when you see it. The orchestra and the public got under their chairs: we didn't. The bomb came down and it exploded. Then the audience got up and sat in their seats, the orchestra got up and started playing, and we went on with the ballet. But there was that interval where everyone did what they were supposed to do, including us – we were supposed not to do anything. We stood there and it was incredible. A wonderful experience.'

# VILE BODIES

I wonder if it is because he was a dancer that Henry Danton spoke so tenderly about the human body. Ballet is the ultimate expression of the body as a poised whole, displayed on a stage in tight leotard, our physical form as a living, breathing work of art. It is as far as one can be from the grotesque vision of men killed by the impact of a blazing bomber falling from 20,000 feet, the charred remains inside a knocked-out tank or the suppurating wounds and viscera of men disembowelled by bayonets.

The state spared Danton's body from the possibility of destruction from the metal edges of modern war. Chance spared him from the lacerations of a window shattered by a German bomb. He spent the war as an embodied man, learning the possibilities and limitations of his form, its subtleties and strengths. This physicality meant he remained sensitively connected to the foibles of the body, and the rough-and-ready way it was managed and cared for in a time of conflict.

Danton was one of a troupe of dancers who took part in an ENSA entertainment tour for servicemen in recently liberated Europe. The privations of wartime meant that the group often had to slum it in dilapidated hotels, military barracks and private houses, frequently sharing beds. Danton bunked up with his friend Celia Franca and, upon arriving back in England, they both discovered they had caught crabs. 'You know what crabs are?' asked Danton from the glow of his screen on the other side of the Atlantic. 'We lay down on these marble slabs, I was on one and she was on the other, and we were painted with this horrible-smelling stuff which killed the crabs. It was down to earth: war was down to earth.'

This incidence of crab extermination strikes me as a beautifully simple way of describing both the forced intimacy of the war years and the rather blunt means by which the medical authorities intervened to preserve public health. The military had the significant task of ensuring that it kept the male body fit and able to fight. The 1934 *Army Manual of Hygiene and Sanitation*, amended and reprinted in 1940, highlighted the fact that, based on statistics from the First World War and earlier military campaigns, 'disease is responsible for from three to four times as many casualties as enemy action during a campaign, and it is only by ceaseless attention to sanitation that sickness can be combated and the Army maintained in a condition to carry out its object, which is to break down the resistance of the enemy.'

The *Army Manual of Hygiene and Sanitation* seems prim and arid compared to the reality of the conditions that it describes, the unwashed armpits and bollocks, stinking feet, blackheads, scrapes and scratches oozing blood, the grim discharge of VD, the fetid stench of all that on men crammed together sweating and farting in the back of a truck behind the front line or stuck for days in a zone of heavy combat. Men were instructed, 'The skin requires frequent cleansing not only to remove visible dirt, but also the salt, grease and dried sweat poured out from the glands of the skin, which otherwise will become clogged. Daily washing should be practised and special attention given to the armpits, crotch, between the buttocks, and the feet, especially between the toes.'

There's a rebellion in how the soldiers of Julian Maclaren-Ross's stories do not conform to the physical standards of the 'normal' male that politicians, medical professionals and military fitness fanatics alike had tried to create. Likewise, there is something gloriously democratic in the 'down-to-earth' masculinity that Henry Danton describes when compared to the fetishised strength and power of the totalitarian soldier. Britain's attempts at fixing the body feel almost quaint by comparison.

In a parliamentary debate on 7 February 1934, Reginald Clarry MP urged rearmament to avert a 'steady decline towards helplessness'. A desire for physical improvement was at the heart of his speech: 'We ought to make a great deal more attractive to the young manhood of this country an augmentation of all the Services, which will at least have the effect of raising the physical standard of our country.' The idea of 'keep fit', summoned once more in our own age of crisis in the grinning form of Instagram fitness coach Joe Wicks, has martial origins, with the slogan 'Keep fit for service' mentioned in *The Long Weekend*.

Even non-militaristic organisations that tried to build a new ideal of the British male body used martial imagery in their branding. In the 1920s and 30s, the Health and Strength League sought to promote physical exercise and conditioning among young men. The League was founded in 1906 from concerns about the state of national fitness. Primarily a working and lower middle-class movement, it had 86,000 members in 1930, and 124,000 by 1935. The League had its own monthly magazine and annual, *Health and Strength*, that featured recommended routines, advice on how to start an exercise club, anatomical articles on how muscles work, yoga techniques, dietary suggestions, how to get a 'perfect physique – without apparatus', the history of massage. The British way of exercise by focusing on working the body itself was viewed as superior to the 'continental method' of using apparatus in physical training. There were also galleries of posing competitions, taut bodies contorted and glistening, nude save for tiny pouches and thongs, some looking not unlike the concrete statue carved and left by German POW Rudi Weber out on the edge of Epping Forest.

In the years leading up to the Second World War, the Health and Strength League frequently emphasised its memberships' connection to the military. Pictured were sailors and soldiers in crisp white underwear, posing, flexing, pulling on ropes, one man carrying another (himself lifting weights) on his shoulder. Another article declared, 'The British Army and the Army of Health and Strength march side by side,' and in April 1938, the magazine printed a photograph of sailors exercising on the sunlit deck of HMS *Ramillies*, the battleship's huge 15-inch guns looming into the frame.

By 1939, the League's membership had increased to over 160,000, the annual exalting, 'Like an oak tree growing from a tiny acorn, the League has grown to its mighty dimensions and is still sending out fresh shoots in every direction.' In the British Library, I found the small, blue diary for Health and Strength League members for that year. On the cover is embossed the motto 'Sacred Thy Body – Even as Thy Soul' with a figure in front of a blazing sun, resting on a sword. It's a tiny book, smaller than a packet of fags, but stuffed with information. There are the words of the League song, to be voiced to the tune of 'Marching Through Georgia', a grandiose medley of exhortation to physical glory: 'Sing the battle to the swift, the triumph to the strong'; 'Sing a perfect Temple for the Spirt and the Mind'. There are sports stats, quack remedies ('Height does count – achieve it easily – short people can be made taller with the aid of a box of Challoner's Famous Formula'), weightlifting routines, advice on sunbathing paired with an ad for nudist magazine *Health and Efficiency*. Inside the back and front covers are four photos of statuary: the ancient Greek *Borghese Gladiator*, *Discobolus of Myron*, Antonio Canova's *Damoxenus* and the *Bowls Player* by August Kraus. Just six years previously, Kraus had signed a declaration of loyalty to Hitler, and had become a member of the Presidential Council of the Reich Chamber of Culture. Members are invited to 'copy one of these poses and win a fine Health and Strength posing cup'. Looking through these pages, so full of the joy of physical exercise, it even makes me, chronically unfit and with a lifelong allergy to sport, feel like I ought to buck up, find some vim and learn 'how to perform the forty-two BAWLA lifts' or try some 'Yogi rhythmics'.

An old, blank diary will always have a haunting aspect, that a life wasn't lived in it that should have been, and this feels especially so given the year. I couldn't help but turn to Sunday 3 September, where on the foot of the page is a line drawing of a man, raising up on all fours 'as high as possible. A fine tonic and massage for the liver'. I looked again at the servicemen featured in *Health and Strength* magazine, men like Signalman Horsefield, arms by his side and a slight pout, or M. J. Opperman in South Africa, in boxing stance and almost naked save for a small cloth and his shiny boots, or Alf Davis of HMS *London*, pulling on a rope. My eyes lingered on their fantastical bodies, the peak of fitness compared to the rest of wheezing, knock-kneed pre-war Britain, and wondered how many had made it through.

I wonder too how the shallow-chested, 'normal' soldiers, sailors and airmen felt about themselves in comparison to their strangely beefed-up comrades, and if there was the same feeling of inadequacy, resentment and dysmorphia that we experience in today's narcissistic age, in which the physical prowess of the developed body is used as a status symbol. Instagram, or the tediously toned torso pictures of dating apps, might be the digital incarnation of the *Health and Strength* photoshoot. Yet the bullet, bomb and shell are great equalisers. So too was this constant presence of other men in all their funk in confined spaces, and the necessity to regularly be naked in order to deal with it.

In a Michael Aspel interview in 1987, Kenneth Williams spoke about his neurosis at showing his naked body to fellow soldiers after he was called up in 1944. 'I used to take the trousers down, put my pyjama bottoms on, and then do the rest. But they rumbled it and said "What, you frightened of showing us your willy?" After that, I became quite uninhibited.' According to Dudley Cave, there was even a class element to nudity among new recruits. Accustomed to changing in front of other men at his private school, once in the Army he recalled, 'I tended to undress quite casually and get into what I was going to sleep in, whereas most of the more working-class boys would carefully wriggle out of their pants being careful not to expose their private parts.'

Nudity and the soldier had been, according to Paul Fussell in *The Great War and Modern Memory*, a staple of artistic reflection on the 1914–1918 conflict: 'Watching men (usually "one's own" men) bathing naked becomes a set-piece scene in almost every memory of the war.' Naked bathers feature in the poetry of Siegfried Sassoon and Rupert Brooke and connect to pre-war visions of male beauty stemming from the Greek ideal. Frederic Manning's poem 'A Shell' makes explicit the violation of the male body by the modern technological horror of high explosive, imagining men 'naked as Greeks' delousing their shirts as a shell rips overhead and lands nearby. Nudity might also be an intensely personal, private moment of escape from the conformity of uniformed life. In Dan Billany's autobiographical novel *The Trap*, Michael Carr returns to his tent one night and removes his uniform, standing naked in the cool the night air: 'When the skin felt as free as this, the soul felt free, too. And after all, this creature so rarely seen was the real me, much more real than the uniform which went out with me inside it.' As a dancer, Henry Danton had an intimate awareness of his own body. Dan Billany's homosexuality, I think, made him more acutely conscious than most might have been of the rituals of concealment that society forces upon our purest humanity.

I find the thought of our grandfathers and great-uncles, naked either communally or alone in some uncomfortable, distant posting, trying to clean or dream away the physical and mental dirt of their service to be a strangely beautiful one. Just as the photographs of uniformed soldiers mugging up for the camera can't really do the reality of their experience justice, so I find the perhaps surprising number of male nude photographs of the Second World War don't quite capture these precious seconds of unclothed selfhood. These collections of candid photographs have been preserved and now appear on historical websites, social media accounts and in high-quality art publications. *My Buddy: World War Two Laid Bare*, published by Taschen, is a compendium of photographs from the collection of Michael Stokes, a photographer known for his nude portraits of contemporary US veteran amputees, both men and women, as well as more traditional erotic photographs of hunky blokes. They are 'found' photographs, acquired from sales and wider collections. As such, the men are reprinted in the book without the context of identity, unit or rank, often even nation. Flicking through these images of cheerful-looking men going about their ablutions, I'm left looking at the materiel and physical surroundings for clues as to where they're from. Men wash one another, lark about at the water's edge, sunbathe nude on the rocks, clean vehicles in the river. These are unconscious, innocent pictures in their way, yet they're more troubling than they might first appear. On one hand, the stripping away of national identity with uniforms makes the cogent point that, naked, nothing really divides these (white) men. Yet I find myself looking for signs as to which might be British. Does that submarine on which naked sailors are being hosed down under a makeshift shower belong to the Royal Navy? Sometimes caps give a clue, or in one snap of a large group of men nude under a gushing stream from a nozzle used to replenish the boilers of steam engines, British third-class railway carriages can be seen in the background.

Photographs are a slippery way of understanding the cultural differences around sex and nudity. In wartime America, for example, military suppliers Common Towels printed luxuriant full-colour advertisements called True Towel Tales, featuring illustrations of groups of toned, sun-golden nude men frolicking with their products. It's hard to imagine something so confident being printed in Britain. There's a different feel to the photos of British servicemen. Where the Americans seem to be all front and confidence, the British images are more humorous – take, for instance, one of a man in his pants crouched in a tub on the deck of a ship, a bucket of water being poured onto his head under the breech of a gun, laughing soldiers and sailors looking on, including, in the background, a blurred officer wearing a gold and blue uniform and a wry smile. They are images that, like Kenneth Williams' words on that television talk show, speak more of bawdy humour than the homoeroticism of all-male 'buddy' culture. Perhaps that's how we understood our naked selves – as awkward and funny, rather than idealised and virile.

Inevitably, nudity ends up lending itself to sex. There's a certain discomfort in the reprinting of these largely chaste photographs taken in a moment of innocent larking around (though there are a few pictures of Americans holding their cocks suggestively) in a way that might now be used for titillation. Something is lost in looking at them with a prurient eye. It robs them of their dignity and their agency in their sexuality, or their performance of it. At the time, intimate sexual thoughts and their bodily manifestation were a matter of state concern.

The saying 'hands off cocks and on socks' has transatlantic military origins, remembered in veteran testimony and appearing post-war in places as diverse as Tristan Jones's faux-memoir of Royal Navy life *Heart of Oak*, Barry Hines's *A Kestrel for a Knave* and its 1969 film adaptation *Kes*, Ken Kesey's *One Flew Over the Cuckoo's Nest*, Stanley Kubrick's *Full Metal Jacket* and British sitcom *Auf Wiedersehen, Pet*. *Health and Strength* magazine's attempts to promote the perfect British male body were accompanied by its embracing of the Victorian struggle against masturbation, often referred to as 'self-abuse'. The 'Man Making' columns of T. W. Standwell obsessed over the intimate practice that risked undermining the very spirit and spunk on which the military depended. These were printed across a double-page spread: the right-hand side featured an essay on a notable feat of bodily endurance, triumph over adversity, and physical and moral fitness; on the facing page, a poor unfortunate's letter would detail his usually sexual problems before Standwell stepped in with the 'cure' – a selection of his books, promised to be posted out discretely in plain envelopes.

On 19 February 1938, Standwell's column brought to our attention case No. 19366, a 31-year-old man suffering from sexual impotence (perhaps it's a case of nominative determinism that a man called Standwell wrote so much on impotence). The man was a sailor in the Royal Navy who described himself as being 'in the wrong boat' (meaning sexual impotence) due to his masturbatory habits. This, he confessed, had begun at the age of 14. His 'self-abuse' was violent until, for a while, 'I tried to pull myself around and be normal.' Alas, the struggle was in vain and, from his teenage years onwards, his habit continued, causing him appalling self-loathing. Even though at the time of writing he hadn't indulged for two years, the desire had had an impact on his marriage. He ended his letter with a plea: 'Is it possible for your methods to restore my normal manhood and to cure this trouble?' Standwell sent him two books – *Do You Desire Health?* and *Sexual Neurasthenia* – which the navy man reports much improved his physical condition, and he now has 'complete confidence in my sexual abilities'. The spread concludes with the summary exhortation of the Standwell Signposts, asking readers: 'Are you striving to be the MAN that you desire to be? If you are a failure, and wish to become Mentally and Physically efficient, the right road is to first stop all nervous waste, conserve the energies, accumulate a good nerve reserve, and build up virile manhood.'

Masturbation was a problem that some of Standwell's correspondents seemed to feel was contagious, writing that they learned it after falling into 'bad company' at school or under the influence of older friends. Solo sexual pleasure and all-male company when conducted outside normal restraints might both be problematic. Standwell's columns are formulaic: they generally feature the same self-debasement of the desperate wanker's first letter, the wonder and gratitude at his cure and Standwell's cajoling editorial – 'It takes a MAN to confess his weakness . . . All who have written to me for help have proved themselves by their action to be MEN at heart . . . If YOU are suitable material for re-making into REAL MANHOOD – write to me to day.'

'Self-abuse' was something that always seemed to have been performed 'in ignorance', suggesting a terrible oppression of desire and the natural view of fantasy and masturbation as an essential part of masculine identity. Yet neither was Standwell's moralising a fringe belief. The *Army Manual of Hygiene and Sanitation* listed 'sexual and alcoholic excess' alongside constipation as a condition that might leave a man vulnerable to heat and sunstroke by lowering 'the vitality of the body'. Excesses of self-love might even be seen as a way of losing one's status in the acceptable mass of 'normal' masculinity. Founder of the Scout movement Lord Baden-Powell had written as much in *Rovering to Success*, what reads today like a self-help book for the young adult male, first published in 1922 and reprinted in a new edition the year before the start of the war. Sexuality was part of Baden-Powell's lesson in how the young British male ought to pursue wary self-control for the greater good. In the chapter on the 'rock of Woman', Baden-Powell is forthright in his discussion of puberty, sexual development, relationships and venereal disease. He writes that emissions of semen (compared to the 'sap' of nature) are perfectly normal but warns, 'don't try and bring it on for yourself; that would be straining and draining it out of your system'. One who doesn't resist the temptation of sex or masturbation risks losing his self-respect: 'it is something low and unmanly. A man who is ashamed is no longer a man; he becomes a conscious sneak.'

For all the strange exuberance of Baden-Powell's prose, there's a looming sense of doom over his dire warnings. All his 'rocks', these issues on which the male might be sunk, seem to intersect – eschewing his suggestions for virtuous activity and staunch endeavour in favour of too much wine might lead to regrettable sex which might lead to shame and guilt and becoming less than a man. For the young chap reading these words, already within the constraints of what was expected of the 'normal' British male, it must have felt as if it were almost impossible not to go 'wrong'.

I don't think Baden-Powell's writing is as outdated as might first appear. We see parallels a century on with the self-improvement and self-help writings of figures like Jordan Peterson, in the membership rules of the American Proud Boys gang and the 'no-fap' online anti-masturbation movement, all contemporary cultural phenomena that sit close to new forms of nationalist and right-wing thought. The self and the nation are barely divisible in Baden-Powell's writing, as is the superiority of the white male over all others – in a section called 'It Is Up to You to Be Master of Yourself', Baden-Powell recommends regular washing of 'the racial organ' and he refers to sperm as 'a sacred trust for carrying on the race'. A man who resists the temptation to masturbate or indulge in casual sex and keeps himself 'pure' 'will have fortified your body with the full power of manhood', not just for himself but for his people and his country.

The disruption of the war, the changing attitudes around nudity and the body that Henry Danton described to me as 'down to earth' must have made these edicts around sexuality seem increasingly arcane to the ordinary men in the armed forces and civilian population alike. When it came to printed material, the quest for titillation would overcome the frowsy judgement of moralising tracts or T. W. Standwell's finger-wagging. The newsagents' stands were sexed up. In the *Punch* cartoon series 'The Changing Face of Britain', one illustration depicts the key difference between pre-war newsstands and the wartime moment as being the increase in erotic publications on sale. It's noticeable that popular wartime magazine *Lilliput*, which featured serious journalism from the likes of Wyndham Lewis, J. B. Priestly, H. E. Bates and Ernest Hemingway as well as pictures by Willy Brandt and humorous juxtapositions of images (Herman Goering on the facing page to large mammals was a popular subject) increased the amount of nude photography they published as the war went on. Dirty books and banter are frequently mentioned in wartime memoirs and autobiographically inspired fiction. In Julian Maclaren-Ross's short story 'Death of a Comrade', a soldier drowns and his pals go through his kit before returning it to his next of kin. Two photos of naked girls torn from a magazine are found in with his civilian shoes, letters, playing cards, a book called *What a Young Husband Ought to Know* and a broken cigarette case. The dirty pics are removed – there were things a young soldier's family didn't need to know, a private erotic life that ought to remain beyond the eyes of loved ones, as it might corrupt their image of their son or partner.

Men looked for visual stimulation wherever they could find it. The ballet might not be the obvious entertainment of choice for a bunch of soldiers, exhausted from the tough advance across Europe, but when Henry Danton was dancing with ENSA in Paris, it was frequently to rooms packed with them. 'They didn't know what they were looking at,' he told me, 'but it was just some kind of relief from their daily routine. And ballet's enjoyable, even if you don't understand anything.' It was also, one suspects, a fine opportunity to contemplate the female form. *Coppélia* was choreographed by Arthur Saint-Léon and performed to the music of Léo Delibes, but its first Parisian run was interrupted by the Franco–Prussian war and Siege of Paris in 1870. Aptly enough, the plot is a tale of misguided fantasy and misplaced lust, after a humble village boy abandons his true love for the sake of a beautiful doll, created by a dastardly inventor. Danton told me that, 'in the last act, three girls run onto the stage and get up onto their toes. As they did it, one of the girls had not fixed her skirt properly, and it fell down, so she was on stage in her panties. The soldiers started whistling and crying and they inflated condoms and sent them blowing down to the stage! I mean, these poor boys, they're probably going to be dead the next day, and I thought it was a wonderful, wonderful expression of human spirit!'

Others took matters into their own hands. John Keston, who had lied about his age to enlist in the RAF aged sixteen and worked as a mechanic repairing Beaufighter attack aircraft in the Western Desert, told me desire even provided a connection with the men they were fighting. His unit took over a remote desert airstrip with a few buildings that had previously been occupied by the

Germans. 'It was a poignant event for me,' he said. 'There was a beautiful drawing of a nude woman on the wall, and it was done by a very good artist, one of the German soldiers. It brought home to me the fact that we were all human beings and we didn't really need to be killing one another.' You can imagine the longing of the German soldier who poured his fantasies into that drawing, his comrades who admired it and the connection that his enemy found with him afterwards, each man projecting onto the penmanship his own ideals of attraction and lust, or thoughts of a lover back home.

There is a gap between the attitude of moralising military hierarchy and societal expectation and the reality of the human spirit for the men in the three services. Yet masturbation still disappears into the silence of history. There must have been hundreds of millions of ejaculations among His Majesty's Forces in the Second World War, intensely private moments. There's a common theme that in POW camps this most instinctual of bodily activities was more obvious and noted upon. In J. H. Witte's warts-and-all wartime memoir, *The One That Didn't Get Away*, he writes in his particularly frank and straightforward way, that in his Italian camp 'the married men were the worst because when their stomachs were full they would spend hours re-living their courting days, the wedding night, the honeymoon and sundry Sunday afternoons on the carpet.' Single men, with fewer rooms in their erotic memory palace to visit, were less fervent, yet some were mocked by their comrades with a colourful range of insults for what seemed to be a compulsive habit. The penis became "the one-eyed milkman" and the hand, "the five-fingered widow".' As a POW on a forced march through Germany, Witte took step with Wanker Bill, a man so prolific that 'it was even said that he wanked between wanks'.

In his Colditz novel *Yes, Farewell*, Micky Burn's character Alan

Maclaran examines how the power of desire for the ordinary serviceman overcame even that of the violence that surrounded them. 'The war was ephemeral. On all the battlefields the soldiers were thinking of love, dreaming of love as they slept beside their tanks and in their lorries [. . .] However vast the battles might now seem, the desire that came over him now was greater.' In the POW camp, Maclaran feels like his time is running out, old at twenty-six. Yet there is an energy and a relief in how, 'His sexual imagination flowed at night. It was the river flowing under the city of his waking life, and though its insistence was painful he was glad of it.' On the other hand, he described the three key ways prisoners at his POW camp tried to deal with the inexorable passage of time as 'smoking, sleeping and self-abuse'. Burn uses the shaming term for what his character Maclaren deems to be no outlet, but took energy, 'doping the prisoners who surrendered to it'. Yet was this the case for all?

I find this idea of POW camps, military bases, ships at sea full of this flow of sexual imagination fascinating. It is feral, unruly, intimate and free from military hierarchy or state control. During the First World War, there were consistent rumours in the ranks that the military top brass were adding potassium bromide to their tea in order to reduce sexual drive. To be sexually curious in the 1940s was to escape the shaming expectations of 'normal' masculinity, yet our modern myths of brave boys doing their bit can similarly erase the rough and ready nature of male desire. Could contemporary Britain countenance the idea of the veteran hero Captain Tom in his younger years cracking one off under itchy blankets, or would it be seen as a subversion of his role as an icon of a national past at war?

For many, a fantasy voyage into the erotic imagination or masturbation must have been a multi-function act. The pleasure of release. A means of relieving boredom, of breaking routine. A connection with a loved one back home. But, perhaps more than this, a moment of liberation in which the man was not merely a number, a rank, a part of the machine of war, but flesh, emotion and once more himself.

# THE CLAP TRAP

One night in the summer of 1943, an air raid alert stopped a train on the tracks between Grantham and Peterborough. In the dark corridor of one of the carriages, RAF pilot Peter Johnson, married with two children, started talking to a stranger whom he would only ever know as Shelagh. They were overwhelmed by a spontaneous and intense attraction: 'the strength of the current which flowed between us obliterated everything else,' Johnson wrote in his memoir, *The Withered Garland*. Desperate that this not just be a fleeting encounter, they agreed to meet in a week's time, at 6 p.m. on the platform at Grantham. Thus began an intense affair in 'stuffy, blacked out hotel rooms' in which no 'I love you' was ever said. Shelagh was understanding of Johnson's marriage, as he was about her sexual relationship with her boss, who gave her money and a place to say. 'How could I mind?' Johnson reflected many years later. 'In war one's vision was pretty blinkered. You saw what you had to see and partly, I suppose what you wanted to see.' The affair ended when Shelagh, an air raid warden, was crushed by a falling beam while trying to rescue a child from a burning building.

The war years witnessed a relaxation in attitudes as many subverted 'normal' codes of behaviour. 'You did things which you would never think of doing if it had been at a different time,' Henry Danton told me. 'I wouldn't say a moral freedom; I would say a lack of something, a lack of taste or a lack of what is good and what is wrong. It was an unreal time where people felt they could do anything because next day, they might not be there, it didn't matter.' Death had an aphrodisiac quality, as 158 Squadron's Harry Lomas found out when he returned from aircrew training in South Africa. While he'd been away, Bomber Command's losses had risen dramatically. This had given RAF aircrew a morbid glamour that set them apart from other servicemen. He wrote that, 'We had the image of hard-drinking, womanising, devil-may-care fellows, and I am sure I did my bit to uphold it.'

Sexual activity was, just as Colin Spencer believed his father had found during the First World War, an affirmation of humanity; the fecund exploration of the human body a reaction, conscious or otherwise, to the possibility of death in industrialised total war. The need for intimate human contact as a fleeting moment of comfort against both the mundanity and the horror of combat meant that sexual norms as defined by society and religion were inevitably to be broken, for better and for worse.

As Quentin Crisp so memorably put it in *The Naked Civil Servant*, 'As soon as the bombs started to fall, the city became like a paved double bed.' So did the cinemas, the riverbanks, the parks and quiet spaces, for men and women, straight, gay and somewhere in between. Air-raid shelters too had something of a reputation. In *The Myth of the Blitz*, historian Angus Calder cites a Home Intelligence report from 6 September: 'In several districts cases of blatant immorality in shelters are reported; this upsets other occupants of shelters and will deter them from using the shelters again.'

Yet in post-war literature, this expression of the human spirit was often lacking in variety. As an avid consumer of war thrillers, I remember feeling anxiously hot when sex scenes slipped in among the tales of derring-do. By and large, the sex was idealised for the male audience – breasts were always perfect, pert and topped with brown nipples, as if they were cakes on Mr Kipling's production line. There'd be some moaning, some improbable prowess on the part of the man, and that's about it. Even *The Cruel Sea*, a book that otherwise introduced me to the gruesome terror and monotony of wartime service, rendered most of its romance in soft focus. A gritty or desperate sexuality, a sometimes knotty expression of the human spirit was absent.

It wasn't just in his frank discussion of masturbation that J.H. Witte's memoir presents a more gnarly side of male sexuality unfettered by war. Witte is no heroic figure, something that the title of his memoir – *The One That Didn't Get Away* – seems to have been chosen to emphasise. Witte was a young man from Southend who joined the Territorial Army aged seventeen in 1936 simply because an hour-long meeting meant an escape from the boredom of office life. He ended up spending seven years and sixty-three days in the Army, including four years in prisoner-of-war camps. In the black-and-white photographs of his memoir he has a cocky, assured air – a handsome man with a moderately large nose, swept-back dark hair and big lips pursed. In another image, he wears a sardonic expression that gives little away, the picture captioned, with typical laconic self-deprecation: 'The downwards chevron on his left sleeve represents two to five years long service (but not particularly good conduct).'

Witte's army career was average at best. He is one of Maclaren-Ross's characters made flesh, cynical and exasperated by the privations of service – 'fed up, fucked up and far from fucking home', as he puts it. From the TA, he joined the Royal Horse Artillery, gaining the jangling spurs and sharp, antiquated uniforms of horseback warfare increased his appeal to the women in the Castle and Swan pubs of Southend, or the public hall used for weekend dances. When that's not enough, Witte and a pal take a trip up town. Proto-Essex blokes, they head to Liverpool Street station smartly dressed in their uniforms, getting admiring glances from the girls popping into the Lyons tea house and gawping back. They get bought drinks by a city gent and end up drunk. A policeman sends the lads on their way with a suggestion of a trip to the Windmill in Soho – 'you'll like that, plenty of leg'. The drunk soldiers don't need a second hint and arrive to be overwhelmed by the pictures of girls in the windows, advertising a 'Mademoiselle Fifi, straight from Paris', naked and putting on a stocking. The Windmill was full of servicemen, cheering along and clapping to acts called things like 'In the Artist's Studio' – the most popular being a blonde in a G-string. (The war even became an element of the eroticism of the dancing girls of Soho. I've seen a photograph of a line of dancers, legs raised under short skirts, all in gas masks. Another backstage shot features three girls, two in transparent dressing gowns, the third in elaborate bra and panties, hair done nicely, also with gas masks on. It's a photograph that might be from a modern fetish magazine were it not for the framed picture of a handsome airman in his uniform on the table next to them.)

Witte is shipped out to the war in the Middle East. In Jerusalem, he visits a brothel called Madame Rose's, where a 'lack of preliminaries' puts him off. Outside, he gives the details and makes up more and talks about how the woman had shaved her pubic hair. 'Cor,' said his pal Mick, 'they're not like that in Leeds.'

Witte finally arrives in Egypt – the land of the four esses 'sun, sea, sand, syphilis' – where he writes of the physicality of discomfort in the desert, the heat, the monotony, the mirages, the constant dysentery due to flies shuttling between faeces and food, the sandstorms that got grit into medical instruments, food, clothes, weapons, not to mention the moist and tender zones of the male face and body. He writes graphically about the sex trade in Cairo. Never mind the wonders of the ancient world, Witte and his comrade Chalky 'were far more content studying female architecture instead of great monuments of the past'. At a barber shop, the proprietor shows him a girly magazine and then sends a 'young lad' to masturbate him under the sheet. He describes lurid adventures in Black Berka, a dangerous area of the city, where a tattooed prostitute sways naked to a drumming rhythm in front of them, taking a cigarette off Chalky and inserting it into her vagina.

In *Sex Problems and Dangers in Wartime*, George Ryley Scott wrote of prostitution that 'men with their feet on the threshold of death reck little of the opinions of moralists and puritans, they care nothing for their own self-respect'. I'm sure this was the case for many, but Witte doesn't seem to be paying for female company out of a fear of his own mortality. He seems to be motivated by a different emotion, the banter and braggadocio of all-male company.

His final role in the British army was driving a tanker full of water around the Western Desert. This he did with average success until he was captured, leading to a long incarceration in both Italian and German POW and labour camps that did little to quell his earthy approach to life and sex. Alongside the excesses of masturbation, he describes the power of pornographic photographs as items of currency when, in March 1945, the railway works at Leipzig where he's been forced to work are bombed. There's a crude juxtaposition of scenes of horror – a screaming German woman looking for the head of her husband and a disembowelled Russian set against his joy at finding a wallet full of pornographic images which he kept in order to trade them for food or smokes. On a long forced march through Germany, Witte ended up swapping them for some fags with Wanker Bill.

This blunt description of a transactional relationship with the carnal extended to the women that Witte managed to have sex with, even as a POW. 'It was a well-known fact that many German girls would drop their slacks for a bar of chocolate,' he writes, though he fails to get an erection for Dolly, naked under her overalls in her factory crane cabin. In the strange atmosphere at the end of the European conflict after his liberation by American troops, Witte wanders the countryside looking for women. He meets a German widow with two children and seduces her with chocolate and food purloined from an American quartermaster. The woman's husband had died at Stalingrad. 'She hadn't had any dick for a long time, although she didn't put it quite as bluntly as that,' Witte cheerfully notes. With unpleasantly lascivious detail, Witte recounts how the widow's resistance crumbles as he plies her with booze, promises of marriage and escape to England. To him, the pursuit of the widow was some kind of game. He wasn't alone in this behaviour. War is a great enabler of prostitution, on the home front and overseas. It also blurs the boundaries between sex paid for with money and exploitation in difficult circumstances when the violence has ceased but the normal order of society had collapsed.

Norman Lewis's diary-memoir *Naples '44*, published in 1978, is a frank account of the amorality of a city that had recently undergone a change of martial occupation. On 1 October, the Italian fascists and Germans were replaced by the British and Americans – thousands of sexually frustrated young servicemen meeting a starving population in a city riddled with corruption. The Bureau of Psychological Warfare estimated that 42,000 women in Naples were engaged in prostitution. On 4 October 1944, Lewis, an intelligence officer, travelled through the blasted city in which the people, in an air of 'stunned indifference', unenthusiastically raised their fingers in a V for victory, instead of the fascist salute they'd given only days before. Outside the ruins of a municipal building, Lewis found soldiers jostling around an American truck full of supplies. Once they'd liberated tins from the vehicle, the men entered the building where a row of women sat, each with a pile of tins beside them, earned from sex with a soldier. 'Faced with these matter-of-fact family providers driven here by empty larders, they seemed to flag,' Lewis wrote. One drunk soldier, egged on by his comrades, goes through with the exchange, but afterwards buttons his trousers quickly: 'He might have been submitting to field punishment rather than the act of love.'

There was worse too. *Naples '44* details accounts of rape by Allied soldiers. Lewis describes girls as young as thirteen being sold by their mothers. He visits a peasant's home where, finding nothing worth stealing, deserters had sexually assaulted the women, 'subjecting them to every conceivable indignity, including attempted buggery'. The only reason they had not indulged in vaginal rape was a fear of contracting VD. A few days later, the father sent the prettiest girl to Lewis with a letter, offering her in exchange for food.

You imagine that for many men, the fantasy of sex in exchange for tins of bully beef quickly faded once they were exposed to the reality. The ribald banter and persuasion of the male group dynamic might only go so far, as Norman Lewis saw. Undoubtedly, though, others were more like Witte, callously exploitative and crudely proud of it. Perhaps some, due to their own experiences of sexual assault in peacetime, or brutalised by the battlefield and ground down by the mundanity of military life, didn't care.

It's a false comfort for us in Britain to try to brush over the sexual exploitation confessed by the likes of J. H. Witte and catalogued by Norman Lewis in comparison to the crimes committed by Japanese soldiers against 'comfort women', the camps of sex slaves often imported from Korea, or rape as means of warfare suffered by Germans as the Red Army moved west. Recent research has suggested that as many as 1.4 million German women were raped by Soviet soldiers, a subject explored in grim detail by historian Antony Beevor in his book *Berlin - The Downfall*. In an interview with the *Sydney Morning Herald* he described it as the 'greatest phenomenon of mass rape in history' and Berliners referred to the grandiose monument to the Soviet war dead in Treptower Park as 'the tomb of the unknown rapist'. It was no wonder many German women wanted to escape. What was left for Witte's widow, with hungry mouths to feed, the loss of her husband in total war and the prospect of years under occupation by a foreign power? Into this desperation stepped a soldier with pockets full of chocolate, a rucksack of food and wine and the tantalising offer of a new life far away from the rapists and the ruins. Liberation in war often comes at a horrible cost, lending sinister meaning to the phrase, 'to the victor, the spoils'.

I'm torn by Witte's memoir. On one hand, the leering boasting, braggadocio and the view of women as merely a leg-up is coarsely misogynistic. Yet, at the same time, there's an unfiltered power and honesty to his words that burns through sensibility and sensitivity to give a matter-of-fact insight into the lives and libidos of some Private Normals. If we're to have a true picture of the masculinity of the war years, then as now, we cannot sweep the more unpleasant aspects of it out of sight in favour of idealised heroes. To deny men their raucous sexuality, however much it might have offended polite society then and a very different moral spectrum now, is to omit a huge part of themselves. In any case, Witte's base attitudes are timeless. I could imagine overhearing words like his at the football, in the gym changing rooms, at the pub or on the train. Perhaps just like the boy who cannot resist picking up a twig to pretend it is a gun, they are part of the uncomfortable truth of what it can be to be a man.

\*

In fiction and historical record, exploitation came along with a perception that women posed a sexual threat to both individuals and the military state. In Alexander Baron's 1948 novel *From the City, From the Plough*, the tough but hapless Major Maddison is revolted by the effect that women have on his men. He admires the German army for its harsh treatment of officer recruits – 'That's soldierliness. That's manhood' – and, like some historical figures of the Second World War, laments the softening influence of cinema and popular music. He sees women through a red fug of misogyny: 'Maddison hated the women whom he saw clinging to the arms of his men; shrill and white-skinned creatures, soft as slugs, stinking of scent; they turned his stomach.' He did, however, like to watch the troops in their showers, 'exultant with emotions which he could not fathom and would walk away flushed with love for these men of his – until, looking down into the lane below the camp, he would see a soldier strolling with his girl and would feel sick and contemptuous once more'.

On 17 December 1939, a magistrate ordered the closure of a Soho nightclub which, according to the *News of the World*, was one of many that had opened since the war began 'simply to "catch" soldiers, sailors, and airmen'. The presiding magistrate said, 'These premises seem to be run in a way which embraces everything one would desire not to exist, particularly having regard to the times in which we live.' When MI5 wanted to create a fictitious spy network for a Spaniard passing false information to the Germans (code-named Garbo, he was previously known as 'Bovril'), one of the 'agents' concocted was a female secretary in the war office who, once seduced, proved a passionate lover. 'She is clearly unaccustomed to attention from the opposite sex,' wrote Garbo, real name Juan Pujol García, 'this made her all the more accessible to mine. She is already delightfully indiscreet.' Both the 'undersexed and needy' and the 'oversexed, predatory' woman were plausible as a risk to the war effort. It's interesting that Harry Lomas referred to the women who solicited in London in RAF slang as 'Piccadilly flak', a grimly humorous comparison of running the gauntlet through Soho and nights flying through bursting anti-aircraft shells over Germany.

It can often feel that the relative sexual liberation of the war years was seen as an opportunity for men, but one that women were excluded from enjoying. In *Sex Problems and Dangers in Wartime*, Ryley Scott blames the weakness of women in the face of the romance of the soldier for bad wartime marriages. 'To the emotional young girl, bulging with patriotism, every soldier is something of a hero [. . .] the majority of young girls are prepared to fall in love with any young man wearing a uniform. So true is this, and to such ridiculous lengths does the obsession go, that in war-time a uniform, whether of the Army, the Navy, or the Air Force, to the average girl, ranks as a fetish.' Scott believed that just as the uniform served its intended purpose in bringing conformity and discipline into the ranks, it also removed the 'ordinary standards, social and otherwise' by which a young woman would be able to make wise judgements as to the character of a potential suitor. It also enabled men to attract women who would not ordinarily be interested. 'The girl marries a glamorous unknown soldier whose inferiority is camouflaged physically by his uniform and mentally by her own disarming patriotism.' What was said for marriage must also apply to more casual, fleeting relationships. Scott's writing is troubling because it seems to accuse women in two paradoxical ways: on one hand, they're seen as weak in the face of martial glamour, but on the other, the war has made them newly sexually voracious. He writes, almost violently, that, 'In recent years much nonsense has been talked about the girl's right to sow her wild oats, of sexual equality with man, of the vanishing of the double standard of morality.' He squarely blames 'the sexual emancipation of women' during the First World War, believing that the conflict 'awakened and intensified eroticism in women'. The man, according to Scott, was a 'Jekyll and Hyde' character, who was at once 'gentleman and a scoundrel', promiscuous but still demanding a virgin for marriage. For women to expect the same was naïve. Women were now 'drunk on sex' and 'the girl of 1939 [who] started where the girl of 1918 left off', seduced by the allure of uniforms, believing herself as free as men, was a danger to the proper order of gender sexual relations.

Fear of a female sexuality 'emancipated' by war and the body as a place of tension over its possession extended to the dread of a so-called 'Dear John' letter from a wife or lover back home. The Army Morale Report of May–July 1942 found, 'A worry which is constantly sapping the morale of a great part of the Army is due to the suspicion, very frequently justified, of fickleness on the part of wives and "girls".' In 1943, the Legal Advice Service for troops stationed in the Middle East was working on thirty new divorce cases every day. These are common themes of war writing. If *The Long and the Short and the Tall*'s brilliance is that in two acts, it manages to touch on so many of the issues that affected British servicemen, then that has to include the constant insecurity that, thousands of miles and another world away from the dripping and terrible greenery of the Malayan jungle, the soldiers' partners were being unfaithful. This becomes banter at its most cruel, an easy way to wind up comrades. In Witte's *The One That Didn't Get Away*, he recalls how, after a fellow POW received a letter from home telling him his wife was sleeping with an American, he acquired a bottle of schnapps, downed it and died of alcohol poisoning. 'The kindly neighbour who wrote to him ought to have known better,' he wrote. 'It was bad enough being a POW without finding out your wife was being unfaithful.'

The prisoners in Micky Burn's *Yes, Farewell* approach the end of the war fearing that women met and married in a hurry not long before their capture would have been surrounded by exotic men of varying nationalities and charms, whereas they'd return nervous and impotent, unable to cope outside the world of routine, hard stone walls and the sole company of men. American soldiers, infamously 'oversexed, overpaid and over here', were a constant source of these neuroses. They were seen as being able to lure British women with their higher wages and gifts of chocolate and tights, hanging about indolently while the husbands and sweethearts were getting on with the dirty work of war in some tough and lonely posting.

On 11 November 1944, George Formby recorded a song called 'Our Fanny's Gone All Yankee' about a woman who has taken on American airs, muttering at night from her pillow about her new boyfriend's jeep, chewing gum rather than saying 'ee by gum', now fond of Spam and hot dogs, wears American stockings and has started picking up the accent. Fanny's sexual activities have even become more overt and less discrete – she no longer waits until the cover of night, but 'does her hanky panky' flagrantly on public transport. Fanny has been corrupted by the malign sexual influence of Americana. Formby was the flat-capped master of the saucy and it's rather tempting to read a double meaning in how Fanny now thinks British Woodbine cigarettes are a joke, and much prefers to suck on American Camel.

This insecurity was exploited by all sides. In 1939, journalist Sefton Delmer visited the vast French defences on the Maginot Line, soon to be bypassed and overcome by invading German forces. A giggling lieutenant showed him a piece of paper printed with a picture of a bold French soldier on the frontline. Held up to the light, though, the paper revealed a second, hidden and highly pornographic image of a British Tommy having it off with the unlucky Frenchman's fiancée. According to the French lieutenant, this leaflet had been distributed by the Germans to undermine their enemy's morale. Sefton Delmer would go on to create what was known as 'black propaganda', broadcasting to Germany the obscene rantings of an invented fanatical Nazi disgusted at the supposed degeneracy of leading Party members. Before the idea was kyboshed by top brass, he'd even produced a doctored propaganda photograph of Hitler with a giant circumcised penis to be dropped by RAF bombers over German cities – a visual companion to the filthy ditty about Hitler only having one ball that we still sang in the playground when I was a child.

Delmer also produced leaflets intended to undermine the morale of German soldiers by making them consider what their partner back home was up to. Crudely punning on the patriotic anthem 'Die Wacht am Rhein' ('Firm stands true the watch on the Rhine'), the leaflet featured a picture of a grave of a soldier, accompanied by another of a German woman having sex with a 'foreign worker'. Delmer, however, didn't believe that such leaflets were effective. The Special Operations Executive ordered thousands, he wrote, 'but ironically not because they found them to be subversive of German morale, but because they found them excellent for the morale of their men distributing them!'

The German Skorpion propaganda units were far more productive, creating leaflets that played with the libido and insecurities of the British soldiers. Curiously, though these leaflets are now highly collectible, they barely feature in academic study. Some are reproduced on a fascinating website by Herbert A. Friedman, a historian of psychological warfare. German leaflets featured nudes on mocked-up covers of *Life* magazine with a skull and crossbones on the back, attractive women having sex with rich Jews in a series called 'The Girl You Left Behind', another titled 'Home Front Warriors' with a drawing of a woman climbing a ladder as her boss looks up her skirt, along with the caption 'A thought crossed his mind'. A particularly detailed leaflet has a distant silhouette of British soldiers trudging to battle, contrasted with a man who sits on a couch with three naked women cavorting and drinking champagne under the caption 'The Americans are lend-leasing your women'. According to Friedman, Allied soldiers were largely grateful for this freely distributed pornography.

State propaganda might have failed to undermine morale with leafleting, but there were still neuroses about a possible threat to the individual and the wider war effort from the wayward sexuality of women. Most famously, there are propaganda posters of attractive women trying to lure men into giving up secrets – 'Keep schtum she's not so dumb', the sexist relation to 'Careless talk costs lives'. It also manifested in unusual ways. One of the first conversations Harry Lomas had heard in the mess at RAF Lissett was about a woman who had had three boyfriends in six months, all of whom had been shot down, or 'got the chop' in RAF lingo. For the men of Bomber Command, if an unfortunate member of the Women's Auxiliary Air Force (WAAF) had been walking out with more than a couple of men who had failed to return from missions, she'd often become known as a 'chop girl'. The lore of superstition had it that men would then avoid any contact with her. In some cases, the woman would have to be transferred out of the station, a sexual Jonah.

This disquiet about sexually voracious women often had racist overtones. In my grandad's letters from the *Andalucia Star*, he refers to a strange companion who seemed obsessed with the 'dangers' of the 'native' women in Sierra Leone. In the occupied Naples of Norman Lewis, one branch of British military intelligence suspected that the prevalence of prostitution in the city was not driven by the desperate need of the population but a dastardly plot by pro-fascist forces to spread VD among the Allied troops. This led to a counterplan by the Allies' A-Force to use some of Naples's most attractive prostitutes (paid with gold coins hidden in their rectums) to spread the south's epidemic levels of VD into the still-occupied north of the country where cases were low thanks to German military medical supervision of brothels.

Whether spread by ordinary sexual activity or devious plots, venereal disease troubled both the state and individual. The soldier's great fear, according to J. H. Witte, was of 'copping a packet'. He wrote about how servicemen could go to the Prophylactic Ablution Centre to have a solution of pomegranate potash squirted down the urethra. On the way out, he'd be given a blue slip that guaranteed no loss of pay if he contracted VD. More effective was a trip to Cairo's Hygiene Museum, which had a display of plaster cast cocks in varying stages of disease. This, Witte felt, was far more likely to discourage men from having sex with prostitutes than any government or military education campaign.

The concern over the prevalence of VD in both civil and military populations came up against a media that struggled to know how to give sufficiently explicit information so as to be useful. In 1943, the Newspaper Proprietors' Association severely edited a government health campaign. The original advert stated: 'The first sign of syphilis is a small ulcer on or near the sex organs'; 'Gonorrhoea first shows itself as a discharge from the sex organs' and 'Professional prostitutes are not the only source of infection'. The final sentence was removed entirely and the first two edited to remove mention of 'sex organs', leading to panicked letters to the Ministry of Health from people concerned they might have been infected. *The Lancet* journal criticised the 'prudery' of the newspapers in printing such misleading information.

The VD epidemic in Italy described by Norman Lewis was a

warning to military commanders as the Allied armies advanced through Europe in the later months of 1944. In September, the 21st Army Group, made up of hundreds of thousands of men drawn not only from British units but also Canadian, Polish, Belgian, Dutch, Czech and American, issued a small leaflet called 'Facts You Should Know About VD'. It warned that venereal disease was a risk to both war effort and society once the fighting was over. It implied that the retreating enemy were to blame for these particularly dangerous and decidedly foreign strains of disease, which were described as 'much more serious and harder to cure than in the U.K.'. Responsibility was firmly, some would say aggressively, placed upon the soldier. 'No casualties from V.D. need ever occur! If they do it is because individuals are reckless and stupid.' I can imagine this typed sentence being barked out, spittle-flecked, by some regimental sergeant major.

The pamphlet makes the age-old differentiation between the purity of the wife at home and the dangerously alluring licentiousness of the woman abroad. It warned that 'The *Prostitute* is the greatest danger, but almost all willing women in Europe are now infected. Because a woman is doing it for food, cigarettes, or chocolate, instead of money, she is no less a risk! The enthusiastic amateur, who welcomes the victorious troops with sexual favours is another great source of infection.' It went on to warn men against registration cards, medical certificates of cleanliness, brothels and, perhaps above all these, the serviceman's own instincts as to what he could get away with. 'Your own judgement is no use! Even if a girl is "nice", "clean looking" and well-dressed or pretends to be "innocent" she may be highly infectious.' They were also warned against alcohol that reduced inhibitions, especially to 'Beware the Wine of the country! You cannot drink it in pints like beer!' It sought too to dispel myths of transmission (of a sort similar to those that appeared with the AIDS crisis in the 1980s and 90s) via clothes, drinking vessels, toilets and washing facilities. The recommended approach to escape VD was to avoid promiscuity and 'stupid sexual risks', the leaflet even giving a hint of carrot with the stick in the promise of the benefits of abstinence – 'all the evidence indicates that it preserves the sexual powers'. The pamphlet misguidedly insists that men can only catch VD from a woman, that 'Other men undergoing treatment are no danger to you!' While a 1944 leaflet would be an unlikely place for the powers that be to suddenly start discussing the VD risks of then-illegal sexual activity between men, I wonder if this silence caused, for no few individuals, a belief that having sex with one another, or male prostitutes, was in fact 'safe'.

It's a curious little pamphlet with all the outraged moral energy of religious judgement. Like the propaganda posters of the early war years, it falls into the assumption that men are frail and easily led, women are temptresses and that careless talk might cost your balls as well as lives. Shame of VD remained for many a private torment. In *The Cruel Sea*, Sub-Lieutenant Baker loses his battle with the cold of the North Atlantic Ocean after the sinking of *The Compass Rose* in part because the prospect of drowning washes away the physically and psychologically agonising symptoms of the venereal disease he contracted while losing his virginity: 'The icy water was agreeably numbing [. . .] he had begun to welcome the increasing cold as it ate into his groin, and the feeling that this loathsome and hated part of his body was at least being brought under control.' Death was preferable to shame. Yet no amount of pamphlets could put a finger in the dam against the giant flood of testosterone, lust, spunk and pus that accompanied the Allied grind through Europe.

Colin Spencer spent his National Service in the grim ruins of post-war Hamburg, working in the Medical Corps treating men with venereal disease. He told me that his motivation to volunteer for this somewhat curious job was because it presented him, a bisexual man, with the opportunity to see 'a lot of cocks'. 'I can remember this bloody queue each morning, and never getting to the end of it in the day. Generally, it was giving injections into everybody's bum. I remember it now, if that's the cheek' – Spencer drew a buttock in the air with his palm – 'you'd have to knock it like that, and get the needle in, and then on the second knock, when they thought the needle had gone in, then you really pushed it.' The queue of men turning up for the buttock jab every day was, he believes, largely due to prostitution. 'That was their main source of sex because it was all fairly cheap,' he said. 'Our notes would get reported to the military police. We didn't hear about same-sex prostitution, that was never mentioned though I'm bloody sure it happened. There were general anti-gay feelings, so you knew they lied about things. I couldn't always spot the ones who had got it from men. Of course, if they liked the look of you, they admitted the truth.' By and large, though, the men with VD were heterosexual, sometimes crudely and demonstratively so. 'I remember these men who had gonorrhoea about five times comparing their pus, who had the thickest, it was disgusting,' he said. 'Did it put me off? It put me off gonorrhoea, yes! The crude humour was part of the masculinity.'

# SODOMY AND IGNOMINY

Colin Spencer's grotty tale of sex in the ruins of Germany reminded me of a passage of writing that years ago shook my expectations of what a man of war could and should be. I came across it, no pun intended, in *The White Guns*, a novel by Douglas Reeman, the kind of schlocky war thriller that I lapped up through my adolescence but has vanished from bookshops today. The men of motor gunboat MGB801 are stationed in the German port of Kiel in the immediate aftermath of the war. A virgin sailor, Lowes, is introduced by a countess to a young woman who seems (that cringeworthy sex writing of the war novel again) 'like a fawn'. Lowes is terrified of the clap but a kiss from the girl make him forget his fears. The kisses go on for several laborious, intricately described sentences until, 'Lowes thought his mind would burst [. . .] he reached up through the thin robe to discover an erection to match his own. He knew he should have been shocked, disgusted, but he was far beyond that now. The boy slipped out of the robe and lay down beside him while they explored each other like lovers.'

I must have broken the book's spine at that passage as I read it over and over, this novel of ships and destruction and men and violence suddenly and unexpectedly chiming with my own muddled desires. By that point, it'd been a long time since I'd built a model kit. I'd grown frustrated at what seemed to be an inability to get anywhere with my hobby, culminating in a furious rage in which I threw a half-completed B-17 Flying Fortress (in RAF Coastal Command rather than American markings, of course) across my bedroom. I'd stopped going to Boys' Brigade, fed up with the cod-military routines and endless football sessions. In the same year as *The Long and the Short and the Tall*, I went on a trip to the First World War battlefields of France and Belgium. The carefree weeks of the summer holiday had ended with return to the oppressive tedium of all-male company, the whiff of Lynx deodorant, petty macho aggravation, and humiliation in store for those of us arriving for the new term in a second-hand blazer several sizes too large. Teenage historians freed from the classroom, we scampered around the trenches and rusting bits of corrugated iron that were supposedly the remains of the British and Canadian front line, now preserved by the Hill 62 museum just outside Ypres. It felt exciting, this site of violence, compared to the sombre melancholy of the regiments of white headstones in the huge cemeteries that punctuate the flat Flanders landscape like ivory dominos abandoned on green baize. I remember the dreich and the drizzle and the falling leaves, our teacher telling us about reliable evidence and primary sources. Someone else said that Fat Jacques, the museum's founder, used to water the trenches for authentic mud and the 'shell holes' scattered through the woodland occasionally had sharper edges, as if freshly touched up with a spade.

Much of the trip was incredibly moving, but the class also did what teenage boys freed from parental constraints tend to do – misbehave, indulge petty prejudice, obsess over girls. Shopkeepers long immune to English lads with artificially lowered voices and fuzzy chins refused to sell us stubby bottles of lager. Some boys tried to work out if they could force the coach loo to emergency discharge as we crossed the border into France, a dirty protest upgrade on xenophobic back-window mooning. The driver was a creep, switching on the tannoy to announce in a voice cracked by regular access to cheap European cigarettes, 'eyes left – lovely bit of crumpet out there, boys' every time we drove past girls our age walking to school, much to the consternation of the teachers.

In the evening, someone produced a handheld Sony games console. It had a TV adapter and we climbed a rickety metal tower, part of some long-condemned adventure playground, to see if we could get a signal, convinced that late-night European telly would be wall-to-wall pornography. As we stood on the swaying scaffold staring wistfully at the small screen of static, I endured the added frisson of a deep and unrequited crush on one of my classmates, his tanned summer face lit by the soft glow. Later, in the youth hostel dormitories that we were told to imagine were barracks for the British Expeditionary Force in 1915, I longed for his body, a bunk away in the darkness.

I was stuck, the innocence of my departing childhood confused by what seemed to be a strange kind of sexual purgatory as, I thought, I waited for my hormones to decide whether I was heterosexual or doomed to be gay. And I mean 'doomed'. Under the Conservative Party's Section 28 legislation, the religion I had grown up with and the laddism reflected both in nineties popular culture and at school, to be gay was something I had internalised to be dreaded. I had absorbed enough homophobia to believe that gay men were weak and effeminate. I started to see my own uselessness on the sports field as a reflection of that. For a while, the Second World War provided me with an escape from my peers, with my weak body, physical ineptitude and confused sexuality, but I was starting to feel that I was nothing like this generation who were held up as heroes. I'd begun to find my masculine role models in music rather than the black-and-white photos of history books.

*The Long and the Short and the Tall* isn't an anti-war play per se, rather, this deep dive into the side of militarism that I had always avoided – that it was all about men, not machines – was part of my turning away from years of fascination. Literature had ushered me along this path too. Kurt Vonnegut's *Slaughterhouse Five* and Len Deighton's *Bomber* were grim reminders of what happened when RAF bombs found their targets. I'd borrowed Dad's copies of Nicholas Monsarrat's *The Cruel Sea* and Joseph Heller's *Catch-22*, books that explored the insane, haphazard harshness of war. There are passages in Monsarrat's fictionalised account of his own wartime service on the Atlantic convoys that affected me more than nearly anything else I'd read of the war. In one, commander of Flower Class corvette *The Compass Rose* George Ericson is hunting what seems on the ship's sonar to be the U-boat that has recently sunk one of the ships in the convoy. As they surge towards the target area, men swimming in the water view the oncoming corvette as their salvation. Yet Ericson has to make the decision to continue the attack at all costs. His ship ploughs through the survivors, dropping depth charges that explode among the desperately struggling men. One is tossed in the air in the cloud of spray and smoke, 'a puppet figure of whirling arms and legs seeming to make, in death, wild gestures of anger and reproach'. He falls back into a sea which resembles an aquarium after everything has been poisoned: 'Men floated high on the surface like dead goldfish in a film of blood. Most of them had disintegrated, or pulped out of human shape. But half a dozen of them [. . .] had come to a tidier end; split open from chin to crotch, they had been as neatly gutted as any herring.'

These books all laid out with uncompromising honesty what happened when metal and explosives met human flesh. They were imbued with a mood of futility, not glory and heroics. As I read them, I started to wonder if I had the Second World War all wrong.

The conflict of a half century before was reappearing in British culture in a new and ugly way. I have and always have had a mild patriotism, the sort that a very left-wing friend once explained to me rather brilliantly. To love your country in the right way, she said, was rather like loving your dad and talking about him at school. You knew you loved your dad more than you could ever love any of your friends' parents because of the indelible bond you shared, yet it wasn't like you thought he was better. He was just more special to you. Back in the mid-1990s, I became uncomfortable with how this was becoming toxified by what was going on in British culture around me.

There had been a lot of flag-waving at the VE Day commemoration in Hyde Park, but I now saw a more unpleasant side to what had previously seemed a harmless bit of celebration of the courage of my country. It was largely entwined with the boorish, nationalistic jingoism that accompanied football, especially around the 1996 European Championships. On 24 June, ahead of England's semi-final with Germany, the *Daily Mirror* printed a front-page cover story featuring mocked-up portraits of England's Paul Gascoigne and Stuart Pearce wearing British army issue tin helmets with the ill-judged headline 'Achtung! Surrender! For you Fritz, ze Euro 96 Championship is over!'. It was accompanied by a front page editorial by the then editor Piers Morgan in the style of Chamberlain's sombre declaration of war in September 1939 – 'Last night the *Daily Mirror*'s ambassador in Berlin handed the German Government a final note stating that, unless we heard from them by 11 o'clock that they were prepared at once to withdraw their football team from Wembley, a state of soccer war would exist between us.'

After England lost the game on penalties, a couple of thousand angry blokes descended on Trafalgar Square to cause havoc, screaming moronic chants about 'two world wars and one world cup' and 'ten German bombers' as they attacked police, smashed windows and set fire to cars. Parliament's all-party National Heritage Committee blamed the war rhetoric of the tabloids for the violence, issuing a statement saying that it 'has decided to express its disgust at the xenophobic, chauvinistic and jingoistic gutter journalism perpetrated by those newspapers which may well have had its effect in stimulating the deplorable riots following the Germany victory in the semi-final'.

The war heroes I loved to read books about seemed tainted by the kind of strutting, self-assured men who now I was starting to fear and feel uncomfortable around. I was very conscious that the Conservative Party, who largely claimed ownership over any form of British patriotism, was a homophobic organisation that had pushed Section 28 legislation on my education. The only homosexual in the public eye I could think of who had been alive in the war was Kenneth Williams who, though a childhood hero for the Carry On films, his readings of *Willo the Wisp* and fantastic monologues on Radio 4's *Just a Minute*, seemed to fit the notion that gay men were absent from the heroic deeds with which I had been obsessed. The stronger my homosexual urges, the less appropriate it was that I should also still be fascinated with war. I looked at the veterans on remembrance parades and assumed that, down to a man, they were upstanding chaps who couldn't be anything other than heterosexual Brits, fathers of my parents' generation. They all looked so *normal*, after all.

I couldn't have been more wrong.

Dudley Cave was camping as war approached. The eighteen-year-old cinema projectionist and his friends packed up their tents in Chichester and drove back to London, struggling against a tide of traffic as people fearing the long-predicted air attack fled the capital. He saw barrage balloons in the sky for the first time over Hammersmith Bridge and felt the conflicting emotions of fear and excitement. Cave was at the local town hall on air raid warden duty when word began to spread that there was to be an important announcement at 11 a.m. An American woman who happened to be in the area had a rare car radio and allowed Cave to sit in her vehicle as the declaration of war was broadcast and the air raid sirens started to wail.

Even before school, Dudley Cave was aware of his sexuality, falling in love with another boy called Denis who introduced him 'to the most exciting game called "tummy pad" where you pulled up your grey Viyella shirts and you pressed tummy to tummy, 'cos it felt good'. Once at a three-guinea-a-term private school, Cave found that same-sex experiences, far from being frowned on, were enjoyed by everyone, and he was constantly falling for other boys, having sex and indulging in mutual masturbation during lessons, though as a religious child he felt it wasn't right to do so during Divinity. The 'sissies' were the more effeminate boys who didn't necessarily indulge in the sexual activity, such as masturbatory orgies in the bath after sport, preferring to just wash and leave. Reflecting in a 1987 interview, Cave seemed to be of the opinion that same-sex experiences were easier to come by, and perhaps more accepted, than in his present moment, despite the law. He believed that 'in those days, being gay was OK'. Cave left school at seventeen to take a job as a cinema projectionist and became active in politics. Appalled by Oswald Mosley's Blackshirts, he would protest their local meetings on Hampstead Heath. 'I was wildly anti-fascist which made me a Communist because you were either a Communist who fought the fascists or you were fascist or somebody who just let it all flow by [. . .] events proved us right, that fascism did need fighting, and fighting hard and early.'

Working in his cinema, listening to fragments of shrapnel from anti-aircraft shells and German bombs rattle on the glass roof, Cave was unperturbed by the months of the phoney war, the Blitz and the Battle of Britain which, counter to the mythology, struck him 'as a pompous title for a few aerial dog fights'. The fighting was less of a concern than more carnal matters: 'We had our priorities right. During the war one tends to think perhaps from literature that everybody was worried sick about being bombed, in fact they were very keen and they were getting their sex life.' Although he preferred to keep his entanglements among his friends (including while on ARP duty), Cave remembered that for gay men 'there was a wonderful time going on. You see, it was quite easy to be picked up and stay out at night, and I believe there was fun to be had in public shelters.'

Cave was initially inclined to register as a conscientious objector, but revelations about the horrors of the Third Reich's persecution of the Jews changed his mind. Aged twenty and three months, Cave joined the Army. After training, which he enjoyed, Cave was shipped out to the Middle East on the ocean liner *Empress of Asia*, but the Japanese advance in early 1942 led to a diversion to Singapore, where the young soldier's war took a turn for the worse. The ship was attacked by bombers and the survivors were pitched into the last-ditch defence of the city. Cave was captured by the Japanese on 15 February.

The physical extremity of wartime existence and the visceral awareness of the male body in all its vulnerabilities run through Dudley Cave's diary letter to his father, written in old school exercise books and, as the years of incarceration went on, on any scraps of paper he could find. It is an account of life without freedom under the brutality of the Japanese, of cockroaches, rats, flies, biting ants, bugs that stink when squished, endless meals of rice and gruel, gut worms, dysentery, malaria, dirty bodies impossible to clean except by endless scraping with the fingernails. He watched his friend Fred Smith slowly die of starvation and later discovered his corpse, opened up for examination, abandoned on a makeshift mortuary table. It was the only time he remembered feeling truly angry at the Japanese.

Cave was forced to work on the Burma railroad, later immortalised in the popular war film *A Bridge on the River Kwai*. His weight before capture – 12st 4lb – fell away to a shocking 7st 8lb. In the horrendous conditions of the Japanese POW camps, Cave's libido vanished. He didn't join in what he called 'the army phenomenon of mates', where two close pals 'would do things for each other' and when one was sent up country his friend would volunteer to go and be near him. Neither did he submit to his captor's practice of using some men as 'concubines', resisting the advances of one Japanese guard who eyed him up while bathing in a spring, remarking that his penis was 'number one'. Yet he still found a strange acceptance of who he was among his fellow prisoners. Once, when he was seen wearing a sarong, someone 'suggested I was a poof, queer, nancy boy'. A cockney voice spoke up, saying that Cave definitely wasn't a homosexual as he had been brave under fire. 'Well, my wonderful bravery was going to sleep when I was scared of being killed. You notice you couldn't be gay and brave.'

To the military authorities, not only was it impossible to be gay and brave, but as deviants from 'normal' masculinity, homosexuals posed a serious threat to the war effort, to be suppressed at all costs using the tools of strict punishment and moral education. On 25 April 1940, while Cave was a cinema projectionist by day and a sexually distracted ARP volunteer by night, a signal was transmitted by the Admiralty in central London, humming around the world to thousands of ships and land bases. Confidential

Admiralty Fleet Orders were command signals to naval units that now sit in bound volumes in the National Archives. In 1940, along-side drawings of German merchant vessels, diagrams of explosive triggers, the appropriate shells to fire at submarines, the location of minefields, updates on pay grades, camouflage schemes on aircraft and all the minutiae of naval combat is CAFO 648 – Unnatural Offences. These are defined as 'offences of sexual immorality between males', including sodomy, 'assault with intent to commit sodomy', indecent assault, procuring, incitement to commit these offences and the startlingly broad yet severe 'uncleanness, or other scandalous action in derogation of God's honour and cor-ruption of good manners'. This, as the Fleet Order points out, is taken verbatim from the Naval Discipline Act of 1661, with the modern note that 'uncleanness' means 'not necessarily sodomy but any immoral or dirty act contrary to nature'. The Admiralty believed that homosexual activity posed an acute danger to the fighting potential of its ships and recommended that 'religious agencies' and officers alike should 'point out the horrible character of unnatural vice and its evil effect in sapping the moral fibre of those who indulge in it, as well as the physical dangers to those who submit themselves to the desire of vicious men'.

The criminalisation of desire also demanded its medicalisation. An examination was required in any case of suspected sodomy. In an appendix to the order, medical officers are advised on checking the anus for signs of laceration, the presence of sperm or venereal disease. The MO is told to examine both men involved to deter-mine 'whether one or other is the active or passive agent, i.e., they must examine both the anus and the penis of both of them'. Medical officers are reminded of their preventative duties in their health lectures, not only from the point of view of venereal disease but that 'such acts [. . .] may lead, as in the vice of masturbation, to very serious nervous afflictions'.

It wasn't just the navy that bound sexuality in law. Section 41 of the King's Regulations held homosexual acts as a crime punishable under civilian law. The Offences of the Person Act 1861 and Section 11 of the Criminal Law Amendment Act of 1885 made even private homosexual acts illegal and remained on the statute books during the war years. The Manual of Military Law counted 'sodomy' as an offence alongside rape and the abuse of minors – the crucial difference being that even if both parties were consenting, it was still a crime. Even though anal penetration was deemed to be the criminal act, the highly pleasurable grey areas of mutual masturbation and fellatio were bound up in the proviso that 'if the evidence upon this charge is insufficient to justify conviction for the full offence, the accused person may be found guilty of an attempt to commit it' while the following point 40 introduced the offence of 'any act of gross indecency with another male person'. Gross indecency, of course, being very much in the eyes of the beholder. The Naval King's Regulations had the punishment of 'Indecent Assaults, or indecent acts of a grossly immoral character' set at the highest level possible – dismissal from the service with disgrace.

There is no question of a need for emotional and physical connection and intimacy between the men of the wartime services, merely assumptions of moral degeneracy and sexual predation. The moral and legal obsession over sodomy, and whether the man took the active or passive role, reduces sex to an act of dominance and power. It is seemingly inconceivable that anyone being penetrated might be taking pleasure in it.

An Air Ministry file, Discharge of Airmen for Reasons of Misconduct, no. A92339/40, contains a minute of 4 September 1940, questioning whether in the light of manpower needs of the time, too many men were being kicked out of the RAF. Homosexuals, thieves who had previously been imprisoned and those who had been jailed for serious civil offences were all recommended to be discharged from the service 'with ignominy'. A letter from the Air Minister to the HQ of 20 Group in Shropshire dated 7 April 1941 states that 'the offences which in the view of the Air Council are so grave or are of such revolting nature as to render the retention of the offender in the Air Force even in war time definitely undesirable are (a) Theft of money or valuables from a comrade (b) Homo-sexual [sic] offences'.

Despite these edicts from the military hierarchy, historian Emma Vickers points out that, of the nearly 6 million men who served in British forces during the war, only 1,813 servicemen of the Army, Navy and RAF were tried by court martial for offences of indecency, with a mere 1,428 convictions. In *Homosexuality in History*, Colin Spencer wrote that many queer men and women he knew regarded the war years as 'a sexual golden era on which they looked back on with a lingering sense of nostalgia'. He told me that we have heard little about this since because 'sex was swept under the carpet – it was English society not wanting to face up to the truth, so you underestimated it, or refused to talk about it'. His slightly older queer friends told him that 'it was certainly a lot more liberated. Of course the blackout was a great boon – I used to hear stories of all you could do in the blackout.'

Dudley Cave wrote in 1995, when it was still illegal for LGBT+ people to serve in the military, 'There were none of the witch-hunts like we have now with the armed forces. Homosexual soldiers were more or less accepted.' Nevertheless, the most accepted were those who presented as more effeminate, as Cave explained, 'The visible gays were mostly drag performers in concert teams. There was never any disciplinary action taken against them. One was renowned for giving good blow jobs.' Similarly, on a trip to London, John Alcock was fascinated to see RAF officers in make-up hanging around Piccadilly Circus. In the bar of the Regent Palace

Hotel, he realised that he was surrounded by officers, including some from his own battalion. He recalled that to realise 'that other ranks were queer the same as I was' was a 'gratifying' experience. On returning to his unit the following Monday, he saw one of queer officers who saluted and said, 'Have a nice weekend, dear, keep it to yourself.'

There must have been countless small acts of turning a blind eye and tolerance during the Second World War, away from the cruelty of the Navy's Fleet Order or Air Ministry belief that the sexual act between two men was, like stealing his watch or money, an act of robbery. Little did these dour, judgemental communiques know that one of the great heroes of the Battle of Britain had been guilty of their crime.

BBC TV series *It's Not Unusual* was screened in 1997 on a Friday night next to *Have I Got News for You*, a comedy show that I watched religiously. A groundbreaking programme, *It's Not Unusual* explored the history of British queer sexuality, stretching right back before the war years. It was not the sort of thing I would have felt comfortable watching at home and I only caught up with the programme when it appeared on YouTube in more recent years. I wish I had seen it earlier, this rather twinkly account of queer life during the Second World War. I am amazed at how far ahead of its time it now seems. For a mainstream and prime-time television series to be centring the LGBT+ stories of the Second World War now would feel like a breathless antidote to the reams of programmes that seem to excitedly fetishise violence and portray veterans as kindly, simple old creatures without the depth that a truly honest and open sexual existence would give them. Yet *It's Not Unusual* begs a question: is it right that the present can 'out' the past?

That's what happened in the testimony of Christopher Gotch,

an RAF fighter pilot who eventually became a squadron leader. At the start of his career, Gotch was sent from his Operational Training Unit to a squadron stationed at RAF Middle Wallop. After three weeks on the base, Gotch was sitting in the mess reading only to feel the 'curious sensation' that someone was staring at him. He looked up from his paper to see that the eyes were those of his Wing Commander, Ian Gleed. Gotch was naturally worried that he'd done something wrong, but the Wing Commander got up and left the mess. Reading done, Gotch headed to his room to find Gleed sitting on the window ledge leafing through an album of photographs from Canada. 'He just leant over and gave me a great big kiss, which took me by surprise but being the product of a public school wasn't exactly strange,' Gotch recalled. 'He then made an assignation for me to join him in his room, either that evening or another evening, and so we started having sex together. He was the first bloke who ever buggered me, and it went extremely well.' Their relationship, transient as the war demanded, was a secret thing. As Gotch explained, 'they were court-martial offences, for God's sake'. They were never caught, though there was once a close call when the two men were in bed in Gleed's room and the Group Captain hammered on the locked door. Gotch had to leap, stark naked, from the bed and hide in a cupboard, where he stood shivering and desperately trying not to cough while his two superior officers planned the next day's operations.

Ian Gleed was born on 3 July 1916 in Finchley, North London, to a doctor father who had served in the First World War. He had an upper middle-class upbringing, attending Tenterden Preparatory School and Epsom College, with enough family money to pay for joyrides in aircraft while he was still at school. Aged nineteen, he began flying lessons at Hatfield aerodrome, the headquarters of De Havilland aircraft – close to where I grew up and where I would regularly go to air shows – getting his licence on 12 July

1935. He joined the RAF the following year, becoming an Acting Pilot Officer on 4 May 1936. Gleed was one of the professional pilots of the RAF at the start of the war, those suave and debonair chaps whom I had so idolised as a child.

Ian Gleed's wartime memoir, *Arise to Conquer*, was published in 1942. In the contemporaneous foreword by Flight Lieutenant John Strachey, the romantic ideal of the Battle of Britain was already taking shape. Writing that Gleed's words are an insight into the motivations and feelings of the young men who flew and fought, Strachey contrasts them with the German and Japanese 'robots', dehumanised and indoctrinated to enjoy killing for their leaders, claiming that the 'young Englishmen' were just the same as their peers on the ground, 'profoundly capable of the normal, constructive pursuits of peaceful existence' and 'intensely individual' by nature, but had still devoted themselves to the cause of aerial combat and defence of their nation.

*Arise to Conquer*, like so many similar books that blur the line between memoir and fiction, is exactly the sort of thing that I would have loved as a Battle of Britain obsessed kid; it's full of dramatic tension, zippily described action, fear, jeopardy and homage to the power and grace of the Hurricane and Spitfire. There's the comradeship too, the nights in pubs, cinemas and fish and chip shops, haring back to the aerodrome in fast cars to be ready to fight the next day.

Gleed's first week in combat was a violent one. He was posted to join 87 Squadron in France on 14 May 1940. Four days later, on 18 May, he shot down two Messerschmitt Bf 110 fighters near Valenciennes. The very next day, he destroyed two Dornier Do 17 bombers and a Bf 109 fighter, damaging another. On the 20 May, he shared credit for shooting down a Ju88 bomber with another pilot. Within just a week, he had shot down five enemy aircraft to become a fighter ace, a time record that no other RAF pilot managed to break. Gleed describes reading novels in the cockpit, waiting for the alert that would send them into battle. At an airfield in France in the hectic days of early spring 1940, the literature of choice for some of his squadron comrades was erotica picked up in the seedier bookshops of Paris, Amiens and Lille. The men would eagerly await the latest saucy picture of the *Daily Mirror*'s pin-up Jane to see if she had any clothes on, listen to gramophone records and build model aircraft, only to use them as target practice for their revolvers. In France, and then during the Battle of Britain, Gleed describes a mode of life that might best be called a right old caper, the aerial combat always a hectic internal conversation in urgent present tense. It's all laced with exclamations that come straight out of the popular imagining of how young English fighter pilots of the Battle of Britain spoke – 'Hell!', 'Damned Huns!', 'Blast you b— —ds!', 'Good show!', 'Wizard show!' and 'Bloody good show!' – and the zippy slang that is always the lingua-franca of young men – 'dope' for information, for example – and for machine-gun fire, variations on the theme of 'brrrrrrrrrrrrrm'.

Gleed's lover Pam is a constant through the book. Following a nasty crash, it is Pam who Gleed telegrammed, along with his parents, to let her know that he was OK. Recuperating afterwards, he and Pam sailed his boat *Spindrift* from Herne Bay to Broadstairs, always 'dreaming happy dreams of the future'. When Gleed was given medical clearance to fly again, he rang his lover to tell her: 'Poor Pam! She would be hellishly upset. She was very brave, and as we loved each other so much, she would be glad for me.' Throughout, Gleed describes the typical relationship between the gallant young pilot and the lover waiting at home. Above all, he worried that combat would take away his chance for a happy life with Pam. 'I loved her now more than ever,' he wrote, 'but life and death seemed very close together these days.' Even when flying out to sea in his Hurricane to the biggest engagement of his war to date, an interception of an estimated 120-plus German aircraft, Gleed was thinking of Pam. She was there too in the strange, ecstatic moments when, after the intensity of battle and the loss of friends, Gleed became acutely aware of the joy of life. The colours seemed more vivid, the air tasted sweet and he fell asleep between rough sheets, dreaming of them together, sailing the *Spindrift*.

When Gleed's family read *Arise to Conquer* they were confused – who was this girlfriend called Pam, who they had never heard of, let alone met, despite passages in which they're described as having spoken to her? Gleed passed it off as being the introduction of some romance for the lads on the airbase. His biographer, Norman Franks, said that it was done at the request of the publisher, Victor Gollancz, to make the book more marketable.

Franks makes no explicit mention of who 'Pam' really was, though the clues are all over the pages of his book. In the late 1930s, Gleed had a much younger friend who I shall call T, with whom he would sail his boat the *Spindrift*. There are photographs of the pair sailing together, both leaning out over the waves to steady her against the breeze. T is ever-present in the role that Gleed in his memoir gave to the fictional 'Pam'. After Gleed joined the RAF, he'd often fly down to Manston airfield to spend time with his young friend. The relationship continued, despite the war, aided by Gleed's penchant for unconventional operations. In May 1941, he led a small force of Hurricane fighters to the Scilly Isles, with a view to being able to intercept Luftwaffe aircraft operating from northern France. While there, he borrowed a yacht and decided to give his 'young friend', as his biographer puts it, 'a treat'. Gleed borrowed a two-seater Tiger Moth aircraft, flew to RAF Northolt, picked up T and brought him back for sailing trips, dressing him in clothes to resemble a pilot. Were there not an emotional relationship involved, it would seem surprising that Gleed would have gone to so much trouble and risk – the clandestine jaunts happened three or four times. With all this borrowing of aircraft to fly to visit his 'friend', Gleed's comrades must surely have suspected or even known a different nature to his relationship – and his sexuality. Perhaps a fighter ace got to do what he wanted.

Nevertheless, Ian Gleed lived a double life, presenting a heterosexual fiction in *Arise to Conquer*, the truth only revealed by Christopher Gotch on prime-time television and by joining the dots in his biography. There are clues, too, in his friendships outside of the RAF, often with men who, like him, had sexual desires that excluded them from the 'normal'. Gleed had spent 1938 sailing in the Mediterranean on a yacht belonging to the writer Somerset Maugham, one of those men who lived in the hinterlands before fluid sexual desire was properly defined. As Maugham once said, 'I tried to persuade myself that I was three-quarters normal and that only a quarter of me was queer — whereas really it was the other way around.' Maugham even wrote about Gleed (though anonymised) in his book *Strictly Personal*, describing how the pilot told him he was going to buy a boat and sail it to the South Seas with his friend, presumably T. They ended their final meeting talking about whether Gleed was scared during his battles. The pilot's response was that fear came not so much in combat but on solo reconnaissance flights, when he felt he was a tiny speck in the sky. He wondered why it was then that he felt so afraid that his knees shook. 'Infinity,' Maugham suggested might be the reason. 'I never saw him again. Perhaps he knows now that there's nothing so frightening in infinity after all.'

From November 1941 until the early summer of 1942, Gleed flew missions over occupied France, attacking and shooting down aircraft including Junkers Ju 88s, Messerschmitt Bf 109s and the fearsome new Focke-Wulf Fw 190. Now a Wing Leader, he was allowed to have his own initials painted on the side of his aircraft rather than his squadron identifiers. There's a fetching photograph of him standing in front of his Spitfire in flying gear and life jacket, the letters I, R and G sandwiching the RAF roundel. In September 1940, he'd been awarded the Distinguished Flying Cross at a ceremony at Buckingham Palace for his service in the Battle of France and Battle of Britain. He was photographed in a smiling line-up with the RAF's Air Chief Marshal Sir Hugh Dowding and other aces of the battle, including Richard Hillary. On 22 May 1942, he received the Distinguished Service Order. The citation read, 'This officer has led his wing on 26 sorties over enemy territory. He has always displayed a fine fighting spirit which, combined with his masterly leadership and keenness, has set an inspiring example.' That July, he was removed from flying and sent to HQ Fighter Command as Wing Commander Tactics but, fed up with desk work, arranged to have himself posted to the Middle East in the New Year.

Christmas 1942 was to be Ian Gleed's last. He spent it with his family in Finchley. He had a final dinner with T before preparing to fly to North Africa, where he was to return to operations. There he flew with 145 Squadron to get accustomed to the desert war. The Air Ministry published a photograph of Gleed on 15 April 1943, sitting in the cockpit of his Spitfire, called Figaro after the cat in the 1940 Disney version of *Pinocchio*. The animal is painted on the side of the fuselage, twisting round at a swastika disintegrating under its claws. Above the artwork, the Spitfire's canopy is pulled back and Gleed sits looking at the camera, desert sunlight showing his features in relief. The goggles on his flying helmet are raised and his face is a strange half-smile. The day after the photograph was printed, Wing Commander Ian Gleed set out on an operation to intercept a flight of Junkers Ju 52 transport aircraft. It seems that he was hit, probably by German fighter ace Ernst-Wilhelm Reinert, and turned Figaro the Spitfire Vb towards the North African coast. If the way he wrote about 'Pam' in *Arise to Conquer* is a close indicator of how Ian Gleed thought, in those last moments, in the sun-blasted intimacy of the aircraft cockpit, the distant coast approaching, the sea glistening past below, the altimeter ticking inevitably downwards, his mind must have been full of those dreams of sailing after the war, the spray on tanned faces, of love. Gleed was just twenty-six-years-old when he died. A friend found the wreckage of Figaro in the coastal dunes sometime later. His body lies in the military cemetery at Enfidaville in Tunisia, with an inscription from Robert Browning's poem 'Epilogue', selected by his mother, on the grave: 'One who held we fall to rise, are baffled to fight better, sleep to wake.' In the *Battle of Britain* film, the pilots' female lovers gaze longingly into the sky after them, sit fretting at home and so on, all the clichés of women whose men have gone to war, perhaps never to return. How T felt is a great absence, for we have little knowledge of how men who loved men were able to grieve.

The cultural memory of the Battle of Britain is full of pilots like Ian Gleed, though generally the handsome and idealised stereotype has them a little taller – his nickname 'Widge' was an abbreviated compound of 'wizard midget', from his habit of saying things were 'wizard' and his five-feet-six height. I don't believe that we should look to Gleed with modern eyes as some kind of LGBT+ icon. We can never know how he felt about the need to hide T and invent Pam against the prejudices of the day, whether he felt any internalised shame and torment over who he really was, or if it was even right that Gotch later outed him on a Friday night TV programme. I see Gleed as a war hero of the traditional sort, who just happened to be gay. His bravery, technical skill and leadership is evidence in the case against the homophobic notion that queers can't fight like other men. Just as the Polish 303 Squadron was the most successful during the Battle of Britain, the fact that a gay man was a fighter ace strikes me as a wonderful counter to those who would bind the struggle of the summer of 1940 into a reductive narrative about a nation represented by clean-cut and wholesome young chaps of a certain sort.

I had grown up with all sorts of homophobic assumptions about gay men of the Second World War. The ones we knew about, Kenneth Williams or Quentin Crisp, hardly fitted the stereotype of warriors. But you can't find much more of a classic British hero than Gleed, remembered and recognised in the decades since the war. I recently made a pilgrimage to my favourite childhood destination, the RAF Museum at Hendon, to see the cockpit door of Gleed's Mk 1 Hurricane. It sits in a display cabinet, a beautifully aged and weathered shade of green, complete with a cartoon drawing of Figaro the cat clawing a bloodied swastika. In the early 2000s, a surviving Hurricane was painted night-fighter black and given the markings of Gleed's aircraft (P2798, LK-A) for its annual tours around the air show circuit. And, in perhaps the greatest tribute, there are various model kits of Gleed's aircraft, including Airfix's top-selling model of the Mark 1 Hurricane in which he fought throughout the summer of the Battle of Britain. I have one in my kit stash now, ready for careful assembly.

I wonder what would have happened to Wing Commander Ian Gleed, DSO, DFC, Croix de Guerre had he survived the war. When he died, Gleed had been working on a follow-up to *Arise to Conquer* in which he wrote the line, now so tragic, 'It's strange how confident I feel that I shall survive this war.' Hector Bolitho, like Somerset Maughan, another queer writer who had befriended Gleed, wrote of him in the 1955 book *A Penguin in the Eyrie*. He recalled a conversation with Gleed the same day two of his comrades had been lost in an ambush by Messerschmitt fighters. Just as he had with Maugham, Gleed talked of his dream of sailing to the southern seas and said, 'I've grown up too fast. I want to be treated as if I were a boy again: it is something that I have lost, and I want it back.' The tone is a long way from the breathless excitement of *Arise to Conquer*. To Gleed, the place of innocence that the war had destroyed, just as the war would destroy him, was on the water, where he could feel the elements around his body. Perhaps had he survived he might have been able to find that peace, love and contentment, or perhaps 1950s conservatism and the persecution of gay men would have caught up with him, as it did for so many. Alan Turing might have become our figurehead when it comes to gay British heroes of the Second World War, but he is almost quite safe – the bookish fellow beavering away with his computer machine in the laboratory. In Gleed, we see a far more traditional kind of warrior, soaring in his death machine with guns blazing at Nazi aircraft, his life ending above the bright water and hot sand of the Mediterranean coast.

# A FLAME WITHOUT A HEARTH

On a Sunday morning in 1939, as a nation gathered around radios to listen to Neville Chamberlain solemnly declare that Britain was at war with Germany, Peter de Rome was naked in a beach hut on the English Channel coast, being fucked for the first time by a lad called Porky. As the prime minister's voice and the sea provided the accompaniment, Peter sang 'I love you Porky' to the tune of 'I Love You Porgy', and air raid sirens began to wail. Reflecting in his memoir, *The Erotic Life of Peter de Rome*, published in 1984, de Rome mused, 'If it is possible to date the chapters in one's life, that siren marked the moment when my boyhood finished and, if not my manhood, then certainly another life began.' The war would take him far from beach huts on the English south coast. It would change him, his relationship with his sexuality, and the precise nature and taste of his desires forever. Though at first, it perhaps didn't seem that way.

After a dispiriting period learning the wool trade in Manchester (where the only light relief came from a brawny mill worker who liked to pull out his gigantic penis and wave it around), de Rome volunteered for active service in the Fleet Air Arm. On his first night at a transit camp, he was accosted by a lecherous Irish squaddie trying to get into his bed and only a desire to be respectable made him resist the advances. De Rome was desperate to fly but an eye defect rendered him unsuitable. Instead, he ended up as a wireless operator, one who would also transmit a carnal knowledge of men who were superficially 'straight' down the decades. These are the invisible men, the thousands who before the war had sweethearts and afterwards had wives, who begat the baby boomers and lived on, perhaps never telling a soul of what they'd done in bunks, camp beds or blacked-out back alley. They appear in the writing and testimony of gay men describing a fertile, open sexual atmosphere, yet leave very little record themselves, a great silence in our collective memory of the Second World War.

Dudley Cave recalled how some of his sexual partners in the early years of the war were not gay men. He had one pal whose girlfriend had been forbidden to see him on religious grounds – she was a Catholic and he was Jewish. In the absence of her companionship, the friend turned to Cave and would come over for 'fairly satisfactory sex' when his father was on Home Guard duties at the local town hall as the Blitz raged around them. When Cave became an air raid warden at Golders Green post L80 and his friend a messenger, they'd spend the night having sex on the camp bed in the warden's post. His friend ended up marrying the Catholic and by 1987 was on his second wife.

That military service and war might cause a blurring of heterosexual desire had precedent. The Guards regiments are among some of the most prestigious in the British army, responsible for the ceremonial security of London's royal palaces. They embody martial British identity and tradition, yet in the early decades of the twentieth century, they had quite the reputation for homosexual activity. Quentin Crisp wrote that in his younger years, guardsmen strutted Hyde Park, available for half a crown. Peter de Rome wrote,

'It was often said that for a small consideration guardsmen would oblige, and the physique and the uniform certainly impressed me.' This behaviour, nearly always of guardsmen involved in sexual relations with civilians rather than other soldiers, was the subject of frequent conferences between the Army and police, and there were regular prosecutions of soldiers and their civilian clients alike.

Montague Glover, a middle-class man who liked, in the parlance, a bit of rough, was a great compiler of evidence of the elusive sexual identity of the Guards. After winning the Military Cross for his courage fighting in Italy during the First World War, Glover took a job as an architect with the Commonwealth War Graves Commission, working on the design and construction of memorials across the battlefields of northern France. Yet it wasn't just in Portland stone that he chose to immortalise young men's bodies. A keen photographer, he spent his life capturing the beauty of the male face and physique, as well as compiling scrapbooks full of images of men cut from adverts, magazines and newspapers – often featuring soldiers and men in uniform. Glover's photographs, collected in a fantastic book called *A Class Apart*, with commentary by James Gardiner, play with the identities of the young men he took back to his flat to capture on film. He'd often dress them up as military personnel in all sorts of uniforms – from the kilt of Scottish regiment to battledress, cockaded hats, sailors caps, tensing swagger sticks – oiled and shirtless. What's so startling is how classily sexy these images are, deliberately rather than accidentally voyeuristic as in the *My Buddy* collection. They might have been shot for Glover's own gratification, but their eroticism still burns nearly a century on. Certain images are particularly striking – a man leaning against a wall in full sun, in riding boots with Brylcreemed hair, another lighting a cigarette for a sailor lying back in a park, looking away under his cap, in his trousers a curving bulge reflecting the distant tops of a row of trees. The most outrageous are the images shot inside the barracks of the Guards regiment. Glover photographed these men in their huge shining boots rising above the knee like fetish gear, tight white trousers gathered around the crotch, jackets unbuttoned or removed to reveal vests over lean physiques.

Quentin Crisp was wary of the Guardsmen, fearing a beating, but wildly enthusiastic about sailors, especially those of lower rank, who were praised for their full-wallet generosity on shore leave, their open-mindedness (those who ran away to sea 'returned with their outlook and possibly their anus broadened') and, to top it all, the flapping of their trousers was considered a terrific aphrodisiac. A popular saying, often attributed to Winston Churchill, though in 1955, he said he'd never come up with it but wished he had, was that for the Royal Navy, 'ashore it's wine, women and song, aboard its rum, bum and concertina'. This tradition and saying has at its heart the belief that groups of men, cooped up for long periods of time without female company, will turn to one another for solace. It's not merely the slogan of lonely yet liberated nautical sexuality, but of compromise bisexuality, the sort assumed to happen in schools, prisons and so on. In *Sex Problems and Dangers in War-Time*, Ryley Scott wrote, 'Wherever the sexes are segregated sexual vice is to be found. It is a law of nature.'

John Alcock, who, as a teenager in Birmingham, mixed work in a munitions factory where everyone knew him as 'a sissy' with gay sex on the banks of the city's canals, reflected after the war that he believed all-male companionship and fear of death were responsible for the amount of action he got during the war. 'You've only got to get a few men together and you've got it anyway haven't you,' he said. 'It was in people's minds that that particular day was going to be their last so if a bit of free sex came along they were going to indulge [. . .] There was a tremendous amount of homosexuality going on amongst the queer men and amongst the heterosexual men [. . .] I remember that I was having sex all over the place in all kinds of situations and having a real ball.' Among Alcock's pick-ups were American GIs, Italian POWs and conscientious objectors, whom he was especially drawn to as they were always more 'smart' and 'gentle' than the 'rough and ready' ordinary soldier.

This connection between gay men and others who sat somewhere in the greyer zones of sexuality but presented to the outside world as heterosexual was frequently a result of the insecure masculine identity ascribed to homosexuals. To be called a 'sissy', as Alcock was in his Birmingham munitions factory, was to not be a complete man. This put him, and others like him, in a terrible bind, as he explained in an interview with the Hall Carpenter oral history archive in 1985. With contemporary stereotypes seeing homosexuals as being more feminine than male, it wasn't the 'done thing' for queers to have sex with one another. Instead, he, and so many other gay men, sought out those seen as 'real men' as sexual partners, something that in later years he regretted. 'Of course, I realised late, you see, that we were really playing it all the wrong way round, we should only have gone for our own kind,' he told the Hall Carpenter archive interviewer. 'I think it was probably the stereotype that had been planted on us. We were queer so we were much more like women than we were like men, and so you had to go with men and not with your own kind.'

Assumptions about the sexual availability of so-called 'sissy' men to sexually curious supposed heterosexuals caused problems for Henry Danton, who was constantly assumed to be gay. At a stop on a tour of English towns, Danton and another male dancer had popped out of the local theatre and, walking down the street, were sized up by some newly arrived Americans. 'One of the Americans said to his friend, "Hey, bud, if you want someone to blow your whistle, there's your chance!"' Danton told me. Quentin

Crisp grasped the matter in *The Naked Civil Servant*. He writes that gay men might appear to revel in frequent and promiscuous sex, but emotionally yearn for 'a real man who desires passionately (as opposed to making do with) another man'. Unfortunately, 'this being, if he exists, is so rare that one might as well enter a monastery on reaching puberty.' Men didn't come any more 'real' than when the desired body was clad in a uniform, whatever the service or the nation. It was as if to have sex with a soldier, sailor, labourer, farm worker or factory hand was to have sex with the idea of 'normal' itself.

The tragic and 'abnormal' gay man, always doomed in his pursuit of these 'real men', was left merely to service them in anonymous sex in just the kind of deep darkness afforded by the blackout. Do we imagine these gay men, broken in their chance to be their true masculine selves, seeking solace in the trousers of heterosexuals only out for a quick release? I don't believe this does either party justice. It makes an assumption that straight men were driven to gay sex by the absence of women, and gay men who played a feminine role for them. I wanted to find out who existed between these two binary identities.

If we have some testimonies from gay men from the war years, we have fewer from bisexuals. It was difficult for men to see themselves as such when the concept barely existed. A search of the Mass Observation archive reveals just one non-botanical entry for 'bisexual', referring to couples, not necessarily even in a relationship, made up of a man and a woman. I spoke to a woman whose father had worked in British intelligence and who she described as gay. Yet he had children and a long marriage to a woman. Was he a gay man in the closet or actually just bisexual? Micky Burn wrote in *Turned Towards the Sun* of how in the pre-war years, as well as affairs with women and Guy Burgess, 'There was nearly always some man with whom I was futilely in love. I kissed girls at dances, scuffled through soft porn in the Charing Cross Road and ever and anon cruised the Parks [. . .] I went out late to wander streets and squares alone, alive, a flame without a hearth.' During the war, he had unrequited attractions for a few of his comrades in the Commandos. Burn was in love with Maurice Harrison, a sergeant in his unit. In a tender poem called 'The Skater', Burn recalls an image of Harrison skating, the elegance of his movements on the ice, until 'the end of his day . . . Lifts, transfigures, and takes him away'. One night, Harrison locked himself out of his billet, ending up sleeping on the settee in his superior officer's bedroom. After the war, Burn published a poem of lament that recalled the night in which 'I said in casual tones / Speaking against my heart / You could sleep in my bed if you chose'.

Find me a bisexual man who hasn't felt the pangs of longing for a dear close straight friend, the loneliness of the knowledge that confessing would destroy a friendship. From cruising to this unrequited love and lust, Micky Burn might have been describing the patterns of behaviour and loneliness I felt when I first moved to London sixty years later. So little, really, had changed. Burn understood the shame that for bisexual men endured beyond the years of supposed sexual liberation. 'I learned how the mechanisms of concealment spun off into repellent side effects,' he wrote. 'Homosexuals, whether practising or not, perforce became practising hypocrites. Merely by remaining silent in the presence of the snigger and the sneer, I turned into an accomplice and felt shame. It shamed me to be relieved that physically I did not look like the general view of "one of those". I did not make up, or sneak out in drag. I was not a limp-wristed teapot.'

For a long time Burn was trapped between a furtive life cruising London's queer haunts and the hope that it might be solved by the revelation of an enduring heterosexual relationship, 'a profound experience with a woman', which would be one of 'the immortal openings into life'. Burn was so desperate for advice that he used his position as a journalist at *The Times* to contact the officer in charge of a case prosecuting the personnel of a gay brothel, arrange a meeting and confess to him. The officer took no action but shook Burn's hand and said he was sure that one day he would find a woman.

His internalised homophobia, the shame at not belonging to either homosexual or heterosexual worlds, are all depressingly familiar, even into the twenty-first century. In my own explorations of these public sexual spaces, nothing really had changed in the physicality of the moment, save for the material of the fabric covering the crotch that swelled under a curious palm. The ostensibly 'straight' men I encountered in them in the 1990s and 2000s were perhaps still in the same prison of shame and self-denial as their forebears in the Second World War. The out gay men had found a liberation, of sorts. The closet cases and sexually fluid remained in the shadows, revealed only by being reduced to the sex act itself by those who found them there.

Peter de Rome might have loved Porky, but that didn't stop his war being not just a fight against Hitler, but a quest for the perfect cock. The fear of exposure doesn't seem to have unduly worried him. Not long after D-Day, his unit's communal tent awoke to see that Corporal Turner, a hygiene fanatic straight out of the pages of *Health & Strength* magazine, who even brought his own bedsheets to France, had a giant erection protruding through his white shorts. It was fondly remembered by de Rome as 'like the obscene purple spadix of the Dragon Arum. A cock, like a flower, can be a lovesome thing, God wot, and I knew at once that I loved this cock as much as any flower!' Turner invites de Rome to have a go. 'The tent had become very quiet, the others aware of the implicit dangers and drama, but equally suspicious of my sexual orientation.'

De Rome defuses the situation by calling Turner's bluff and the offer – or order, given he's a superior – is withdrawn. 'I've sucked better cocks than that,' de Rome says, to applause from the rest of the tent. De Rome wrote that he had a 'good time' throughout the war, always easily finding 'suitable diversion'. The first of these was the 'hero' of the squad, a tall and 'ruggedly handsome' soldier: 'He was the all-rounder, the one to whom it all came easy.' Thus did Peter de Rome come easily too, in late night showers where they'd soap up and rub themselves together.

The second affair was with a Mauritian called Papillon. Even in the most violent, tense periods that he found himself in, combat had an erotic crackle to it. De Rome writes that shortly after D-Day, 'I remember one idyllic afternoon with Papillon's prick in an apple orchard near Bayeux when I persuaded him to take all his clothes off and we lay naked in the grass while the muffled sound of gunfire rumbled from the front line only a few miles away.' There's a joyous fruitiness to de Rome's words, a glowing sexual freedom under the shadow of war and death.

The appeal of American sexuality was not just felt by women. De Rome's lifelong lust affair with American manhood began when he was posted to Paris as part of an RAF liaison team preparing for Operation Plunder, the crossing of the River Rhine. He seduces the none-more-American Chuck Olsen by helping him send some perfume back to his wife, asking for a big kiss in return. The ensuing relationship became an 'idyll' in which Chuck was the dominant partner. 'He said he had never been with a man before – an assertion that I always find hard to believe – but I had no reason to doubt him. Chuck didn't know how to lie.' Through de Rome, we consistently encounter men who, back in civilian life, lived as 'straight', but during wartime were only too happy to make a temporary accord with another man's hands or mouth.

For de Rome, the war also provided his way into the arts that would become his career. Inspired by visits from Noel Coward and a touring theatre, he became an entertainer himself, relieved of the monotony of his normal duties to join an entertainment unit that visited RAF stations in newly occupied Germany. A fellow member of the troupe was Grena Thornton, the only woman with whom de Rome had a sexual relationship. Eventually, in Berlin, he chose to go to a party with Chuck over her and realised that he was desperately unhappy at his impossible situation: in love with a married man and living a lie in a heterosexual relationship with Grena. Nevertheless, under the prejudices of the time, 'The truth eluded me. But I would soon have to learn what it was about. Would soon learn that I belonged to that minority I had seen and despised [. . .] That I was no different from them. That I was queer. And would end up being a queen, just like them. But that was something I didn't want to think about. Not just yet, anyway.' Peter de Rome eventually followed the American penis across the Atlantic, where, as well as working on films including *Star Wars*, he became an acclaimed creator of Super 8 gay pornography, released on boxset by the BFI in 2012. There's a curious parallel between Montague Glover's photographs and the films that de Rome shot in 1970s New York. Like Glover, he had an eye for the working-class men of the city, especially those from the African-American community. In his films, and Glover's photographs, there's a special tension between the model and the lens, as if the subject is taking a steely pleasure in becoming an object.

It wasn't just de Rome who had an eye for the Americans. When they arrived – tight of trouser, loose of wallet, liberal of nature – it was a moment of wonder for Quentin Crisp, who fell for their utterly disarming forwardness and simple charms. For Crisp, the war made London a magical place. He had equated the quest for danger that was evidenced in his extremely obvious homosexuality with the desire, as soon as the Blitz began, to seek to 'embrace disaster' as, during the blackout and air raids, he 'started to search London for my own true bomb'. He describes a city in which the darkness had changed all the rules, where hands reached out from the gloom, 'in dimly lit trains people carried on as they had once behaved only in taxis', including the not infrequent occurrence of men in railway carriages whipping out their old chaps in the hope of a quick pleasuring. The usual haunts for anonymous gay sex – the Putney towpath, Hampstead Heath, a certain cinema that showed war films – were abandoned as the blackout rendered the entire city a place of convenient hook-ups, though Crisp himself eschewed such entanglements 'less from purity than vanity'. Peace comes on a 'terrible evening'. GIs are now in short supply, 'love and death become rationed' and Crisp 'who had once been a landmark more cheerful looking and bombproof than St Paul's Cathedral, had ceased to be a talisman'. Were American servicemen, so far from home in a strange and uptight land, or those who exposed themselves to Crisp in murky rattling railway carriages, hoping for suck or succour purely out of a desperate need for release? Were they only attracted to men or did they also have female sweethearts? Was Peter de Rome's Chuck a closet homosexual living a lie with a wife at home or a man who was exploring his true bisexuality? It's easy to assume that the war created an atmosphere in which men felt that anything would do, that Crisp, prowling the dark streets of London, was taking advantage of a compulsive need for sex and a moment of intimacy against the prospect of death. Yet I think of my own bisexuality and know that this doesn't sit right with my identity, or that of bisexuals generally. It reduces us to desperate sex-obsessed beings, undermines our agency, and removes our longing for the freedom to hold both men and women in our arms and hearts.

Gay men like de Rome and Crisp had an acute awareness of the fluid nature of sexuality during the war years. As de Rome wrote in his memoir, 'I believe that sex can be liberating, inspiring, ecstatic, transporting, exquisitely agonising, painfully boring, wonderfully stimulating, drearily repetitive, totally addictive, completely erratic . . . It can become obsessive to the point of sickness; it can be sublimated to the point of self-destruction. In other words, it is not only a part of life; it is life – integral and indivisible.' He had a better grasp of matters than most of the post-war sexologists and psychiatrists who tried to make sense of what had happened during the war years. In their records we find only sadness and shame.

Post-war studies of sexuality continued to divide into the binary assumption that men in relationships with women who also had same-sex desires were gay or straight men in denial of themselves.

When peace came, there were concerns that transitory homosexual experiences could in some way be permanently damaging, that after 'indulging', men might not be able to return to what society expected for them. In Richard Hauser's *The Homosexual Society*, published in 1962, he acknowledges that his own wartime service meant that he believed that, 'The unofficial history of the war would include an important chapter on homosexuality.' He subscribed to the common view that the absence of women and seeming fragility of existence were the main reasons why servicemen had homosexual experiences, with most returning to heterosexuality after the war ended or when they were home on leave. He wrote of the idea that homosexuality is something you can fall into and get stuck, describing the case of a man who comes back from time at sea infected with VD and continues to have sex with 'young queens'. The young sailor asks, 'Do you think I will ever be able to go back to women and start over again and settle down?' Another man told investigators how he had only had relationships with women, and never even considered sexual or emotional entanglements with men. However, while he was in the Army during the war, he went drinking with an American officer and ended up sharing a hotel room with him. One thing led to another and they had sex. 'That night – I was thirty-five then – I found out the truth about myself. I have never gone back to a woman though I am still fond of them and we like each other's company. But the normal sex act with women is disgusting to me now.' Normal, again, that simple little word that holds so much shame and pain.

I wonder, though, if there is an unconscious bias at play here. Psychiatrists were more likely to pick up cases of men who were seeking help to be 'cured' of their affliction. Many more must have continued to explore their bisexuality in silence. The homophobia of the post-war years might in part have come about because so many men feared their wartime sexual experiences and their transgression from the 'normal' male identity. Even if these activities had been evidence of their true bisexual selves, it's not surprising that they would deny them. Even in our modern times, and in my own life, it can and has taken years to accept that there is nothing shameful or abnormal in a sexual desire that flickers between men and women. The overwhelming otherworldliness of wartime conditions allowed many men to access their true bisexuality in an environment that was far more accepting than that which surrounded them in civilian life, with less of a fear of being discovered *in flagrante* and where the pangs of guilt at betrayal of a wife or lover back home were dulled by distance and time apart.

In the eulogy at the funeral address for former fighter pilot Michael Schofield in 2014, journalist Rupert Morris said that it was the experience of the Second World War that had led him to devote the rest of his days to 'overcoming prejudice and furthering the cause of understanding and tolerance'. In *Society and the Homosexual*, published in 1952, Schofield (writing under the pseudonym Gordon Westwood) was one of the first to argue that sexuality was a matter of degree, writing that 'over the population as a whole there is an imperceptible gradation from wholly homosexual to wholly heterosexual'. He acknowledges this more fluid sexuality as separate from adolescent experimentation or what he termed 'pseudo-homosexuals', heterosexual men who would prefer a woman but simply found it easier to be with a man, or who thought that homosexual sex would avoid VD or pregnancy, or who just had an extreme libido. Westwood here breaks down the assumption that men who have sex with men do it out of convenience, or just because they are in the all-male environment of the military unit. He undermines the simplistic idea that part of male sexuality is to eventually become so frustrated, seedy and needy that any hole's a goal, as the crude saying goes. I find Westwood's writing radical because, no doubt after the experience of witnessing same-sex desire in the RAF and during the war years, he seems to have acutely understood that bisexuality exists and isn't, as it is still so often seen even now in the twenty-first century, a perversion or indulgence of the promiscuous.

In his writing, Schofield cites numerous reports from POW rehabilitation centres in which men discussed their same-sex activities while in captivity, often involving men who were otherwise ostensibly heterosexual. While Westwood's interest was in examining whether these homosexual experiences 'altered' the sexuality of men in a long-term way, he acknowledges that they're part of a desire latent within most men. Colin Spencer certainly believes that the Second World War allowed many men to access a sexuality that was fluid in a way that they simply couldn't in peacetime. 'My theory is that everybody is bisexual, given the chance and opportunity,' he told me. 'When I was growing up, the view was if you're bisexual you're really heterosexual. I was insistent that that was not necessarily true at all, but I was very alone in that. It was also said that it was men who were in denial of their homosexuality; but if you were gay you really weren't allowed to like women at all.' Of his own sexual experiences in the immediate aftermath of the war, Spencer said, 'One got tired of hearing, "I'm not really gay, but I'm enjoying this." I saw a lot of that in the Army. I never met a soldier who wasn't happy to have sex, however heterosexual they might appear.' He remembered an old sergeant with a huge walrus moustache who picked and chose whichever of the new recruits he fancied for sexual escapades, something that seemed to have been going on back into the war years, despite the soldier being married. 'He was quite open about sex, he certainly wanted to seduce me, but I didn't want to be seduced by him,' Spencer told me. 'I said no, because I didn't like that moustache very much.'

For Micky Burn, the post-war years brought resolution of a sort. While a prisoner at Colditz Castle, he had become close to Norman 'Dusty' Miller, a working-class sailor and something of an autodidact. Burn desired him intensely but Miller was heterosexual. Where love failed a lifelong friendship grew, in part due to their opposite backgrounds and natures – Dusty envied Burn's education, Burn the sailor's 'easy masculinity' and success with women where his own life had been a catalogue of failure with both sexes. The two men spent many hours discussing Burn's hopes for his romantic and sexual existence after the war had ended. Riffing on Augustine's prayer to 'make me pure, but not yet', Burn said his wish was 'make me heterosexual, but not yet'. His hope through those war years was that after a 'bout' of homosexuality, he would be able to 'go straight'. It couldn't happen.

While on leave in October 1941, Burn spied 'the most beautiful woman I had ever seen' across a nightclub dance floor. She didn't see him, they didn't speak and Burn supposed that he would never set eyes on her again, just another potential something lost in the whirl of London and war. The next evening, visiting Brigadier Charles Haydon, his superior officer in the Commandos, he was shocked when the same woman answered the door. Mary Booker was a forty-eight-year-old divorcee with two daughters and worked as the London manager of the Miles Aircraft company. That night they had a short conversation, but then Burn's long years in German POW camps after the St Nazaire raid intervened. Once liberated and returned to England, he sought Mary out and they began a relationship that was frank from the off. Burn told her of his conflicted sexuality, writing to her, 'There is a challenge, and it is physical only physical.' Their first night together was not a success, but the second was 'ecstatic' and Burn supposed that his 'former desires would now evaporate'. Again, so familiar, this hope that bisexuality might just be a moment through which to pass into the 'normal' side of desire.

In Burn's memoirs and letters to Mary Booker is the torment of a man who is not permitted to understand his own sexual identity by the accepted rules of science, culture and his day. He wrote, 'had I given rein to my "natural impulses" more frequently, I would probably by now have found myself either in hospital from disease or physical attack or in prison or all three.' Burn wrote of an idealised love he described as 'the whole nature of totality'. For bisexual men, this so often feels vulnerable to the 'petrifying possibility' that we cannot ever entirely commit to one or other aspect of our desire. Burn's honest words are precious because they are so rare. His is one of very few accounts from the mouths or pens of bisexual men of his time that grapples with this eternal conundrum, that leads so many of us into self-sabotage, that denies us love. There must have been many other men whose wartime same-sex experiences left them for years afterwards in a state of unease, of in-betweenness, a silent loneliness, a cold war in their own desire.

Before the war, Burn had received an awkward question from his father about his sexuality. After his ecstatic night with Mary, he felt it was possible to tell the old man that yes, there had been a 'problem' with homosexuality. His father replied that something must be done as to be homosexual was terrible for a career, and sent him to consult with a Harley Street specialist. This double-barrelled doctor questioned Burn on his sex life, examined him naked and told him there was nothing to worry about – he was 'completely normal'.

Nearly twenty years after Burn's death, in a time where a fair amount, though not enough, has changed, I feel a sadness at the familiar wrestle in his essays, memoir and poetry, his struggle to find his place as a sexual outlaw in this dramatic and profound period in British history. I see Burn's writings as a barometer of feeling, sometimes set fair, frequently stormy and often in between. As bisexuals, our struggle is often to be blown between extremes of self-doubt and recrimination. An analysis of Burn's life could even be that his shifts from sympathy with fascism to Communism and then to Catholicism is the political being dragged by the tumult of his sexual desires, his love for Mary, the pressures of the society around him. When, in old age, he wrote of a Christian faith that, unmoored from dogma, was personal in a way that echoes my own, there's a sense that Micky Burn's wanderings of the self had reached a more solid terrain. His poetry to Mary and to his male partners, is of a bisexual sensibility of love that is tender, moving, honest, himself.

# PEOPLE ARE PEOPLE

What strikes me most about the accounts of same-sex love and lust during the war years is just how few there are, intimate moments glimpsed through the hopeless void of time and public memory. The relative ease with which a tiny subset of queer men were later able to speak about their sexuality illuminates not only the lives of those who loved within their own gender, but also gives a vital impression of masculinity in its wider sense. Those who left records were often dispassionate and frank about their experiences and emotional inner lives. Yet they were outliers, often (like Colin Spencer, Peter de Rome, Dudley Cave) men who were eventually defined by their sexuality, in activism and in art. This presents something of a quandary. While they tell us that, to an extent, the war years were far more open and queer than our popular, heterosexual myths of a certain kind of Britishness would have us believe, they create more questions than they answer. In the need for companionship and closeness in this torrid time, their open sexuality is the contrast from the default position: gay men who loved and slept with men but remained in the closet, and those who I believe were for a while able to be their true bisexual selves. They also give an insight into a further group within the population who defied the ideas of 'normal' British masculinity perhaps more than anyone else – those who subverted it entirely. As Micky Burn was to reflect many years after the war, part of the 'new candour' he believed had followed it was the acceptance that, 'We have had enough of exclusivities [. . .] There is male in women and female in men.'

The popular conception of POW camps that has come down to us via the cultural filter of the films that use them as a setting is of a masculine toughness – football and the brave tunnel builders of *The Great Escape*; the tricky subject of defiance versus collaboration in the brutality of *Bridge on the River Kwai*; the derring-do and rebellion of the officer class in *The Colditz Story*. Less well known is how men who had been without the company of women for months and years went to extraordinary lengths to play convincing female roles in plays and other entertainments. In *Society and the Homosexual*, Michael Schofield, writing as Gordon Westwood, cites the case of a twenty-one-year-old homosexual prisoner who used 'incredible ingenuity' to make not just women's clothes, but 'manufactured some exotic scent which he spread all over his body', grew his hair long and walked and talked like a woman with the object to 'arouse erotic excitement in his fellow prisoners'.

Dudley Cave remembered how in the Changi POW camp, before malnutrition had led to diminished libido, one man answered to the name of Clara and lurked at night in the mangrove swamp, pleasuring prisoners who sought her out. Clara was known for the catchphrase 'Oh! the size of the thing', which inevitably featured in a POW theatrical entertainment in which she played a housewife being interviewed about a bomb in the garden. When Clara uttered her signature motto it 'brought the house down'.

Men frequently seemed to distract from their attraction to these feminine characters with humour. At a psychiatrists' conference in

October 1944, one Captain Mustardé gave a talk called 'Adjustment and Maladjustments', that included his prisoner-of-war experience. He wryly remarked that following one show in which a soldier was 'made up as a rather fast piece of female goods', the editor of the camp magazine wrote, 'Private Jones gave an excellent representation of flowering womanhood; so excellent in fact that it made you want to go to the lavatory and think.' This rather English habit of giving a knowing wink seems to me to be a way of defusing the intensity of the emotions involved and ignoring the seriousness with which the cross-dressers went about their craft.

That acute though crude observer of human sexuality J. H. Witte recalled in his memoir that in the Italian POW camps cross-dressing was rife. 'The girls really looked like girls and anyone of them would have given Danny La Rue a good run for his money,' he wrote. 'Dutiful swains used to wait outside the theatre for the girls to appear after the show. They couldn't take them for dinner so they took them, instead, to quiet places in the compound. The boy friends used to get very jealous if you so much glanced at their girlfriends.'

Typically, it is Micky Burn who deals with the subject most sensitively. In his novel *Yes, Farewell*, he describes a play put on by the prisoners in Colditz. A soldier, Tony Masterman, has been persuaded to play the part of the heroine. He arrives on stage moving awkwardly to the catcalls of the assembled POWs but, as the performance went on, 'Gradually he slipped into the part. His movements became consciously feminine. Many eyes followed him. He seemed to know that he had some power over the prisoners.' After the play, prisoner Tug Wilson said that 'all my worst instincts were roused', yet alas he couldn't get near the cross-dressing thespian, so besieged was the stage door by amorous admirers. Later in the novel, during a conversation about dreams, another prisoner admits to rarely having sexual dreams about his wife, but often about Tony Masterman in drag. 'I don't know how I shall explain it when I get home,' he says, face reddening. When Burn's central, autobiographical character, Alan Maclaran, later reads a book full of prisoner's dreams, it's clear Ferguson was not alone. By the end of the war, the fictional Masterman, his name so over-the-top masculine, has been made more feminine by his repeated roles as female characters in plays like *Rookery Nook*, *Private Lives* and *The Importance of Being Earnest*. Maclaran finds Masterman's metamorphosis refreshing, as he moved around the castle with his long hair, fitting his slender body into elegant dresses for theatrical productions, during which his audience could 'really imagine that he was a woman, without any sense of the abnormal, and were grateful for the illusion'.

Even outside POW camps, servicemen sometimes seemed partial to escaping the expectations of gender. Dudley Wrangel Clarke, an intelligence officer involved in the founding of the SAS, was arrested in Madrid in October 1941 for going out dressed as a woman – the Spanish police sent photographs of him in drag to Churchill. There is a series of images that I often see doing the rounds on social media of British soldiers manning an artillery position on the Channel Coast on full alert. All dressed in women's clothes, they rush to their posts, manhandle shells around the guns and traverse their long barrels, pointing out towards the German foe. 'Jimmy' James, consultant psychiatrist to the Middle East Force, wrote after the war that in 1940 he had come across a unit in which a large number of soldiers from all ranks were involved in cross-dressing, which they explained away as 'rehearsals for a play'. The fact that one of the officers involved had a 'splendid fighting record' meant that they were largely left to their own devices. The men who dressed as women had partners among those who didn't and were 'particularly contented', until the war meant opportunities for dressing up were reduced. James had to admit, 'The military work of the unit was at a high level and there was very little drinking.' The cross-dressing was clearly not merely the result of thirsty high jinks.

I wonder if these frequent accounts represent more than just men craving female company after so long away from home. Perhaps, just as the confines of military service allowed men to explore innate bisexuality, it also permitted some to temporarily escape the confines of their gender. While male gender codes, rules and norms were heavily reinforced by the expectations of military dress, the war had a profound impact on how women were able to present themselves. Some of the men who enjoyed cross-dressing were merely responding to the vast shift that was occurring in society around them, with women entering the workplace and auxiliary services in their millions.

For Quentin Crisp, the war had given him not only the thrill of sex in the blackout, but an entirely new perspective on the attire of others as well as his own. 'The women of London had gone butch,' he wrote in *The Naked Civil Servant*, remarking on how, all of a sudden, it was not just practical for women in uniform to be wearing trousers, but fashionable too. Crisp, who in later life said he felt he was transgender, was often indistinguishable from a woman. This was no complete liberation for Crisp but caused problems, for, as a policeman had told him, 'people did not like that sort of thing'. On a tube, a group of men came and stood around Crisp to loudly remark at his clothes and physique, one eventually grabbing his crotch to confirm whether he was a man or woman. The group chased him out of the tube and beat him. On another occasion, as Crisp was returning from an evening class in Willesden, an Australian soldier sat behind him on the bus and carefully combed his hair.

Just around the corner from Crisp's Soho haunts – the cafés of Charlotte Street, the Wheatsheaf pub – was 5 Great Russell Street, home of Enid M. Barraud, Mass Observation diarist. Barraud had volunteered to be a Mass Observation diarist after reading an article about it in the *News Chronicle*. She responded to the organisation's regular requests for information on a range of subjects because she enjoyed observing other people and herself.

Mass Observation offered the opportunity for ordinary men and women to give such a huge amount of detail on their daily lives that to read the diaries now can be as vivid as watching a documentary. In the years before the war, Barraud worked as a clerk in the office of an American insurance company based in the City of London, near the Bank of England. It was a dull, ordinary sort of place and for twelve years she toiled at her desk under a boss who had fought at Gallipoli in the First World War and was a terrible snob. Barraud's Mass Observation day survey report of 12 July 1937 describes travelling to work on a stifling tube, her colleagues and the minutae of office life, eating a shrivelled kidney for lunch while chatting about death. The tea is strong at the 3:30 afternoon break, she has a massage after work, talks with friends about sexuality, then dinner, bath and bed, and a final note about her lover, 'the most real person I know'.

E. M. Barraud's Mass Observation entries, appearing occasion-ally in the archive into the war years, are confident and forthright. She is a piquant observer not just of the routines of London office life, but of sexual and gender identity. She describes herself as an 'invert', a term to describe homosexuality that had made the leap from sexologist textbooks to the relative mainstream via its use in Radclyffe Hall's novel *The Well of Loneliness*. Yet while Hall described the invert's 'terrible birthright' and persecution so strong that 'bombs do not trouble the nerves of the invert, but rather that terrible silent bombardment from the batteries of God's good people', Barraud appears to be comfortable with her identity, even proud of it. She describes herself as 'technically, single, but "married" in a permanent homosexual relationship with another woman' and 'homosexual. (Physically female, mentally etc. Male)'.

In response to an April 1939 Mass Observation directive on personal appearance, Barraud wrote, 'I am in a half-way position, being officially a woman, yet dressing and regarding personal appearance from a mainly masculine point of view.' She says that she spends nothing on personal appearance except a monthly haircut (in a short Eton crop) and brilliantine, has never had a manicure in her life, uses no cosmetics. She answers a further directive on clothes again from a male perspective, discussing her tailored suits and shirts, vests, overcoats and shoes all purchased from menswear shops. Replying to Mass Observation's request for views on different genders' response to the war in March 1942, Barraud wrote that she would respond both as a woman and a man as she didn't approve of the differentiation between them: 'People are people, not specifics of a gender.'

As often as she could, E. M. Barraud liked to get out of London to work on a farm down in the Kent countryside. She was weary at the approach of war, tired of errand boys singing patriotic songs like 'There'll Always Be an England' and, when she was sacked from her job, joined the Women's Land Army and fled with her partner Bunty to the village of Little Eversden in rural Cambridgeshire. 'I cannot help feeling that while anything in life is worthwhile, it may be worth fighting for, dying for, even killing for,' Barraud would later write about her decision, 'I abhor war as the last suicidal insanity and I deliberately chose the Land Army as my form of war service because it offered one of the very few constructive jobs in a madly destructive world.' She was on the farm when war was declared and saw it as a 'boon', providing an escape from the drudgery of office life.

In January 1946, Barraud published *Set My Hand Upon the Plough*, a now little-known work of nature writing and memoir about the five years she spent in the Women's Land Army and the strangeness of the British countryside at war. Vita Sackville West's review in *Land Girl* magazine praised the 'authentic voice' exhibited in Barraud's writing, which she regards as evidence that the author had had years of intimate connection with rural people and their way of life. She concluded that, 'Her book is one which every true countryman will recognise as being the real thing.' The fields of Cambridgeshire seemed to be where Barraud found herself. According to a history of the village of Little Eversden published after the war, she was known not as Enid, but John. The book has as a frontispiece a poem that in vivid, almost pagan language evokes an awareness of her body as being neither male nor female, but a form and identity that came from toil and the land:

My shadow is ten yards high;
I am as big as the Giant of Cerne Abbas
Or the Long Man of Wilmington.
I march astride golden shocks of cut corn
And between my thighs is all the fruitfulness of the earth.
I am the farm worker going home at evening

As the skies overhead thundered with bombers on their way to attack Germany, Barraud's body has been redefined by the war. She writes of a life transformed and seems to exalt in the changes brought on by her escape from work as a clerk and the tedium she'd painted such a vivid image of in her Mass Observation diaries of the late 1930s. 'When I have time to look in the glass nowadays I see a figure that is two stone lighter, hair that the sun has bleached, arms that the same sun has tanned, hands rough and horny.' The experience of working in these traditionally male occupations for the duration gave women a newfound intimacy with their own bodies. 'Those were the days when every fresh job meant a fresh set of unused muscles to break in, till I began to think I should never come to the end of the possible pain and be able to say, "Now there isn't another inch of me to discover."'

Barraud gets called 'mate' or 'buddy' as much as 'gal' and refers to herself as a 'townsman' and 'new boy'. Only once is she called 'miss'. While mucking out pigs, she keeps a cigarette going to block out the smell, and argues with Stone, the farm manager, who, as a pigman, thinks the porcine pong is clean and healthy, whereas calf muck is foul. 'I, as calf-man, maintained the direct opposite.'

This is a world, as depicted in the black-and-white plates throughout *Set My Hand Upon The Plough*, of wicker baskets and wooden barns, of future hopes of the arrival of electricity, of magical healers within living memory, children who speak 'BBC English to strangers and Cambridgeshire in their home', horse-drawn carts laden with hay and steam-powered threshing machines clacking in the fields. Her writing is full of the joys of her move to the country and vivid descriptions of the farming landscape: at the end of harvest 'there lay the sheaves like corpses after some great battle as the sun went down'. She restores an old German air rifle, which she calls Herr Heal, and shoots sparrows, which she skins, guts, cooks on the open fire and eats with a slice of toast.

Despite Barraud's easy physical and mental adaptation to the rigours of wartime rural life, she was fully aware that as a member of the Women's Land Army, old assumptions died hard even though she chose to present as masculine. The farmer told Barraud that that she wasn't suitable for the hard work that was coming and sacked her. She was so angry at this sexist firing that she refused to work out her notice.

Despite this, there's another change too, to someone who seems to have found a great ease within herself thanks to her war work. A photograph of Barraud in *Set My Hand Upon the Plough* shows her in a wintery scene, standing in wellington boots and voluminous britches, a jumper on with spearpoint collar shirt and tie, her hair fixed back with pomade. Under her arm is a rifle – in another context, she might have been a bold member of a resistance group.

The body is merely a vessel for an identity, one that can be repaired, amended. E. M. Barraud exulted in her calloused hands, her tan, her developing muscles. For others, physical change enabled by the war became even more profound. Conflict promotes both staggering advances in military technology to destroy the body, and the medical procedures used to return the wounded back to some semblance of life afterwards. Sometimes this could have unintended consequences.

In Roberta Cowell's 1954 memoir is a photograph of a family taken in the early 1920s, a typically formal image of a strictly religious patriarchal family headed by a military surgeon. The father, in a jacket and bow tie, sits looking dotingly at his youngest son. The mother and eldest daughter stand at the back, portly and slightly severe. The eldest boy, Robert, sits front left, slightly apart with a straight fringe. He wears a similar shirt to his brother, and shorts, but, unlike the rest of his family, his clothes are plain. Young Robert had torn off the frills. As a child, he loathed anything that felt 'sissy'. He dreamed of being a fighter pilot or a racing driver, took up smoking and drinking, learned filthy jokes to spread around the RAF Cadet Corps at school and cut his long eyelashes. Anything homosexual revolted him and, when aged sixteen, he was hit on by a tennis partner, his reaction was violent and physical. Cowell failed in his initial attempt to join the RAF in the mid-1930s, and instead went into racing motor cars. When war came, he tried and failed again to fly, and was put into the Army, becoming a captain in charge of mobile workshops – the exemplary soldier male, good with machines, good with his hands. The picture of 'normal' masculinity was complete with marriage and two young children.

With demand for pilots increasing, Cowell finally earned his transfer to the RAF. At his training aerodrome, he saw group photographs of each of the previous intakes to which additions had been made – a drawing of a bowler hat or a halo. The bowler-hatted men had failed to complete the course, the haloes had been killed. Posted to his squadron, Cowell noticed the louche masculinity of the other pilots who dressed 'for comfort, not without a certain studied inelegance'. Finally realising his dream of flying a Spitfire, Cowell was always convinced that he would follow his friends to death, yet this didn't affect his enthusiasm for his job protecting civilians on the ground from enemy aircraft. Off duty, Robert played like any other RAF officer, all booze and banter. At a local theatre one night, he excitedly told his fellow airmen that he'd met an 'extraordinarily nice' girl who was taking part in the show. When the second half began, the same woman appeared in front of a banner proclaiming 'Salute to the RAF', wearing nothing but an Air Force cap. For an age afterwards, Robert was asked if he had met any more 'extraordinarily nice' girls.

After a period of rest following his first tour of operations, Robert returned to squadron for D-Day, flying high-altitude operations at 40,000 feet. During one of these, his oxygen supply failed and he entered a strange, trance-like state, and had to be gently talked down back to base. Despite this narrow escape, his morale, like that of the squadron, was high and there were regular flights to England to return with drop tanks (usually used for extra petrol) full of beer. And then, on the final mission of his second tour of operations, Robert Cowell was shot down far behind enemy lines, taken prisoner and sent to POW camp Stalag Luft 1.

There, he encountered the usual transvestism and sexual fluidity that so many men wrote about in their memoirs. It was a joke in the camp to say that men would be 'home before Christmas or homo before Easter'. As often had happened in his past, homosexual men assumed that Cowell was one of them, and asked him to play a female part in the theatre. In his school play, to wear skirts had been compulsory, but here Robert 'refused without hesitation. I was still clinging to my masculinity.' Such were the privations in the camp that Cowell resorted to eating cats to stay alive, but survived until he was liberated by the Red Army, having lost 23kg and becoming ill with scabies.

After the war, Cowell set up in motor engineering and started racing again. Yet there was never any satisfaction, no matter how successful he became in business or wealth. He had constantly sought to achieve in ways that felt like an assertion of masculinity – motor racing, flying Spitfires, success in business, a home and a family life – but it all left him feeling hollow. A visit to a Japanese garden, and the rich symbolism of its layout with areas called Turning Points and Garden of Peace and Contentment, had a profound effect on him, as did a trip to the cinema to see *Mine Own Executioner*, a war film in which the main character is shot down. The film had been realistically made and 'for a moment I was back again in the cockpit [. . .] As the aircraft was hit and crashed in flames I felt all the pent-up emotion released that I must have experienced when my own plane was shot down; but this time I was an observer, and was not so preoccupied with what I was doing that I could feel no emotion. Now I felt the full impact of stark terror. Fear that I would be burnt alive, fear that I would be lynched by the soldiers, fear that I would be terribly injured by the crash.' It took Cowell an hour to be able to leave the cinema.

Although Cowell was writing long before it was defined, this seems to be a description of the symptoms of PTSD. In 1948, his marriage broke up and, unable to cope, he went to see Freudian psychiatrists to finally unpick a true sense of self. Cowell had expected to find that he had an unconscious fear of losing his masculinity, but 'I did not expect to find that, free of repressions, I was psychologically a woman.' Cowell considered suicide, drank, took amphetamines, withdrew from other people. He started to realise that his body and his mind were both telling him that he was in the wrong physical form. Cowell played squash with a Wing Commander friend at the RAC club and, in the changing room afterwards, the officer said, jokingly, that Cowell might try to wear a bra. This banter led Cowell to try to find out how physically feminine he really was. It was also the last time he used a communal male changing room.

A sexologist examined Cowell and found that he had 'quite prominent feminine sex characteristics', wide hips, 'female type of pelvis', small hands and feet and no Adam's apple. 'Once I realised that my femininity had a substantial physical basis I did not despise myself so much.' It was a revelation and an intense relief, but Cowell soon knew that he was unable to continue as he was. 'It was most desirable that I should allow some of my innate femininity to express itself, but I had not the slightest desire to become effeminate, which was an entirely different thing,' as he puts it in his memoir. Cowell took up dressmaking and spent time in a more artistic milieu of effeminate men and 'mannish' women – the latter were fine to get on with, but Cowell still felt an intense dislike of homosexuals. It seemed likely, doctors said, that Cowell was intersex. This, Cowell believed, was a 'grim joke' of nature and explained the years of trying to compensate by performing an aggressive masculinity.

Cowell started taking hormones and noticed that people began to treat him differently. Old ladies told him off, one saying that *she* ought to be ashamed going around dressed in trousers and with hair cropped short. He often heard children speculating as to his gender and developed the ability to blush when offered a seat on the tube. In 1950, trans man and surgeon Michael Dillon performed the then illegal operation to remove Cowell's testicles. She legally became a woman in early 1951, waiting for further operations and continuing with both dressmaking and motoring businesses.

No doctors had ever managed to conduct a transition from adult male to female, but advances in medical technology made during the First and Second World Wars had finally made it possible. Twentieth-century warfare often resulted in horrific burns, especially among aircraft, ship and tank crews, confined in a metal casing in close proximity to highly flammable substances. In the First World War, a New Zealand surgeon called Harold Gillies had built on existing French and German research to develop new techniques of rhinoplasty to recreate the faces of terribly wounded men, constructing noses, lips, eyes to replace burned and necrotic flesh. As the prospect of conflict returned in the late 1930s, the military authorities revived their interest in rebuilding the male. Archibald McIndoe, another New Zealander, had worked with Gillies until a rivalry developed between the two men. During the war years, McIndoe furthered the research of Gillies and set up a hospital in East Grinstead that treated men who had been badly burned in action, specialising in RAF aircrew, including Richard Hillary. The patients referred to themselves as the Guinea Pig Club.

Despite their professional differences, following the war, Gillies and McIndoe joined forces to set up the British Association of Plastic Surgeons. Gillies, who had performed trans man Michael Dillon's pioneering phalloplasty operation using techniques developed to repair the genitals of injured male servicemen, agreed to take on the challenge of performing Cowell's vaginoplasty, an operation that had never previously been attempted. He attracted controversy by 'practising' on a corpse in a morgue. His rival, Archibald McIndoe, had developed the McIndoe Technique, an operation which is still used for trans women today. The two uneasy colleagues and rivals who had reconstructed so many men brutalised by fire and bullet during the war set to work on making Roberta Cowell her true self.

The operation was a success. As soon as Roberta transitioned, everything changed. A childhood fear of medical 'monstrosities', the mysterious specimens in jars she'd been terrified of in museums, vanished. She felt less angry. She became more tolerant of effeminate men, writing that 'had I met one I would have refrained from actually kicking his spine up through the top of his head, but only with an effort'. The strong and powerful instinct to perform the masculine role by racing cars or flying receded. She began to take more of an interest in what society around her told her were more feminine pursuits, such as cooking or her work as a dressmaker. She soon attracted the attention of men.

I like to imagine the scene in a London pub of the early 1950s, early evening sun angling in through a plate-glass window into great clouds of cigarette smoke. A man, brash and confident, pint in hand, has spied Roberta Cowell and likes what he sees. He bowls over, orders her a drink – a gin and lemon perhaps – and, inhaling a gulp of ale that leaves wisps of froth on a statement moustache, starts shooting the line about his illustrious wartime career, giving it the old up-diddly-up-up, 'ratatatatat' at Jerry, 'wizard show' and all. He sups away as his story reaches its climax, a tale of combat against a dastardly foe, hands waving away to illustrate the skill of his manoeuvres, until bang! his hydraulics are shot away, meaning he can't lower the flaps on each wing that slow the aircraft down . . . he's going to have to crash land his Spitfire at a terrifyingly high speed! I imagine Roberta Cowell, RAF pilot of two tours of operations, taking a sip of her gin and asking this fool who had taken another's bravery as his own, what was so special about *his* Spitfire that made it different from every other one in the RAF, which had pneumatically, not hydraulically, operated flaps.

In the photographs in Cowell's memoir, there is a hint of the gender expectations that even this pioneer was made to follow. In 1951, Robert is pictured behind the wheel of a racing car, moving fast in front of a blur of spectators. A few pages later, there are two further photos. One captioned 'Cooking was unexpectedly exciting' is of Roberta in the kitchen in a nice dress, the picture of 1950s domesticity; in the other, captioned 'Back at the wheel again', she's in a car, but this time a dodgem. To modern eyes, there might be a tragedy in her conforming to the gender roles of the conservative post-war years, yet there's a striking difference from the images of Robert Cowell as the stern, macho racing driver and Spitfire pilot. Her face is split by a beaming smile.

# BREAKING THE CAGE

Heterosexual love is ubiquitous in the cultural and psychic terrain of the Second World War. In numerous films and the over-written romance of war novels, wet-eyed women stare up at their uniformed man for one last, tragic time. We see the fruits of it in the baby boom of the post-war years, the war brides who followed love overseas, their offspring growing up in America and Canada, far from where their mothers were born. But heterosexual love of the war years wasn't always as dramatic or romantic as those cultural artefacts have it. I find a great tenderness in how my grandad refers to letters from home as being 'like food', but aside from his regular mentions of thinking of his family at a certain time each night, there are no grand displays of romance. Yet even in that simple daily ritual, there's more than we can ever know from the thousands of gay and bisexual men who loved one another through those six long, tough years. When we hear massed voices rising along with Vera Lynn in 'We'll Meet Again', that warm hymn to hope of love enduring against death, do we ever imagine it sung from man to man?

If, as Dudley Cave, Micky Burn, Christopher Gotch, Peter de

Rome and others have told us, there was a certain tolerance of gay sexual behaviour, what about love? Queer love as recorded in the written word is so hard to find and often, as in the case of Ian Gleed disguising his lover T as 'Pam', it is also a code to decipher. There are further glimpses. Michael Schofield, who, after the war, would go on to try to understand queer sexuality in his work in *Society and the Homosexual*, had his first love affair with a fellow pilot of his night-fighter squadron. When his partner was tragically killed in action, the commanding officer ensured that Schofield was informed first, even before he wrote to the man's family. In 2008, a collection of 600 letters were purchased by Mark Hignett, curator of the Oswestry Town Museum. Initially assumed to be between a heterosexual couple, it emerged that they had been written by Gilbert Bradley, an anti-aircraft gunner, and Gordon Bowsher, an infantryman. The two wrote to one another using only their initials to avoid detection, and in one letter, Bowsher, afraid, asked Bradley to destroy them.

Less circumspect was Montague Glover, whose camera captured so boldly the queer masculinity of the interwar years. His partner Ralph, born in 1913, was the archetypal working-class object of desire and looks incredible in Glover's photographs. We might now refer to him as a 'twink', glowing with youth he had thick full lips, waving hair, a solid jaw and cheekbones – immensely attractive no matter how Monty shot him, which included sitting on the bed, legs apart, fully nude. The pair lived together in London and Warwickshire until Ralph was called up and joined the RAF. He looks most natural of all in his uniform, sitting on a wall during leave early in the war, his hair neatly billowing back from his forehead. He wrote sweet and affectionate letters full of 'my darling' and 'my dear' and wishes of goodnight and love, cries over recollections of when they first met, and imagines Monty working in the garden. I wonder what Ralph's comrades thought of him, whether they knew. Ralph certainly passes on that they enjoyed a cake that Monty sent, yet there's a feeling of loneliness: 'I have not got much to say about the lads here my dear,' he wrote on 1 December 1940. 'It's all women down here my dear I go out on my own and think of the lads my dear.' Further letters from Ralph come from a ship at sea and I'm struck by how similar they are to those my grandad sent from the SS *Andalucia Star*, en route to Freetown – the heat of the tropics, the flying fish, the stars in the sky, shifts keeping watch from submarines, the odd night of drunkenness. Whether it was to Dorothy in Loughton or a friend of Dorothy in Warwickshire, men wrote of the very same things.

The pair had an unconventional relationship; in Glover's archives are letters from various privates, leading seamen and so on thanking him for his hospitality and 'intomat [sic] moments'. A soldier in No.1 Company of the Welsh Guards wrote on 25 May 1943, 'I am sat in the Salvation Army with the horn up to my neck, so I guess I'll just have to go and have a come off on returning to camp.' Despite this, Monty and Ralph remained together through the war and beyond, pottering around their garden and decorating the bathroom in a rather unique way – above the taps was a painting of a handsome young sailor in knee-high boots, a warship sailing between his thighs. They'd been together half a century by the time Monty died in 1983. Heartbroken, his lover followed four years later. Movingly, *A Class Apart* ends with a pair of Monty's photographs of Ralph sitting in front of the same fireplace, both as a young and then an older man.

There is one testament to queer love that has come down to us from the Second World War that is not only a remarkably innovative work of literature, but, in its immediacy and its relationship to actual events and parallels with letters sent home, documents the complexity of falling for another man. As he advanced through the ranks of the Army, from Private in the Royal Army Service Corps to Lieutenant in the East Yorkshire Regiment, Dan Billany had already published a bestselling detective novel called *The Opera House Murders*, as well as *The Magic Door*, a children's story featuring the class he taught in Hull. He'd also started to address his homosexuality as something tragic, unwanted, doomed. In an unpublished short story called *The Cow on the Roof* that he wrote around the time of his officer training, he described it as 'the sort of love which damns a person [. . .] a sort of love which, in the world as we know it, could not be made public. One might rather commit suicide; some have done.' The character Mrs Valentine, a blackmailer of a gay man, had turned 'the very honey of his life into poison to buy her brandy and run her Daimler'. In 1936, he wrote a poem called 'The Pseudo Man', a rejection of the corporeal feminine and 'heterosexual fires' in favour of the cold, unreal, asexual beauty of the male form as seen in Greek statues.

Seemingly a man clouded by the difficulties of his sexuality – the lot of so many of his time – Dan Billany left the UK for his military service in North Africa on a luxury liner, RMS *Mauretania*. Like my grandad, he wrote letters home of the extravagant food and booze on offer, such a change from the rationing back in Britain. Similar descriptions appear in his first war novel, *The Trap*. Billany's biographers believe that the events described in *The Trap* are only slightly fictionalised versions of what he himself had gone through in his military service. Certain characters, such as a troubled young soldier who Billany tried to look after despite a violent incident during the passage out, appear in both the novel and his letters. That his writing was close to life was sensed at the time, with a review in *The Listener* praising *The Trap* for being 'raw', with a narrative that didn't appear to have been corrupted by foggy memory or nostalgia.

Billany's experiences of the dehumanising process of sinking into a military identity are reflected in his grim evocation of army life in the desert. He describes a landscape in which 'there was nothing nothing nothing nothing except khaki khaki khaki khaki, sand sand sand sand and flies flies flies flies'. Lieutenant Dan Billany took command of a platoon in the 150th Infantry Brigade, defending a 'box' of this desolate terrain on the Gazala Line that stretched south across the desert from the Mediterranean sea. When Rommel moved the Panzers of the Afrika Corps against the British in late May 1942, Billany was ordered to withdraw but, cut off, was captured after heavy fighting. In *The Trap*, he describes the moment in familiar fashion – the steel helmeted German soldier rising from his armoured vehicle to say 'Kommen Sie her [*sic*], Kamerad. You Kaput, for you the war is over.' The war, perhaps, but for Billany a great love was about to begin.

In June 1942, Dan Billany was sent to Italy and Camp 66, a sprawling network of huts, compounds and barbed wire to the north of Naples, in the foot of the Apennines. This was intended to be a processing centre but the Italians had so many prisoners that it took a long time to move them on to more established POW camps. Bored and waiting for the transfer to who knows where, Billany began to record the events of recent months, from training in England to command and combat in North Africa, in what would become the manuscript for *The Trap*, writing home asking for pens, ink and exercise books. Corporeal sustenance came in food parcels sent by the Red Cross, which were distributed to syndicates of five men, who would build stoves, cook and eat together. In Billany's syndicate was David Dowie, a twenty-three-year-old lieutenant who had been evacuated from Dunkirk with the Royal Northumberland Fusiliers, sent to North Africa and captured at Tobruk. The two men stayed together in late November 1942 when they were finally transferred from Camp 66 to Rezzanello, a castle complete with four romantic turrets. There, the friendship seemed to bloom.

The two men learned French, German and Italian; David studied hygiene and sanitary engineering. Billany took part in a production of *The Importance of Being Earnest* and made ink portraits of fellow prisoners, while Dowie excelled in the camp's sports competitions.

Billany was so taken with David Dowie that he wrote to his sister Joan on 8 January 1943 'on an important matter affecting your future'. This was that she ought to marry David; she should ignore the attentions of any glamorous flying types in favour of his friend who, he wrote, is *'very* attractive, intelligent, generous, and in every possible way nice'. There was the small matter that Dowie was 'already slightly engaged' but this wouldn't necessarily be a problem. 'You see how I think of you!' Billany wrote in his tall, never joined-up, neat pen, '(I'm not entirely haywire in this matter.) You'd like him: have shown him yr photos.'

In April 1943, the men were moved again, this time to a former orphanage in Fontanellato, a village near Parma. On 16 May 1943, Billany sent another, even longer letter which begins as an intense critique of Joan's fiancé Ken. He is 'not as sensitive, as intelligent as you need, and there isn't any real depth to his character. I think you've already seen right through him and out the other side.' Ken is physically not good enough, and 'inhibited' with 'the spirit of a schoolboy'. It continues, until Dan suggests his alternative of the ideal man for Joan – 'good-looking, physically charming and strong, a graceful mover – dancing swimming, sport. He must have a sense of justice . . . [be] kind, merry, truthful, self-knowing, self-respecting, absolutely courageous.' Billany continues his parade of virtues before saying, 'there's one man I know, here, who fulfils these conditions.' In the near violence of the invective against Ken and the idealised portrait of David Dowie is a terrible sadness, the words issuing a blazing intensity of feeling, that the only way he could keep the man he was falling for close was to try to unite him with his sister.

Or perhaps there was another way they could become intimate – a love made immortal in the written word. On 30 May 1943, Billany wrote to tell the family that he and Dowie were about to embark on a project to write a book together. He promises that 'it's going to be a corker – a jewel – and a strong selling line'. The news of the book came with a reflection on his own state of mind. Referring to his marriage advice for Joan, Billany remarked that he didn't know whether it would be helpful and admitted that perhaps his sister would be better suited to advise him, than the other way round. Nevertheless, 'one can see certain principles clearly. One is, no half measures: another, don't wait about, life flies.' It was this philosophy that provided the determination to complete a beautiful and tragic account of queer love at war.

On the title page of the manuscript for Dan Billany and David Dowie's collaborative book *The Cage*, which they had intended to be called *For You the War Is Over*, is a drawing of their life in the Italian POW camps. Two men sit on upturned boxes, facing away from the reader. Their heads are bowed. In front of them is a tall fence of strands of barbed wire, through which are line drawings of everything that might be found out there, in a world at war – a train puffing smoke, tanks zooming along, a newspaper, a telephone, a cyclist, old ladies gossiping and a woman with a pram walking cheerily by. The drawing depicts their camp life as almost morbid, in flat grey lines compared to the drama and energy of what lies out beyond the wire. In a reversal of the image, the words within the book are vivid, alive, full of an intense human drama like no other.

Dan Billany and David Dowie wrote *The Cage* through the spring and summer of 1943. It is a hybrid book that dances between diary entries by David, vignettes of camp life, pen portraits of particular fellow prisoners, introspective reflections, letters back home and intimate dialogue that feels like a script for a radio play.

It describes the relationship between three key characters, Dan, David and a third man called Alan Matsen, who has a biography – the working-class errand boy working his way up to become a teacher who has radical views on the education and upbringing of children – very similar to Dan Billany himself. A publisher's note at the start of the first edition remarks that 'he is perhaps a symbol of distress, perhaps, in part, a self-portrait'.

*The Cage* begins as any POW novel might, with the minutiae of life under headings such as 'Little-Known Facts About Bed-Bugs', 'Scatology, or the writing on the wall' and 'Our Daily Bread'. It has the smells and the ennui, the tensions and petty dramas, child-like feuds and banter common to the genre. The monotony and boredom is punctuated by a bell (a square brew can) to be rung whenever there was a new rumour – on the progress of the war, the likelihood of Red Cross parcels, a new medical inspection, the possibility of being moved. The men eat endless meals of macaroni soup. When women pass the camp outside the fence, all eyes turn to the cry of 'Bint!'. The collaged narrative heightens the disloca-tion, the feeling of bodies contained on a hot rectangle of Italian soil. The dialogue is often fast and lurid, especially in one passage about the night-time shenanigans in the rowdiest Hut One, an unusual mixture of high camp and banter.

So far, so life behind the wire. There were so many such books when the manuscript was first sent to Billany's publisher Faber & Faber that they rejected it on the grounds of a crowded market. They missed a trick. As the incarceration continues, Alan develops a deep infatuation with David, one he struggles to understand. He gives David all of his cigarettes and bread and even offers him his shaving kit and underwear from parcels from home. He follows him around the camp, desperate to engage him in deep conversation. The attention becomes so relentless that David feels he needs to speak to Dan about him. David's continuous rejection of Alan's advances are tough, at times disparaging. As well as a dog, he sees him as a parasite, spineless, pitiful. What must it have been like for Dan Billany to read them as they worked on the novel together, both scribbling away in their notebooks?

The agony of the one-sided desire, made more intense by the confinement of the POW camp, leaps between internal monologues from each of the three men and conversations presented as scripted dialogue. Conversations between Alan and Dan about the situation feel like an articulation of the tortured internal narrative within the real Dan Billany's mind: oddly enough, the honest version of what he was writing when he desperately told Joan that she should marry this wonderful friend. It's as if the character of Alan was invented to deal with the complexity of the real-life relationship that Billany could only write about askance in the letters back to England. The real Dan Billany is split into two characters: Dan, outwardly just a sensitive, intelligent, bookish man, and the unhappy Alan, the doomed homosexual. Dan asks Alan how he feels about women, if he's ever been in love with one. Alan is, 'Scared of them. Don't understand them. Frightened. Don't like their breasts.'

David takes regular walks around the camp grounds to clear his head, but his exercise is ruined by the constant presence of Alan and his 'utter servility'. One of the diary passages of *The Cage* records a stroll on 17 January. The two men discuss sexual experience in which, David writes, 'my honesty on the subject shook Alan considerably'. Alan's desperate need for David seems to be part infatuation, part belief that this strong-minded, physically capable man might bring him the fulfilment that he cannot find in his loneliness. The character of Dan is aware of this, telling Alan that what he wants from David is affection, the sharing of 'the burden of your life as it must be shared'. He advises Alan not to lie to either himself or to David: 'Let him see what's in your heart, give him your confidence, and believe me, he won't laugh at you.'

Alan unburdens himself on David with the agony of his failure. 'I'm just the same shivering kid dressed up in the flesh of a man. Not a man. I daren't come out of my armour. I daren't get myself free and come out in the open air. I'm scared of life.' He believes that 'buried pretty deep in my being, something that I can't see, but it won't let me live'.

I don't feel that the character of Alan was invented to conceal the writer Dan Billany's sexuality from readers after the war. Instead, the character's journey tells a story of the time. From Alan's initial lack of awareness of what drives his obsession with David, to the eventual, almost erotic passion of his desire, it seems to reflect the struggle of gay men to allow themselves to love others, but also, by doing so and understanding the true nature of their sexuality, to be able to love themselves too. Alan had spent his youth trying to be normal, yet had felt as if he was always in a prison, even before he arrived in this cold castle with tantalising views to the distant Alps. In fact, it was meeting David there that had freed him, with his eyes that 'melt ice that's been frozen round my heart all my life'. Alan is relentless in his desperation. He can't bear the thought of an armistice because it would inevitably lead to him being parted from David. In an intense, lonely soliloquy of torment and frustration, he imagines his life as the song of a nightingale: 'Ringing, ringing life, power and strength and lust – bursting, brilliant, sobbing with life and lust, and joy beyond imagination. And I here – still, strangled. God, God, I do not have to die. I am dead.' Even the light of a lamp shining on David's hair feels overwhelmingly intimate. But that is as close as he can be.

Eventually, Alan decides that his obsession with David is merely the result of him never having grown up, a manifestation of a desperate need for comfort still lingering from infancy. This chimes with Billany's own history, as he frequently wrote of being unable to stop feeling as if he were still a child. Perhaps this is because the prejudice of the time meant that he was never truly able to accept the sexual urges that came with adolescence. The spell is broken when David, in a moment of pity, finally takes Alan's hand. It seems to create a balance between the two men, the weakness of Alan and the strength of David flowing down their arms into one another. They speak about their miscommunication, the jealous neediness that for so long had pushed David away. He can finally find empathy and, on the book's final pages, decides, 'I would take his hand. I would lead him back to the world of life.'

The real Dan Billany seems to have confessed his love to David Dowie and come to an acceptance when it was rejected. Inside the cover for the manuscript of *The Trap* is a poem Billany wrote to Dowie that feels like the missing link between the story as set out in the novel and the coded version that Billany's family read about in their letters home. It is both humorous and full of desperation at the unrequited affection, saying that he could no more relinquish his love than he could control how the blood moved around his body, and proclaimed that this love would endure until death. Nevertheless, he ends the poem by hoping that despite the imbalance of emotion between them, they might return to their former, easy friendship.

In one of the last letters Billany sent from Fontanellato, there's a reflection of the emotional equilibrium that seemed to have been reached in the book. On 1 August 1943, he writes that he thinks David will marry but wants the family to meet him 'so that you can see my idea of the right type' and then, tellingly, 'He knows what I think.' He writes too that he needs help from his family in whom to marry. Despite everything, Billany was still in the cage. Perhaps instead he should have listened to the words of advice the character Dan wished he had given to Alan and David, that 'true escape is not a flight, a running away. It is only when the prison walls drop, drop away from around you, that you truly escape.'

*

When news of the Armistice of Cassibile between the Allies and the Italian government reached the camp on 8 September 1943, the prisoners at Fontanellato wandered through the fence and dispersed into the surrounding countryside. Trying to avoid the German soldiers and Italian fascists still determined to continue the war, David Dowie and Dan Billany took shelter with the Meletti family, who farmed land on the edge of Soragna, a nearby village. For weeks they slept in a hayloft by night and lurked in nearby woods during the day, all the while working feverishly to finish their book. The fruits of the joint creative endeavour ripened as Italy passed into autumn. Once their work was done, Billany and Dowie entrusted the pile of notebooks containing both *The Cage* and *The Trap* to Dino Meletti, who promised to post them to Dan once the war was over. With German troops actively hunting for former POWs in the local area, it was too dangerous for them to stay any longer. They paid a final, sad farewell to their Italian protectors and struck out towards the Allied lines, many hundreds of miles to the south, and vanished. Nobody knows what happened.

Dan Billany's sexuality remains in the shadows. We can never know the true nature of his relationship with David Dowie. The Meletti family, who eventually returned the manuscripts to the Billany family in 1946, never mentioned anything out of the ordinary about how they were together, even when a BBC documentary crew visited them to make a film about the disappearance in 2010. It does seem unlikely that Dowie would have embarked on the innovative writing project of *The Cage* with Billany had he been as frustrated with him as his character in the novel, still less that he would have joined him on the long and dangerous journey towards freedom. Jodi Weston Brake, Billany's niece, daughter of Joan, and very much the keeper of his flame, believes that the two men were in a relationship by the time of their disappearance.

It's not just this final mystery that makes *The Cage* so compelling. It is because the writing is so urgent. If there couldn't be a consummated or requited love between the two men, then those agonies became the written word and still feel so alive on the page. This was a book created in a state of high focus, clearly such a vital endeavour to them that they delayed their departure by a month longer than most of their fellow prisoners.

In my 1949 first edition of *The Cage*, the cover flap carries an 'IMPORTANT NOTICE' asking for anyone who knew the whereabouts of Billany and Dowie to contact the publishers. Their photographs were printed opposite the title page, with the line 'whose fate are unknown', giving the air of both a work of art and a missing persons appeal. *The Cage* is a near-perfect example of the slipperiness that often exists between wartime fiction and memoir. To be able to read the intense desperation of Billany's love in both novel and letters home gives the account of the love affair an authenticity. Eyewitness evidence corroborates this.

George Mathieson had been part of the same POW camp parcel syndicate as Billany and Dowie, appearing in *The Cage* as a character called Henry. After the war, he went through the novel, easily spotting the real people and events that the two men had written about, and remarking that the greatest fiction was the Alan Matsen character, who, unlike the rest, didn't have an obvious inspiration among their fellow prisoners. However, he felt both that some of the elements of Alan were recognisable from Billany's life, and that the Dan of the novel closely resembled the Dan he knew. He believed the story of Alan and David was 'quite credible'. Both George and the fictional Henry seemed not to have spotted the true depths of the relationship described, with Mathieson noting, 'Dan ascribes to Henry a blissful ignorance of "Alan's" problems and his character reading is entirely accurate!' Even in the intimacy of the POW camp, the true nature of how men felt for one another was not always clear.

Was it clear to Billany himself? Writing seems to have been fundamental to his search for who he really was. In a note on the original manuscript, he wrote, 'How shall I get the essential, nagging soul of me, the truth itself, out? I don't know what's inside me. The chaos when I look into my own personality. The conflict.' He feared to 'write down in ink the essential that I live for'. I'm so happy that he did. More than nearly anything else I've read, *The Cage* seems to get to the core of the depth of passion and complexity of love that two men might feel for one another during the war years in the hinterlands between friendship, desire and comradeship, and how the one-sided nature of these infatuations must have been torture for one and awkward for the other, while both remained aware that it was happening against the framework of a culture that despised it. That David Dowie never rejected or felt shamed by Dan Billany's love and was happy for their friendship to continue perhaps speaks of an acceptance of his homosexuality and a kind, generous soul.

The last anyone knows of Dan Billany and David Dowie is a chit given to Italians in the village of Capistello on 20 November 1943, 500km south of their shelter with the Meletti family and tantalisingly close to the Allied lines. Signed by the two men and a third, Alec Harding, chits like this could be presented by Italians to any Allied officer as a reassurance that 'The bearers of this have given us food and a place to sleep at some danger to themselves from the Germans in the vicinity.' After that scrap of paper, no trace of the men was ever found. The Billany family kept sending hopeful letters out into the complex postal systems of the military, the Red Cross and the Italian authorities. They put advertisements in the newspapers and contacted the families of other prisoners to try to find out what had happened, but to no avail. George Mathieson wrote to Billany's father on 18 July 1946. He said that he hoped that his words would not give him pain, but that during his own journey south through Italy, he had heard stories from Italians who had found the bodies of British soldiers up in the mountains, limbs entwined and clasped together, in a final attempt to stave off death from exposure. 'That always suggested Dan and David to me,' he wrote. 'I mention this [. . .] as indicating the impression Dan and David's friendship had given me.'

These were just two of the millions of men who disappeared without trace in the Second World War. That their story has reached us at all feels like a miracle. The Meletti family who sheltered them could have been caught by the Germans, these manuscripts taken, mislaid or destroyed. *The Cage* should be cherished not just as a memorial to Dan Billany, but for all those men who loved like him, and whose struggles and self-loathing, whose moments of overwhelming love were never told. Some of those died in the war. Some, perhaps, only a few years ago. In the twilight of their lives they remembered an intimacy that their time would not allow them, wondering what could have been.

I am sure that Dan Billany would have found a contentment in the impact that his writing and his memory had on the family he so loved back home. Jodi Weston Brake, Billany's niece, told me that her mother, Joan, who the writer had so wanted to marry David after the war, lived her life inspired by the brother who had disappeared and the books he left behind. Jodi grew up in a liberal house, where gay men and women were welcome. It shaped her own, unconventional path too, some of it spent living on the site of the Glastonbury festival in its hippy heyday. I find this rather beautiful, the thought of the spirit of this kind man who spent his final years behind barbed wire living on in the British post-war counterculture in a lush Somerset field.

# THE DEMOCRACY OF DEATH

On the day before the St Nazaire raid in March 1942, Micky Burn instructed his men to prepare for the possibility that they would be killed. They were told to write their wills in their army service pocketbooks and to pen last letters to their families back home. It was an uncommonly warm day and members of Burn's troop had spent it on the decks of the *Princess Josephine Charlotte*, a ship anchored in the calm waters of Carrick Roads, the Cornish estuary off the town of Falmouth. In his memoir, Burn recalled looking across the bucolic surroundings and over his men of No. 6 Troop of No. 2 Commando until he had 'a hideous shock. For a moment I saw Bill Gibson's face, and I knew that he would be killed.'

Dated 24 March 1942, William Gibson's letter to his father is a heartbreaking read, even in reproduction in Burn's book. I can barely imagine what it must be like to put into words your last testament to the man who raised you, who had known you from your very tiniest, most fragile and delicate breaths, had been woken by the lunging intensity of your nursing screams. Gibson thanks his father for the ideals he has inherited and writes of his hope that their dangerous mission would have some greater purpose.

I sense in his words that he in some way knew the firmament of life was slipping under his feet, like the tide beneath the *Princess Josephine Charlotte*. To the young commando, everything on that March afternoon feels so vivid, so real. He tells his dad that he's just finished his tea, that 'God's lovely sunshine is streaming in through the portholes', and that he and his comrades had been sunbathing all day. Spring is in the air and 'with everything looking so beautiful we only now appreciate how lovely everything is; almost like condemned criminals'. He writes that he will go to his first Holy Communion, that 'I know God will help us all he can and I pray Dad, that he will help you. My will has been made out – it seems so silly but we all have had to do it.' He hopes the letter will be a comfort rather than the 'dreaded plain telegram' that was all officialdom would have seen necessary to mark his death. The letter concludes with the hope that his dad will not be too unhappy, that he should 'remember what you always told me to keep my chin up', that he had tried to do his duty and that by his death, future generations might remember them and gain something from what was done. He finishes with the sorrow that he has been unable to do the things he had hoped to do. He gives thanks for the start his family gave him in life and offers a hope for peace, a promise of love.

William Gibson was killed on Motor Launch 268 and has no known grave. He was twenty-two years old. I read his letter over and over in a silent library one winter afternoon, three weeks after the birth of my own son. The dying young man calling for his mother is almost a cliché of war films and histories, so much so that the image has lost some of its power. But this letter to a father, so tender, so accepting, brought tears to my eyes that earned me worried looks from the person sitting at the opposite desk.

To imagine myself in war, behind the controls of a Mosquito or Lancaster bomber, driving a tank or wielding a rifle in my hands,

I realised after reading Gibson's words, was not a dream I could really have any longer. It was, after all, best relegated to teenage fantasy, where it provided a bitter escape from what I perceived as the persecutions of masculinity. I couldn't imagine waiting in the fragile surroundings of a wooden motor launch, clutching a deadly weapon as German artillery and machine guns sent steel and explosive towards me from a hostile shore. I could, however, picture myself sitting on a ship's warm deck in a perfect English spring, breathing air that tasted of both water and woodland, writing a letter to my dad telling him thank you, goodbye, that I loved him. I could now also contemplate the singular, griping horror of receiving such a letter, of reading it in the voice of my son. The machines were stripped away. It was not war that had fascinated me for so long, but these lives that moved through and sometimes ended within it.

Lance Sergeant William Gibson's name is inscribed on panel 14, column 2 of the Brookwood War Memorial in Surrey. His greatest monument though is in that letter he wrote to his father, and Micky Burn's sensitivity in sharing it. Lives lost in warfare have given us our history not just in their roles in battles won and wars lost, but as archaeological evidence, clues as to the cultural relationship different societies had with themselves, through their hierarchies and understandings of gender, violence, death, mourning and the afterlife. Buried weapons illustrate advances in metallurgy and art. The human body itself becomes a discrete time capsule which might be analysed, the cut marks on bones symbols to be decoded, smashed skulls and traumas the echoes of a historical act. The remains of those killed in conflicts illustrate our understanding of the past and, in their use in trials for crimes against humanity, can help to bring justice and peace to the present. The Second World War is still recent enough that to rummage in old bones, unless for the purpose of investigating war crimes, remains taboo.

Shipwrecks and bomber crash sites alike are designated war graves and must not be touched.

Western traditions of burial are a form of sanitisation, protecting the living from the pungent reality of the process of dying. This is especially so in the case of violent death in war. The British marked each grave with bright white stone familiar from any photograph or film of a military cemetery, carefully maintained by the Commonwealth War Graves Commission. They look clean and hygienic, like hundreds of thousands of mortuary slabs that gleam as if they had been scrubbed for an eternity. Burial hides the final agonies, the reduction of the soldier, sailor or flier from human being to proteins and matter.

Often, there was little left for the men who had the grim task of clearing up after combat to bury. The historian John Keegan quotes as a source a novel by Eric Lambert in this grim description of the remains of men in armoured vehicles in the Western Desert: 'Inside each wrecked tank a putrid blackening paste on the walls was what an armour-piercing shell had left of the men who manned it.' It would have been someone's job to scrape that away, to try to give the person it was some dignity in burial. Other men simply disappeared into the land, the sky and the sea. There are haunting photographs from explorations of wartime wrecks of pairs of boots, lying on the seabed, showing the final resting place of the bodies of sailors long ago lost to the endless hunger of nature. For many left behind, their man passed from life as a final memory before they departed overseas, in a last letter, or in the barely there weight of a brief government telegram printed on wartime paper that *regretted to inform*, etc. For gay and bisexual men, there was no acceptable, open way to express grief at the loss of a lover.

In war and in peace alike, our rituals of grieving frequently involve the creation of myths around the life departed. This occurs in many ways: the printed tribute in the newspaper, the memories gossiped until the name slips out of mind, the mourner in their loneliness forever conjuring a romantic vision of the person who was lost. As the state buries and immortalises the dead of its military adventures, it has immense power over who and how to remember. It can create mythic, heroic narratives, not just at the time of the conflict but in the years afterwards, when the survivors, with their thousands of individual, thorny truths, begin themselves to slip away.

After the Second World War, the men of Bomber Command squadrons like 158 were forgotten more quickly than most. The destruction of Dresden and other German cities became a source of shame and the politicians who gave the orders to drop the bombs distanced themselves from their responsibility. The men of Bomber Command took the rap, never being awarded the type of unique service medals given to other units and branches of the British military. In memoirs and personal testimony, many of the aircrew who risked their lives on operations across Occupied Europe are understandably resentful at this collective amnesia. As arguments continue to rage over whether the destruction of German cities was strategically and morally justified, I fear we risk losing sight of the courage of the likes of Bertram Warr and the other men of Bomber Command who made the ultimate sacrifice. If the metal of their melted down aircraft is an unseen memorial on the atomic level all around us, how they have been officially recognised is more complicated.

'Bomber' Harris, the man whose obstinate belief in the area bombing of Germany caused so much destruction, got his own monument in the form of a statue by the artist Faith Winter. This was erected outside St Clement Danes church in London's Aldwych in 1992, the centenary of his birth. Formal and austere, it looks like a relic of another age and – although the plaque at the base of the statue reads, 'In memory of a great commander and of the brave crews of Bomber Command, more than 55,000 of whom lost their lives in the cause of freedom. The Nation owes them all an immense debt' – was it right that a ruthless commander was commemorated over the 55,573 of his men who died?

Eight of those men made up the crew of 426 Squadron's Halifax LW682. None of them had completed more than three operations before, on the night of 13 May 1944, they were all shot down and killed by a German night fighter. The wreck of their aircraft was retrieved from a Belgian marsh in 1997, with some of the metal and parts going to a Canadian project to restore another Halifax brought up from a Norwegian lake. Much of the rest was melted down into 390kg of ingots. When, after a long campaign led by figures including Bee Gee Robin Gibb, the men of Bomber Command were finally given their own war memorial, these ingots were made into an aluminium alloy. This was rolled into tiles, given a bronze-coloured coating and used to make part of the roof structure. When I visited the memorial on a hot summer day, it was being used as the backdrop for a fashion photoshoot by three Japanese girls, just another London tourist attraction that might look cool on Instagram. As the teenagers pouted and snapped away, I looked up at the curves of the recycled metal roof, designed to reflect the geodesic design of the Wellington bomber's fuselage, which looked graceful against the sharp, bright blue square of sky in the middle. Yet with its thick pillars, solid walls of Portland stone, from which lions' heads sprout, almost at random, the rest of the memorial feels grand, pompous. At its heart is a sculpture by Philip Jackson of seven aircrew in full flying gear. Realistically cast in bronze, they loom 2.7 metres above their plinth. An informative board explains who they all are: the flight engineer raises his hand to shade his eyes from the sun. The pilot rests his chin on his hand. They are all shoulders back, determined, their faces handsome, chiselled and stern, archetypal warriors, except one. On the right, the wireless operator stands shoulders slumped, mouth open, staring at the ground, even cast in metal giving the air of a mind distressed by the life he has volunteered to lead. He is the only one I can believe. When the monument was unveiled by the Queen on 28 June 2012, the Battle of Britain Memorial Flight's Avro Lancaster roared overhead, showering Green Park with hundreds of thousands of red poppy petals.

I don't doubt the sincerity of the motives behind the Bomber Command memorial. It clearly means a lot to the veterans who survived to see it, and to their families now. Yet despite the beautiful touch of the recycled bomber roof and the harrowed expression on the one statue, I find it overbearing. I would imagine a memorial to men who took to the sky at such huge risk to be built to create a sensation of grace and light, but this is a classical, martial structure. The men are perplexingly both too realistic and too grand, hardly a representation of the varied identities of the thousands of men who flew and died. The location of the memorial is peculiar too. It sits on the edge of Piccadilly in a part of London associated with Parliament, monarchy and aristocracy, frequented largely by tourists and the international mega-rich. Nearby are a scattering of other memorials, to the Duke of Wellington, men of the Commonwealth, the Royal Artillery and so on, that together sit in the context of state power and British historical pomp rather than as a reflective commemoration of collective sacrifice and individual lives. Standing there as London's traffic thunders by, I wanted to feel a context to their bravery, but the metal was cold, the thought beyond reach.

By contrast, the subtle war memorials in our town and village centres are often effective interventions into the bustle of daily life, giving the opportunity for a momentary thought of the local men who never came home. There are others that you might need to hunt for on the map – monoliths, sculptures, the remains of aircraft, ships and tanks – many idiosyncratic and all unique, that commemorate specific events, military bases or units. They are intimate interventions in the landscape that take us back to when their locations would have witnessed the coming and going of men finely balanced between life and death.

Every September, the 158 Squadron Association holds an annual reunion in Bridlington, the seaside town that hosted the bomber crews as they tried in those evenings when they were not in the air to forget about it for a while, to smooth the edges of their trauma with beer and girls, dancing and song. I'd been in touch with Chuck Tolley and Tony Frost, two people with seemingly unending knowledge of the young men, including their own relatives, who had taken to the skies with 158 Squadron. Tony's uncle was Bertram Warr, whose youthful vitality and energetic poetry had so captured my imagination, and he'd been generous in providing me with copies of his wartime poetry, notebooks and diaries. Chuck and Tony's hours of diligent research that went into creating biographical files on as many aircrew as possible seemed in itself to be a ritual of remembrance. They invited me to come up for the Squadron reunion service and lunch, on the first Sunday in September. It was time to return to RAF Lissett.

As I arrived at the village church, on the other side of a small field to the guard hut Tommo and I had explored a few weeks previously, a cheery vicar was setting up chairs and a PA system. In the grassy churchyard, the Canadian and Australian flags had been raised alongside the British. Not wanting to get in the way, I wandered again along the old concrete of the former entrance to the airfield, past the guard house and padlocked buildings, and out onto the perimeter track. This time I followed it east, toward the sea. I passed a turkey, hobbling weirdly over the site of the former hanger where the 158 Squadron Halifaxes were once patched up from everyday wear and tear, flak and fighter cannon damage. It was a morning that felt more like early spring than Indian summer, buzzards soaring in the thermals and birdsong loud in the fading green of the trees. The former taxiway kinks sharply at the end, meeting the final rectangle of the old main runway from which 158's Halifaxes roared into the air. Even after eighty years, the airfield's imposition on the landscape is startling. A red admiral sat sunning itself, gently opening and closing its wings where the edge of the concrete slabs dropped off to a field of recently harvested wheat like a miniature cliff.

Back at Lissett Church, the smartly dressed congregation took their seats out in the churchyard. Using the order of service to shade our eyes from the low autumn sun, we sang the 158 Squadron hymn and heard the roll of honour of those men who flew with the unit, survived the war and had passed away since the last service, pre-Covid in 2019. After the time I'd spent immersed in the words of the writers of 158, the Last Post that morning was one of the most moving renditions I'd ever heard, resounding off the ancient church walls just as once did the noise of engines of the Halifax bombers as they warmed up for flight on the nearby airfield.

As people milled around after the service, reconnecting and catching up after two years away, something struck me. Although there were plenty of people with grey hair present – I was one of the youngest – there seemed to be nobody of an age to have actually served with the Squadron. In fact, most of the association was a similar age to my parents now, very much in the same age bracket of the veterans I remembered from church and Remembrance Sundays of my youth. I was introduced to one elderly gentleman who had lived near the airfield during the war and was surprised to learn that, during those years, he'd been a small boy. It was a sharp reminder of just how fast the war was slipping into the intangible past. The sensation of time moving inexorably forward was overwhelming.

After the service, the congregation moved to a proper old-fashioned lunch at a seafront hotel in Bridlington – sliced ham and beef, jacket potatoes, coleslaw with just the right amount of onion. Harry Lomas writes beautifully about his experiences of a 158 Squadron reunion in *One Wing High*. After many years, he and his pilot Keith Anderson returned to RAF Lissett, from where they had flown so many dangerous operations. 'The present receded in a bittersweet memory of youthful days,' he wrote. 'Could this really have been the setting of these momentous days? Had it all been just a trick of the memory? Could this be a place of pilgrimage? Driving home, we didn't talk much. We had been overtaken by the past. Nostalgia can breed its own sadness.' Yet, looking around at his former comrades, these fortunate survivors, many of whom he would never have known during his active service, he reflected that although they had been sorely tried by a youth dominated by the Depression, and then by the war that had disrupted what they might have expected from working and family life, 'The years had not treated these people harshly [. . .] It was almost as though nature had compensated them in their later years.'

Lomas wrote that as they chewed over their memories at the reunion, these ageing men were 'all together in the nostalgia business'. But it strikes me that this is not a nostalgia as we often see it today – about as far from blokes in Second World War uniforms or a Blitz-themed tea party as you could possibly get. Lomas knew that outsiders would have 'misconceptions' about a reunion of veterans, expecting 'beer-hall bacchanalia or jingoistic jamboree', but the reality was 'little in the way of proceedings which is in any way militaristic; there is no glorification of war, no stories of bravado or derring-do, no divisions of former rank'. Instead, the men were gathered to remember those they had lost, to touch the memory of missed youth, to recall the old stories – a man trapped in the WAAF accommodation, a sheep dressed in a RAF tunic appearing in the mess. These are the moments that give history its character, that raise it above mere facts and figures, the strategic concerns, the profit and the loss in lives and machinery.

It was only then, on a visit to the Yorkshire Air Museum, that Lomas found out about Operation Gisela, the Luftwaffe infiltration raid on 3 March 1945 that targeted bombers as, with tired crews, they approached their home airfields. Many aircrew were killed not just in sight of the relief of their simple Nissen hut homes but the end of war itself. We've now had so much Second World War history in the form of television, yards of military history books and latterly the internet that it's striking that the people who actually fought in the war spent most of their lives not knowing the wider context. Their bombers, ships, tanks and tired boots drew lines on the map; they saw mundanity and horror, but often knew little of what they were a part of. Theirs was an experience heightened by its specificity and I wonder if subsequent generations know almost too much. We now have the kind of overarching insight that in the immediate post-war years would have been only available in sealed files or the memories of the very highest commanders. Achieving an encyclopaedic knowledge of tactics, strategy, historical events, the intricacies of the workings of missions and vehicles might act as a barrier to seeing the war in intimate and ultimately human terms. Heroes as ciphers slot better into these vast narratives than the ordinary and every day.

And what could be more ordinary and every day than men of a certain age gathering for a buffet in a hotel in an English seaside town that has seen better days? Their uniforms switched for civilian clothes, hairlines receding, waistlines expanding, each year fewer of their number able to attend. Just as during the war years, they'd often only know who had failed to return from operations from the photographs pinned to the intelligence hut's wall. As time went on, the roll call at the Lissett memorial service would be of names that could not be put to faces. And so, their numbers dwindled until that Sunday afternoon in September 2021 and a room of people who were themselves no longer young but looked like the photographs of their dads and uncles printed in memoirs from the 1980s, 1990s and 2000s. Another generation might be slipping by, but the spirit of thinking, of care, still echoed in the Bridlington walls.

Kevin Bryett, current chair of the association, rose from his chair and the room fell silent. He confirmed my earlier thoughts and said that this was indeed the first reunion at which there were no veterans present. Those still alive were unable to travel, or felt it unwise due to the risk of catching Covid. This, he said, put the association at a crossroads. The veterans had always said that once there were none of their number able to come to the reunion event, it was up to the next generation to decide what to do and whether to carry on. I sincerely hope they do. The association not being connected to an existing squadron is appealing in its civilian nature. It isn't part of a martial heritage, a symbol of esprit de corps to bolster the morale and sense of tradition for an active squadron. Not that there's anything wrong with that, of course, but there's an eloquence and sensitivity to the way 158 Squadron Association go about preserving memory that feels unique and important. Most other bomber and fighter squadrons of the wartime RAF are forgotten now, most Royal Navy ships too, army units disbanded, their records hidden away undigitised in the vast collections of the National Archives. I am happy that this little human story lives on.

Over coffee, there was discussion of next year's service and things to do, of newly unearthed material to be deposited in the squadron archive, of plans to delve deeper into the biographies of the ground crew who sustained the aircraft and the men who flew them. I wonder if the patient determination of these members of the association is also stirred by the memorial that sits near to the RAF Lissett runway where I'd stood in the bright warmth of that morning's sun.

'I think we're blessed that the obscurity adds to it, that it's the back of beyond,' said Peter Naylor, designer of the 158 Squadron memorial, as we parked up in the lay-by next to it after the lunch had ended and the people dispersed. Up a slight incline, the silhouette of seven men in flying gear stands out against the puffy clouds and blue sky. A board by the edge of the lay-by gives a history of the squadron and the aircraft commemorated by each of the wind turbines spinning in the distance. Peter had recently returned to the north east after twenty-five years living in Saudi Arabia when his wife showed him Novera Energy's open competition to design a memorial to the 851 men and one woman (Sergeant Olive Mary Morse died in an air crash in September 1943) who perished on service with 158 Squadron during the Second World War. Despite not being a professional artist or sculptor, Naylor – an enthusiastic, funny character – was hit by an idea overnight. 'I thought you could do these figures in plate steel and cut the faces out; there'd be seven men, bomber crew, coming towards you,' he told me. 'The great thing about silhouette is that it's a perfect analogy of what these guys did; they went in two directions. They're facing Germany and they're facing home, and that's why we have the convex side: there's a little bit of almost bravado about it, chests out, heading out. And then, on this side, you get the concave and there's a little bit more huddled intimacy, as if to say, "Thank God we've got back".'

Peter got through to the final three and, granted a small budget for research and development, tried to work out how to bring his initial sketches to life. After speaking to a London-based engineering company, he decided he wanted to build the memorial in CORE-TEN steel, which is durable but weathers to a beautiful patina. The steel is so tough that most manufacturers told Peter that he wouldn't be able to carve the names of those who died into the memorial and suggested that he instead put them on a plaque nearby. But Peter was adamant that the names had to be present on the steel itself. He eventually found W Campbell & Son Limited, based in Hull not far from his home, who worked out that by reducing the amount of garnet sand they put in their water cutter they'd be able to etch the metal, rather than slice through it. Company founder Walter Campbell and his wife Vera, it transpired, remembered Lissett airfield in the Second World War and used to come to visit one of the men who farmed the surrounding land.

The concrete in the ramp up to the monument binds together small stones and pebbles with dividing lines between the slabs at regular intervals, a deliberate echo of the runway surfaces of the old RAF station. 'It was designed for the veterans, so that it'd open up memories of the very runways that they were crossing,' Peter told me as we walked up it that Sunday afternoon. The steel forms of the airmen loomed before us but, despite their sharp metal outline against the sky, they still have a remarkable humanity. 'What I didn't want to do is make them gods,' Peter said. By designing the memorial so that visitors can walk around and touch the figures that are only slightly larger than life-size, he wanted to reflect that 'This is you and me, this is my dad, these are ordinary guys, they're all in it together. I keep calling it the democracy of death – some were lucky, some weren't.'

It has an entirely different atmosphere to the Green Park memorial, where the figures of the airmen might indeed be deities to be looked up to. The late summer clouds pulled back, the sun sending the shadows of these everymen onto the concrete, the dying grasses and seed heads of the wildflowers growing all around. They whispered in gusts of wind. The way in which the names of the dead are etched into the memorial contributes to this strange atmosphere of transience, of lives held for moments within engineering. From directly in front, in bright light, the letters disappear back into the steel. But move around the sculpture, so that the carved grooves are put into relief, and they suddenly appeared black, bold. This was deliberate. 'So many of these guys literally disappeared into thin air,' Peter said, 'they were just blown to kingdom come.'

As we walked round the memorial, the names faded and sharpened, appearing and disappearing into relief. I mentioned the speech given by Kevin Bryett at the lunch earlier in the day and Peter pointed to the inscribed letters that spelled out Harold Kevin Hornibrook. Known by his middle name, Kevin Hornibrook was a twenty-one-year-old Australian pilot who flew with his best friend, bomb aimer Alan Bryett. On a raid over Berlin, their Halifax was hit, caught fire and started to fall to earth. Hornibrook's final act was to push his friend out of the escape hatch of the doomed aircraft, saving his life at the cost of his own. Alan Bryett's parachute opened and he floated safely to the ground. As he watched the bomber crash, he vowed that if he ever had a son, he would call him Kevin in memory of his best friend. Seeing Alan Bryett and his son touching the name of Kevin Hornibrook had been a powerful moment for Peter. 'It was just fantastic,' he said, 'his best friend, who saved his life [on the memorial] that's going to last for 200 years. It's been the joy of my life that I've been able to bring this to these people.'

Peter got back into his car and drove home towards Hull. I stayed a while, thinking of his parting words: 'The turbines were built in the very cities that these men bombed the bejeezus out of.

It's gone full circle. Who of these guys in 1944 would ever have imagined that there would be German turbines on the very spot where they were taking off?'

There was one man in particular I wanted to find on the memorial. In Peter Naylor's democracy of death, there is no hierarchy or alphabet. You have to search hard for the name of the dead airman that you're looking for. That slowing down of time, the names clocked as eyes scan the metal, brings home the sheer number of the dead. And there I found it: Bertram Warr, the twenty-five-year-old with a lifetime of words still to write, who, on 3 April 1943, lifted off into the dusk in Halifax F-Freddie just above where I stood, never to return. Now his is one name carved into one memorial in one tiny corner of England.

At any one time, as many as 1,442 men and 351 women lived and worked in this landscape, a bustling community of youth and the doomed. Despite the best efforts of the 158 Squadron writers and now archivists, what we know of them are just fragments. Their words and thoughts, desires and dreams of eighty years ago have vanished into the dark earth and sky. I thought of how, of those thousands of men, some would have been gay or fluid in their sexual attractions yet left no record of this behind them. For them, perhaps this windblown expanse of Yorkshire countryside was especially lonely.

As I looked around me, RAF Lissett no longer felt hidden in the East Yorkshire fields. There was an absence of men and machines, a contrast to the busy fashion parade of heavy metal at Tankfest, or the gleaming, mean exhibits in our war museums. In the distance, on the other side of the lane away from the main airfield, I could see the remains of some of the accommodation blocks from which aircrew would have walked to the operation briefing room, its curved corrugated iron roof still visible on the far side of the hedge and the lane, to learn of their target for tonight. From there, they would have walked along the lane to the main entrance of the base, or maybe down a path that from old plans and crop marks on contemporary aerial photos seems to have entered the airfield just near to where I stood. Like the decaying guard hut, the lane was the threshold between their semi-civilian and entirely military lives.

I stared down the old runway towards the wind turbines, such beautiful symbols of the essential battle against climate change that is the heir to the troubles of the 1940s. It struck me that two pairs of turbines ploughed the warm, late summer air like the engines on either side of a Halifax's fuselage. The landscape crackled in my eyes, almost psychedelically so. The steel-cut sculpture of these seven ordinary men became an anchor point to the entire base, coming almost alive to speak out and say *Look around you, this landscape, these turbines, these fragments of concrete, all of this is a memorial, not monumental or nationalistic, but all of this ought to make you remember*. I thought of a line the young poet Bertram Warr had written in one of his notebooks in typically dramatic, florid pen scrawl: 'My eyes must die directed to the evening sky.' I could spend hours here, imagining the crops peeling back, the full length of the concrete runway revealing itself once more, the sound of engines revving up to full power as, one after another, Halifax bombers thunder down it, gently lift off over the sleepy lane into the coming darkness of evening, wheeling away over the fields, then sand and surf, to be swallowed into the night over the North Sea.

# MR THWAITES' BRITAIN

Just like the warped metal in the Imperial War Museum and the anti-aircraft fuse I'd found, the steel sculpture, wind turbines and Yorkshire landscape around RAF Lissett were another unorthodox memorial to those who died in the Second World War. To me, these uncanny objects and spaces make far more fitting totems of remembrance than the aggrandising and monumental. I thought of how Siegfried Sassoon had criticised the Menin Gate, the memorial on the road out to the killing mud of the Battle of Ypres, calling it a 'sepulchre of crime'. I thought too of a diary letter Dudley Cave wrote to his father from his POW camp on 29 May 1944. He and his fellow prisoners had been talking of 'afterwards' – release and the return to civvy street. Some of the men speaking, Cave thought, would never make it back, 'but they will be remembered, I expect in bronze, marble and granite, immortalised in stone battle-dress [. . .] at attention with a carved Short Lee-Enfield, standing on everlasting guard at Whitehall or the Park watching the grey hairs come to those heads which have substituted the trilby for the cap. Watching *us* in *their* civilian heaven.' He wrote that he wished instead that these 'civilians-in-uniform' ought to be remembered

278

as they would have wished it, in civilian clothes. 'Let them out of the Army now that they are dead. Give them their discharge and the Future a chance to see soldiers as ordinary mortals – only too mortal – and not as heroes of glorious battles.'

Grand memorials are an expression of the naivety that the most recent war might be a final one. They function as means for the state to honour the victims of war while abdicating responsibility for creating them, and as a panacea against enacting the serious societal change that war so often brings in its wake. In 1945, there was great hope for a better world, just as there had been in 1918. My grandad's diary letters seem to convey a sense that the war might have a positive impact on his future. Reflecting on the third anniversary of the declaration of war, he wrote, 'I had doubts three years ago and was afraid. Today I have hopes and feel a certain confidence.' Listening to the radio that night, he thought of home and added, 'hope we soon meet and celebrate and resume the happy lives we knew, stripped of doubts and fears. Three years is a long time . . . perhaps it has done us all good in some strange way and helped us to find ourselves. I trust the test won't be too long.' In his words, I hear the voice of a man who believed that the privations of war demanded a better future.

There was certainly a hunger for improvement across the armed forces. The Army Education Corps and Army Bureau of Current Affairs ran thousands of courses and published informative magazines on subjects including modern farming, town planning and the 1942 Beveridge Report that laid the foundations of the British welfare state. Micky Burn did his best to educate the men he commanded, taking the effort to find out what they wanted to do after the war and suggesting courses they might take to help them achieve it. In his first POW camp, Spangenberg, Burn's lectures on the poverty he had seen in England before the war led to his being branded by one officer as 'slightly to the left of Mr

Attlee'. In Colditz, Burn might have been admitted to the camp's own Bullingdon Club, but his lectures on what post-war Britain might be like were considered so radical that Battle of Britain hero and my childhood idol Douglas Bader forbade RAF prisoners from attending. Burn even claimed that another officer wanted him prosecuted for treason.

Micky Burn's Colditz novel *Yes, Farewell* was reprinted in June 1974 as *Farewell To Colditz*, in part to capitalise on the success of the BBC TV series about the POW camp. In a foreword to the new edition, Burn wrote that 'thousands returned from the war and voted for what we thought would become a more humane society'. Burn explored this in his poem 'Until That Night', about the training of the Commandos and the raid in which so many of his men, and his friends, died. In his notes to the poem, Burn wrote that the 'Commando Spirit' had taught him that 'nothing worth accomplishing, whether on a much larger scale or in individual obscurity, is impossible'. There were two lines he added, many years after the war, 'in times of nationwide disillusion', that reflect on the dreams that had led him to believe that the young, masculine energies stirred up by the responsibilities of war would usher in a better world. 'Wild-wagered youth, call, cause, crusade / What a world we might have made!' Sadly, recent history and memory tells us that 'might' is the operative word.

Burn's reflections on the war and the lost potential for change afterwards have stayed with me. We are often lectured on the values our forebears fought for as being absolute and unchanging, and usually with an assumption that they were conservative, nationalistic. Post-war generations cannot ascribe values to those who fought without also considering what they voted for immediately afterwards – as Burn put it, a more useful question than 'What did you do in the war, Daddy?' might be to ask 'What did you think?'

I find it strange when I see the memory of the Second World War being used in conservative arguments, with both a big and small C. I see the war's upheaval in the lives of men as provoking a mass thinking, a curiosity, a chaotic wondering at nationhood and manhood, and where the two connected in sex, love, fear and how we remember. The dissolving of moral codes, the subversion of gender roles, some acceptance of queer sexuality, the arrival of pioneering transgender surgery – I see these sitting alongside the more frequently cited creation of the NHS and welfare state as profound legacies of the Second World War. Against the trauma of what had just happened, perhaps it was impossible for these radical sparks to endure.

After 1945, society tried to fit men back in the roles that had been ascribed for them. Private Normal put on his demob suit and went back to civilian life with the promise of a new deal in the relationship between the individual and the state, the prospect of the body that he had risked in service for his nation being preserved until his grave by the new National Health Service. Like their fathers from the First World War, these men often brought the psychological scars of conflict back with them, leaving them stuck in a hinterland between the military man who was asked to kill and the civilian he had been before.

Powell and Pressburger's 1946 film *A Matter of Life and Death*, the most poetic war film ever made, often strikes me as reflecting this. David Niven's Squadron Leader Peter Carter represents the idealised British fighting male, handsome in his RAF uniform and pencil moustache. 'Age 27. Very important,' he tells June, the American wireless operator listening in on his final transmission from the shattered cockpit of a burning bomber, plummeting to earth through an English fog as he sums up his life before he was turned into a servant of war. 'Education violently interrupted. Religion – Church of England. Politics – Conservative by nature,

Labour by experience.' 'What's your name?' June asks. 'I cannot read you. Cannot read you.'

*A Matter of Life and Death* was ahead of its time in more than cinematography and the hallucinatory scriptwriting. Squadron Leader Carter seems to have survived the crash of his bomber but ends up on trial to decide whether he can stay on earth or must disappear up a huge staircase to another place (not heaven, exactly, but something like it), full of servicemen of all nations. As the trial looms, Carter's experience of the world is all askew – he tries to take a drink but the drink vanishes. Everything seems unreal.

Watching the film, I am struck that so many of the confusing symptoms experienced by Squadron Leader Carter – hallucinations, nightmares, flashbacks, constant self-interrogation – are similar to those of post-traumatic stress disorder. PTSD was defined in 1980 by the American Psychiatric Association, based on research into the post-war afflictions of Vietnam veterans, Holocaust survivors and civilians who had experienced terrible events. It remained controversial in British military psychiatry circles but eventually, the need to understand what was happening to veterans of the Falklands War, as well as the victims of peacetime disasters, led to a wider awareness of the disorder, and the development of therapeutic treatments. Powell and Pressburger's fictional Squadron Leader Carter is, like those suffering from PTSD, caught in the limbo of a life haunted and disrupted by the trauma of the war experience. In autobiographical novel *Flesh Wounds*, David Holbrook compares the life-changing impact of seeing the carnage of metal against the human body on the beaches of D-Day with another symbolic moment in male identity. The sight of a blazing tank with corpses laid out alongside it triggers a physical sensation, a 'dreadful taste' that is 'the first full flavour of machine warfare'. Holbrook writes that for a man, the loss of his virginity is a moment that leaves him changed in a new understanding of life and love. The sight of violent death on Normandy sand did the same, but instead left men 'for ever to be a little deadened'. In the symptoms of PTSD, this deadening was not just a quiet psychological blankness, but externalised in the sort of disruptive patterns of behaviour Derek Jarman had experienced from his RAF father.

A few months after I took part in the VE day celebrations in London in 1995, a woman wrote to the *Guardian* as the anniversary of the end of the war approached. She described how her dad had suffered terribly in a Japanese POW camp, returned from the war and quickly married her mother. Her own birth, she believed, was 'the much-needed evidence for my father that the depriva- tions he had suffered had not rendered him infertile'. The war was a taboo subject and never discussed, and the family lived in terror of the father's anger, depression and constant criticism. 'Perhaps the only way to ease the pain was for the victim to regain his lost power by becoming the persecutor,' the woman wrote. 'The victim became the tyrant.' He suffered all the symptoms of PTSD – the hallucinations, nightmares, paranoia – and was only, eventually, freed by the onset of dementia. Her words are a weary echo of those of Colin Spencer, Derek Jarman or Micky Burn discussing the impact of the First World War on their own father's lives.

A different kind of trauma, I discovered, had hit my family too. My Great-Uncle Reg had worked in an RAF bomb disposal unit during the war, afterwards joining the Inland Revenue and moving to a bungalow on the edge of Cheltenham, where he lavished time and attention on his garden. On the morning of 30 November 1958, the forty-four-year-old clerk told his wife that he was going to his shed to 'do a little job' before heading out for a ride on his bike. That evening, an engineer putting up electricity cables found his body hanging from a tree on the edge of a field two miles from his home. In that garden shed, Reg had left suicide notes in which, the local newspaper reported, he said he had no financial worries and attributed no responsibility for his death to his wife. My dad remembers it as the only time he ever saw my grandad Percy cry.

My family tends towards melancholy and worry. Reginald and Percy's uncle had died by drowning aged just eighteen, and I still haven't been able to discover whether this was by accident or design. Was it the trauma of working in bomb disposal that brought Reg to the point of no return? His unit's war diary is lost or buried in an archive. There are no letters to get an understanding of what he went through during his time in uniform. We have a vague family story that suggests that newspaper report wasn't entirely accurate, and that a love affair with a Norwegian woman he'd met during the war had overshadowed his post-war life. I know from the records of his service sent to me from RAF Cranwell that he had indeed spent time in Norway in the later years of the war, but can find out nothing more.

Yet trauma and suicide can manifest like this – not in one simple moment, but as a tapestry of hurt and depression that finally becomes too much to bear. It would hardly be surprising if the intensely dangerous work of disposing of high explosives, a doomed love affair which he was never able to get over, and other factors which we can never know had all contributed to Reg deciding he could no longer remain alive.

The decade in which Reg died was one of tough readjustment to peace, dominated by the straitened conditions of austerity. British culture started to look inwards as the great roar and thrill (however grim) of the war years, and the great hope of the post-war Labour government and welfare state, slid into a threadbare greyness, decline and personal and national poverty. In films like 1951 thriller *Port of London*, we see Thameside streets that had once welcomed the world to the heart of power still blitzed and broken, the sky soot-stained, barges sailing downstream to dump the waste of a capital full of gaudy drunks and petty criminals onto oily, dank marshes. Peter de Rome summed up the feeling in his memoir when he wrote of his reasoning for emigrating to the United States: 'I had fallen victim to the fashionable feeling of disillusionment that seemed to have assailed London in the post-war years. The vital days of the war were recalled with regret, the lingering restrictions were accepted with weary resignation.' The freedom he'd felt as a queer man and noticed all around him in the liberal atmosphere of the years of conflict had dissipated. 'Few people realised that a social revolution had taken place, silently and bloodlessly, while the war had been going on; and that in the interim, while the country grew slowly and uncomfortably used to the fact, England was a very dull place indeed.' In victory, we had lost the opportunity to undergo radical, enduring cultural change. The birth of the NHS, rather appropriately, can feel like a sticking plaster over this wound.

Patrick Hamilton, the alcoholic novelist who bequeathed to the dictionary the concept of 'gaslighting', captured better than any other writer an atmosphere of English shame and seediness that runs counter to the heroic myths of the mid-twentieth century. Of the many appalling characters to whom he gave breath, none is more curiously, recognisably modern than Mr Thwaites, the terror of the shabby boarding house called the Rosamund Tea Rooms in Thames Lockdon, the setting for his 1947 novel *Slaves of Solitude*. Like *Dad's Army*'s Walmington-on-Sea, the town is an everywhere place, sitting in the gloom of the blackout which feels, as Hamilton puts it in one of his brilliantly evocative yet simple phrases, 'like moonlight gone bad'. The pages are gloriously heavy with the airless purgatory of lost souls wandering in a never-ending cycle from dining room to brown-painted lounge to bedrooms 'in a state of almost complete stupefaction, of gas-fire drunkenness – reeling, as it were, after an orgy of *ennui*'. This is a micro-society of people from differing walks of life thrown together under one roof by the war, but instead of some bright unity for the national effort, the air is as thick with resentment and tension as it is the scent of heavy steamed pudding and custard and farts (at Christmas, the 'odour was the odour of turkey and stuffing experienced after one had eaten turkey and stuffing'). *Slaves of Solitude* represents the war years in a way that's the polar opposite of the sort of nostalgia porn we often see these days, anywhere from our TV screens to '1940s days' at heritage railways or 'vintage' festivals. Though it is set during the war, it seems to capture the atmosphere described by Peter de Rome of the years immediately afterwards, a nation unsure of itself, closing down and failing to progress. Mr Thwaites is both a boor and a bore, and in him is embodied an English archetype of narrow-minded masculine unpleasantness who thrives today.

Miss Roach, who has a minor job in publishing and has ended up at the Rosamund Tea Rooms after her former residence in town was bombed, is trapped with Thwaites' gruesome presence in interminable after-dinner conversations on cigarette smoking, whether hot water bottles were a sign of decadence and different versions of the card game Patience. Where there is solidarity in the boarding house, it is only against the powerful energies of Mr Thwaites. He occupies space, both physically and spiritually. He dominates the dingy pink dining room with a voice that 'resounded, nasally and indefatigably, with a steady health and virility' and in whom 'could be discerned the steady, self-absorbed, dreamy, almost somnambulistic quality of the lifelong trampler through the emotions of others'. He is full of entitlement in his correctness: 'Ah – I knows the Law', a misogynist describing the women who were his chief victims as 'old frumps' and 'desiccated spinsters'. Like some of the harrumphing buffoons and young fogeys of our own day, he adopts arcane linguistic forms – 'Dost thou not forgather, of a Saturday morning, with a certain dame of Teutonic origins?'. He is a pompous oaf whose gender and financial privilege allow him to fire bullying, unopposed broadsides into the other residents over their bread and dripping.

For Mr Thwaites, the war in which he does not fight is to be approached with a 'test match spirit' enthusiasm. It often feels as if we're now living in a Britain that has evolved in the image of Mr Thwaites, who lives on in the baby boomer who didn't fight in the war but will insist on using a specific narrow take on it to shore up a particular brand of conservative 'patriotism'. His spiritual descendants have an enthusiasm for citing the war in a manner that removes all nuance and context, that loses the richness of lives like Dudley Cave, Henry Danton, Peter De Rome, Bertram Warr, Micky Burn, Roberta Cowell, and even the coarse masculinity of J. H. Witte.

As the wartime generation has passed, so remembrance has become an increasingly politicised and controversial British ritual. I used to feel so deeply moved going to buy my poppy from the old boys at the station, standing with their boxes of paper petals and pins, medals on their smart jackets. I'd sometimes awkwardly thank them for their service before putting my coins in the tin and shuffling away. For a few years, though, I'd stopped buying one. As the twenty-first century began, so the poppy became a conflicted symbol. I had felt contradictory emotions at how some of the conversation around the so-called 'war on terror' seemed to co-opt the language of the Second World War. According to US president George Bush in his State of the Union Address on 29 January 2002, the Axis powers of the Second World War – Germany, Japan, Italy – had been replaced by 'the Axis of Evil' – Iran, Iraq and North Korea. The September 11 attacks on New York and Washington were referred to as a 'new Pearl Harbor' and criticism of military action denounced as a new appeasement. The 'special relationship' between the USA and UK, revived as a political force, had its roots in the cooperation between the two countries during the Second World War. The difference now was that Britain under Prime Minister Tony Blair seemed to be a deeply subservient partner, meekly doing America's bidding.

At the time, unlike most of the people I knew, I wasn't opposed to the war on Iraq. I'd seen British military intervention in Sierra Leone and the Balkans as having achieved positive ends. On the way to a music festival in Novi Sad, Serbia, we had to cross the River Danube on a temporary bridge, the original having been bombed by the RAF. Didn't locals resent us for this, I asked nearly every Serb I met. No, came the answer, because the war had been the catalyst that removed the dictator Slobodan Milosevic. This fitted the narrative that I had absorbed from my life immersed in war culture, that British military intervention was sometimes necessary to remove tyrants and oppressive regimes. This led me to, if not support the invasion of Iraq, then not exactly to oppose it either. I have sometimes felt since that my interest in British military history was to blame, that I'd been duped.

Many I know continue to refuse to wear the poppy because they see it as a symbol of British Imperial violence, and our involvement in the wars in Iraq and Afghanistan. I don't agree with this view but can understand it, given how toxic much of the discourse around the poppy has become – the flower that was once a symbol of peace now deployed as an emblem of British nationalism. It has even become co-opted into the old, homophobic notion that somehow queer people have no right to lay claim to the memory of the war. Brexit Party candidate Nicholas Goulding criticised an LGBT+ rainbow poppy in 2019: 'It should be there to unite everyone in the country. If you take an emblem and use it for political controversy, then you are undermining a symbol for the nation.' An echo, yet again, of those pre-war beliefs that the homosexual was a threat to the supposed sanctity of nationhood.

There are perennial arguments over whether or not TV present-ers should be made to wear the paper and plastic flower, something that should surely be a personal choice. As if to make up for those who don't, there is a growing culture of poppy excess. Examples of more outré personal and corporate 'tributes' are shared on a Twitter account called Giant Poppy Watch. I am sometimes a little wary of how it mocks the tasteless, if heartfelt, efforts of ordinary people who choose to mark remembrance by dressing their homes and front gardens in tableau of the Western Front or D-Day, complete with dummy soldiers, bunkers and barbed wire. Less forgivable are the corporate and merchandising tie-ins that appear every November. Last year, I saw porn stars posing in front of memorials and tradesmen with vans painted up with poppies, wartime slogans and war machines. There's tacky merchandise too, from beer glasses to Covid masks and poppy thongs. In 2021, the Royal British Legion was forced to apologise after a public outcry at a 'pull the pin' grenade-themed bottle of rum.

Who owns these symbols, these memories?

The Second World War, and specifically the Blitz spirit, are fre-quently invoked in times of crisis – severe weather, terrorist attacks, government-mandated austerity measures and, more recently, the Covid-19 pandemic. The moment the war was declared was a cliff edge from which there was no going back. The lives of everyone involved were irrevocably changed by that moment. I can think of very few circumstances since the 1940s where there has been such a society-wide crisis until the first Covid-19 lockdown of 2020. But just because, as a nation, we walked off a cliff edge, it was not the same cliff. Nevertheless, Boris Johnson, Health Secretary Matt Hancock, Vera Lynn and the Queen all made comparisons between the 1939–1945 conflict and the pandemic, summoning the 'spirit' of the war years to boost morale as if in the absence of vaccines or effective medical treatment, it might be imbibed as a potion, a twenty-first-century version of the spices and dried flowers in a Medieval plague doctor's sinister beak. Then Prime Minster Boris Johnson saw himself as the political descendent of Winston Churchill, but where Churchill was a workaholic with a level of attention to detail that his aides in the war effort often found infuriating, Johnson missed key COBRA meetings. On the libertarian right, politicians and pundits railed against the restrictions imposed to slow the spread of Covid-19, complaining that pubs and public spaces had been closed when they'd remained open throughout the war, displaying quite the ignorance of the different ways in which bombs and diseases do their killing. Meanwhile, the British death toll – the highest in Europe – crept upwards towards the total number of our civilians killed during the war itself. Medical historian Paul Weindling of the Wellcome Trust gave the war-summoning tendency short shrift, saying that the habit of referring to the Second World War was evidence of all not being well in the nation. 'A patchwork of historical metaphors poorly hides defects in provision and planning as Britain vegetates in its prolonged lockdown.'

This peculiar atmosphere in which the war years and the current crisis were intermingled reached its apogee around the seventy-fifth anniversary of VE Day on 8 May 2020. The Queen gave her address from a desk on which sat a picture of her father, King George VI, in his naval uniform, summoning his memory and that of the war in the struggle against coronavirus. 'When I look at our country today and see what we are willing to do to protect and support one another, I say with pride, that we are still a nation those brave soldiers, sailors and airmen would recognise and admire.' I wasn't so sure.

The VE Day anniversary took place in the middle of a lockdown when most gatherings were forbidden. A WhatsApp group set up for mutual aid and emergency support in my local area, pinged with chat about bunting and someone playing ukulele for a doorstep singalong of songs from the era. The BBC reported from Hilary Avenue in Cosham, where people ('All here for a bit of fun!') waved dainty flags and someone sang 'Pack Up Your Troubles in Your Old Kit-Bag' through a karaoke machine. They were all standing, despite the claims of the correspondent, far closer together than the two metres required by the regulations designed to stop the spread of the disease. The focus seemed to be less about the struggles of those who fought than the possibility of a boozy knees-up to distract everyone from this very modern crisis. The *Guardian* printed an image of the front of a house in Kent where two boards had been painted – one with a union flag, the other with the slogan WE'LL MEET AGAIN, drooping poppies and the words 'FAMILY' 'VE DAY' 'KEY WORKERS' 'NHS'. The *Sun* welcomed the news that Britain's pubs might soon reopen with a front-page picture of a pint and the jaunty headline 'ALE MEET AGAIN', a cheap reference to Vera Lynn's song 'We'll Meet Again'. A Spitfire with 'THANK U NHS' painted on its underside and the names of doctors and medical staff written all over its aluminium skin in exchange for a charitable donation toured the country to do flypasts of 255 hospitals. Its pilot, John Romain, later recalled that there was a common misconception that this was 'Boris Johnson's Spitfire, paid for by the government' when in fact all the flights were funded by the aircraft's owners themselves. On the news, the Red Arrows were shown triggering their red, white and blue smoke trails as they passed over central London. The thunder of their jets rattled around a deserted city, an empty Mall, an abandoned palace.

Covid-19 was just the latest moment which saw the Second World War co-opted into our culture wars – another being around

Brexit. As the academic Thomas Colley wrote in 2019, the Leave campaign had the power of myth on their side: 'Brexit advocates could invoke the spirit of Churchill, calling forth brave heroes who stood strong to protect Britain and the world from tyrants, many of which emerged from Europe.' This was clearly evident to the German ambassador to Britain Peter Ammon, who, on leaving his post, told the *Guardian*, 'History is always full of ambiguities and ups and downs, but if you focus only on how Britain stood alone in the war, how it stood against dominating Germany, well, it is a nice story, but does not solve any problem of today.'

In 2017, a year after the Brexit referendum, three British war films focused on this part of wartime history – two about Winston Churchill (*Darkest Hour* and *Churchill*) and Christopher Nolan's *Dunkirk*. In July 2017, Chief Brexiteer Nigel Farage tweeted a picture of himself looking solemn next to a poster for the latter, urging every 'youngster' to go and watch it, as if to tell the generation who largely voted to stay in the EU that this was evidence a gutsy escape was a better course. During the campaign, Farage drove into one rally in support of the Leave vote in a double-decker bus playing the music from war film *The Great Escape*. When Farage was a pupil at the prestigious Dulwich College, he concerned his teachers with 'racist and neo-fascist views' and, while playing soldiers at a Combined Cadet Force camp, 'marched through a quiet Sussex village very late at night shouting Hitler Youth songs'. Farage denied these. The movement he led used a very narrow view of the Second World War as part of the argument to leave the EU. In a BBC interview, Mark Francois MP angrily attacked the German CEO of Airbus for saying that leaving the bloc might result in closed factories, declaring, 'My father, Reginald Francois, was a D-Day veteran. He never submitted to bullying by any German and neither will his son.' The Vote Leave campaign was forced to apologise for tweeting a picture of Angela Merkel with the slogan 'We didn't win two world wars to be pushed around by a Kraut', while Boris Johnson wrote an article in the *Telegraph* saying 'Napoleon, Hitler, various people tried this out, and it ends tragically. The EU is an attempt to do this by different methods.' The British tabloids were in on the rhetoric, the *Sun* responding to David Cameron's pre-referendum talks to wring concessions out of the EU with an attempt at humour in a *Dad's Army*-themed front page and the headline 'Who do you think you are kidding Mr Cameron?' Matt Hancock MP launched his failed bid for the Conservative leadership on 10 June 2019 by citing the D-Day invasion and saying that to prorogue Parliament over Brexit 'goes against everything those men wading onto those beaches fought and died for. And I will not have it. They made that sacrifice so we could create a better world and we have.' Three years later, on 6 June 2022, as Boris Johnson faced a vote of no confidence on the eighty-eighth anniversary of D-Day, Tory MP Michael Fabricant retweeted a commemorative post by the US National Parks Service with the added comment 'June 6th The Longest Day 1944; and 2022 (in a different way)', crassly equating the opening of the campaign to liberate Occupied Europe from Nazism with the prime minister's desperate attempt to cling onto power.

In the face of all this, it's perhaps understandable that people who count themselves as progressives have ceded the legacy and psychic impact of the Second Word War to the right, or politically undefined reactionary forces. But to do so is to risk losing an understanding of how we got to where we are. It also sacrifices the memory of those who served and fought and died to those who might abuse it. I think of the men and women of the Second World War and feel deeply uncomfortable that the propagandists and bilious keyboard warriors of the political right believe that they are writing for the dead. It is as if they are claiming ownership of their ghosts.

If trauma extends down the generations, within individuals and families, disrupting even our minds and thought patterns, then the same might happen with a country and its people. Britain is living in a state of unresolved trauma from the Second World War, never having come to terms with what it meant for us as a nation. Instead of a necessary processing, a readjustment, a redefinition as a post-imperial island that ought to have learned from the terrors of its past conflicts to forge closer relationships with Europe, the jingoistic memory of the war gives a boost to a national selfhood that is gaseous and unsustainable, forever on the edge of – and perhaps now finally – collapsing into hubris.

During the late 1940s and early 50s, Mr Thwaites-esque boorish conservatism had a destructive energy, the consequences of which were felt by the gay and bisexual men who had experienced a brief glimmer of freedom. It was the war that allowed some to understand who they really were. For all his pre and early war same-sex experiences, Dudley Cave had assumed that it might be a passing phase. When, despite the reduced libido due to malnutrition in the Japanese POW camps, the feelings didn't subside, he went to see the MO, who referred him to fellow prisoner and sexologist Philip Bloom. He told Cave that it seemed he was a homosexual, lent him a copy of Havelock Ellis's *Sexual Inversion in Men* and told him to come and see him in Harley Street after the war. That was beyond Cave's means, so he went to see another army doctor. 'I told this colonel I was homosexual,' he recalled in an interview years later. 'He said "what?" and I repeated it, and a little vein in his neck started throbbing and he went quite a purple colour at the thought of this dreadful thing they'd been nurturing to their bosom all these years. He said, in a slightly choked voice "better see a psychiatrist".' A consultant at Sutton hospital, enlightened for 1946, told him not to worry, but to try to find someone similar to settle down with. Not long afterwards, Cave met partner Bernard Williams – a teacher who had been in Fighter Command during the war and who had seen his lover shot down – in gay haunt the Fitzroy Tavern. They would spend the rest of their lives together. Few were so fortunate. Although Michael Schofield's writing in 1952 book *Society and the Homosexual* sought an understanding for gay men like himself, he still had to write it under the pseudonym Gordon Westwood, and throughout refers to homosexuality as a 'problem'. He notes that, 'When it becomes impossible to avoid discussing the problem of homosexuality, the very word engenders any amount of blind prejudice and extreme emotional reaction.' Once again, the homosexual is set against 'the normal man and most are careful to hide their abnormality from the rest of the world'. The private intimacies and snatched liberations allowed by the war years feel so very remote from this terrible fear, the 'mental anguish or the feeling of guilt common to all homosexuals'.

As Matt Houlbrook wrote in *Queer London*, societal homophobia and prejudice against gay men in the post-war years was a continuation of the belief that to exist outside of 'normal' heterosexual masculinity was a threat to the state: 'The queer, a predatory and lustful danger to the nation and its manhood, embodied a wider post war crisis of Britishness.' The early years of the war culture that I had so eagerly absorbed – the films, the comics, the model kits – made into fantasy and play the idea of a heroic past that would put a veneer over the crumbling reality of the present, part of which was a rising homophobia.

Mass Observation's General Attitudes to Sex survey in 1949 – popularly known as 'Little Kinsey' after the ground-breaking American Kinsey Report on sexual behaviour of the year before – found that though 12 per cent of respondents had had physical same-sex relationships, 'popular feeling against it is very strong', and a third showed 'very violent reactions, calling homosexuality "disgusting", "terrible" and "revolting"'. Quentin Crisp wrote with bleak wit that 'the horrors of peace were many'. Dudley Cave fell victim to the homophobia of the time, thanks largely to his own good intentions. He'd caught staff at a cinema he was managing engaging in homophobic bullying. Cave spoke to the young lad who was being terrorised, telling him not to worry and that plenty of famous men had been gay like him. Unfortunately, the next time the bullying happened, the lad retorted that some of the best people in the world were gay, including Dudley Cave of the Majestic cinema. The senior management got wind of what had happened and, despite the backing of a number of the staff – some of whom Cave had fooled around with, including having 'wildly vertical' sex with a projectionist behind the screen as a film played – he was sacked.

What Micky Burn described as 'the old hateful need to conceal and lie', was not unusual in the Great Repression that followed the Second World War. He himself was the victim of a blackmail from a young man he'd met cruising London parks. Around the same time, Colin Spencer, torn between his attraction to his wife Gillian Chapman and his lover John Tasker, ended the queer relationship to try and make the heterosexual work. He told me that he felt that the homophobic atmosphere of post-war Britain was partly to blame and in his history of homosexuality went as far as writing that for queer men of the time, 'Britain had become a police state'. Mass Observation diarist 5122 wrote that he found it 'alarming' to see a dramatic increase in stiff custodial sentences handed out to gay men. In London, incidents in which men were prosecuted for homosexual acts at the Metropolitan Magistrates Courts and City of London Justice Rooms increased from 251 in 1937 and 211 in 1942, to 637 in 1947, 583 in 1952 and 491 in 1957. In the decade after 1945, the number of prosecutions for homosexual behaviour rose from less than 800 to over 2,500. John Alcock remembered it being a time of personal and community terror. 'I personally became very frightened,' he said in 1985. 'I thought that every policeman was coming up to me in the street and was going to arrest me. I always looked over my shoulder when I was bringing a gentleman home to entertain [. . .] The newspapers were full of it. I got so frightened I came home and I burnt all my love letters [. . .] the temperature of the time was quite unpleasant.'

Yet Colin Spencer believed that for queer people, the Second World War had been a 'revolutionary process within their lives' that could not be stopped or contained when peace finally came. This would be a slow and painful revolution, via the 1957 Wolfenden report and the decriminalisation of homosexuality in 1967. Gay liberation in the 1970s achieved much, only to be met by the horror of the AIDS crisis in the 1980s and 1990s that swept through a generation of young men as brutally and at times arbitrarily as the bullets from a German MG-42. Slowly, gay and bisexual men had to fight back for their voices, their freedoms, while trying to bring society with them. In the changes that these men wrought there is a counter to the stuffy, retrogressive and jingoistic ideal of an old England that never was, one that sucks vampiric on the memory of those who gave so much. I look at men like Peter de Rome, Ian Gleed, Micky Burn and Dudley Cave and do not see them in some ghetto, to be fussed over by activists and labelled as 'queer heroes'. Instead, they are men who allow us to see beyond the bunting and understand what the Second World War really was. Perhaps some involved in the left-wing politics that surround gender and sexual identity see war as an aspect of a history, society and masculinity that they would rather not embrace or be part of. I look to Dudley Cave and know that they are wrong.

In later life, Cave became an activist. In 1974, he was on the founding committee of the Gay and Lesbian Switchboard. Down crackling telephone lines, he heard of the loneliness and grief of queer men and women of his own generation who had lost loved ones, and in 1980 he set up the Gay and Lesbian Bereavement Trust. For all that he had suffered at the hands of the Japanese, he sought to promote peace and reconciliation with his one-time persecutors, frequently travelling to the site of the railway he had been forced to build. Takashi Nagase, a Japanese officer who had worked as an interpreter on the construction project, built a temple for peace on the banks of the River Kwai. Members of Cave's church funded the making of a bell to hang in the temple and he took part in a 'Handshake on the Bridge on the River Kwai' during the fiftieth anniversary commemorations of VJ day in 1995.

On the home front, Cave was the figurehead of a difficult and controversial campaign to ensure that the lives of LGBT+ servicemen and women received their due respect in our ceremonies of remembrance. He wrote an article in *Capital Gay* magazine on 5 May 1995, a month before the VE Day commemorations. He recalled that 'as the country was threatened with annihilation by the Nazis and in those circumstances, there was no fuss over who [the military] accepted'. Cave had known gay men who had been killed in the war, including a private who had died on the River Kwai and an RAF Squadron Leader who had disappeared into the English Channel with no known grave. Yet some within the military establishment were all too eager to forget their service and sacrifice.

In the early 1980s, a Royal British Legion branch had refused to parade if an LGBT group was also allowed to join in. Cave, via his Unitarian church organisation Intergroup, had written to the Legion's Group Captain D. J. Mountford to ascertain the stance of the organisation. Mountford replied saying there was no official guidance. 'Our members attend Remembrance Services throughout the length and breadth of this country in order to pay their respects to those killed in two World Wars and for their own survival,' Mountford wrote. 'As a result most are staunch supporters of the Church and look to it for guidance on moral issues. Recently leaders of the Anglican and Catholic Churches have spoken out against homosexuality; it is only a few liberals in all walks of life who attempt to weaken our society by insisting these unfortunate individuals should be accepted by the community. If they wish to follow a lifestyle which is repugnant to many people they must not complain because they are ostracised.'

Mountford's assertion that gay and bisexual men and women would 'weaken society' was akin to the language of the pre-war years, when to be 'normal' was seen as essential for the continuing security of Britain. Responding to this bracing homophobia in Intergroup's publication *Internews*, the editor – perhaps Cave's partner Bernard, who had been in the Air Force during the war – wrote, 'Where have I heard those words before? Oh yes – of course, it was Adolf Hitler who prevented the weakening of his society by making sure that the naughty Jews and homosexuals were not "accepted by the community". Just a minute, though – wasn't it Hitler that Group Captain Mountford and I didn't like much, when we were in the RAF? Perhaps I'd better ask the Group Captain's church about it; they'd know who Jesus wants to ostracise.'

The row continued until the end of the twentieth century. In November 1998, *Outrage!* announced a Queer Remembrance Day to commemorate LGBT+ men and women who had fought in the military and those who had died in Nazi concentration camps. The Royal British Legion had attacked the previous year's ceremony as being 'distasteful', 'offensive' and 'bound to offend many former soldiers'. Cave spoke at the event and laid a pink triangle at the Cenotaph, and a statement from Ian Gleed's one-time lover Christopher Gotch was read out to the crowd. The ceremony was intended not only to highlight the military authorities' continuing refusal to recognise the contribution of gay and bisexual men and women to the war effort, but also the injustice that homosexuals were, at that point, banned from serving in the military. In 1999, Cave would tell Peter Tatchell, 'They used us when it suited them, and then victimised us when the country was no longer in danger. I'm glad I served but I am angry that military homophobia was allowed to wreck so many lives for over fifty years after we gave our all for a freedom that gay people were denied.'

To me, the necessity of this long campaign speaks of a depressing shabbiness as to how the LGBT+ men who fought in the Second World War were treated. They could have marched silently, anonymously alongside their heterosexual comrades. They could have not made a fuss, hidden themselves for fear of causing offence. Yet in the moment of rising queer consciousness amid worsening discrimination on the grounds of sexual identity, Cave and his comrades were right to take a stand. By laying a pink triangle wreath at the Cenotaph, as he would do at later remembrance ceremonies, Cave was reminding the world that homosexuals and bisexuals were among the persecuted of the Holocaust, that the pink triangle is our star of David. Yet it was also a symbol of defiance against a conservative society, an assertion that the war had been fought for the values of liberalism and freedom, and that gay and bisexual men had not just been passive victims but had participated in that fight as courageously as anyone else.

I bought a poppy in 2021 and spent Remembrance Sunday visiting friends in a quintessential village of 'Deep England', the mellow Cotswold stone of chocolate-box houses glowing with the yellow and orange of a particularly fine late autumn. 'Are you of the village?' a posh lady asked as I approached the crowd gathered around the simple war memorial, a cross on a plinth featuring the names from the First World War and one of the Second who never returned from the fighting. After the two-minute silence, a prayer and the Last Post played through someone's iPhone, the congregation moved off down the lane to the local church. Inside, places in the pews had been taken up by figures cut out of Perspex, each with a poppy on the Bible shelf in front of them, a simple gesture that reminded me of the Lissett memorial. The service, with readings from Job and the Book of Revelation, was gentle and traditional. I was the youngest person there. Part of what makes the remembrance service so affecting as a ritual is how its basic elements – the Last Post, the two-minute silence, the 'They shall grow not old' – are the same wherever they're heard or experienced, be that in a village church or some lonely military cemetery with its rows of identical grave markers. They are, or ought to be, an expression of collective memory and solidarity, a reflection on sacrifices made and lives lost that can unite and heal.

It felt wonderful to know that, back in London, in the 100th year of the Royal British Legion, LGBT+ veterans and serving men and women were an official part of the commemorations at the Cenotaph for the first time. It's sad to have to say that 'of course' this did not go down well in all quarters. It felt like a significant moment in which those who marched, some of whom had served in more recent conflicts, represented the LGBT+ people who had gone before them, at best merely unrecognised, at worst fearing persecution, ostracisation and shame. Intolerance and prejudice were not merely ills fought abroad, symptoms of the Nazi disease that died with Hitler in his bunker in April 1945, but have deep roots at home. The struggle against them continues. This most recent victory at the iconic structure of national mourning felt as if it belonged to Dudley Cave as a representative of those unknown queer men and women who have fought in our nation's wars.

Those who survived carried the memories of the comrades

they lost with them for the rest of their lives. It is in them that I truly understand that old line about 'they who shall grow not old'. In their eyes, the dead forever live on, as people who knew fear, comradeship, banter, purpose, regret, love and lust. When Peter de Rome returned to England, he was met by the cruellest blow. Porky had been killed, just before the end of the war, not in combat, but in a flying accident. 'Most of my other friends had come through. Porky, the closest and sweetest of them all, was the only one I would have missed.' Those billions of intimate moments by which we hold onto our friends and lovers – a certain laugh, a tic, a flick of the hair, how a man drinks his pint or pulls on a cigarette – endured after the war was over, perhaps not spoken about, but surely always present in memory, before the gentle yet inexorable erasing of time wiped them away.

Just because it can often feel like reactionary voices speak for the memory of those who fought in the war, I don't believe that this is an argument for letting it fade into a forgetful past. We might instead pick up the kaleidoscope and look back to a richer history. I don't want to see the men who lived through the Second World War as heroes, though I do believe they were brave. To elevate them to the heroic removes their potential to be flawed, and therefore entirely human. There can be a tendency now in some LGBT+ circles to believe that our predecessors, because they were persecuted, were unblemished, noble. This is obviously not the case. In so many memoirs of gay, bisexual and transgender men and women of the war era I find language that today would be beyond the pale. There is bigotry, racism, fetishisation of dark-skinned men, frequent celebrations of pederasty and the teenage body. Despite this, I accept them with those flaws just as I accept any – shall we say, 'normal' – person who grew up in a time and a context beyond our understanding.

*

Embracing these sometimes contradictory individuals threatens the simple narratives that easily become an orthodoxy of heroic or stoic identity. Myths are fine at a distance. They shape our culture, our understanding of who we are as individuals, nations, groups. There's something about the proximity of the Second World War to the digital age that has made its myths fast and slippery, so easily exploited and still so relevant in our own time. My fascination with the war was underpinned by the belief that it was naive and foolish to think that this could never happen again. History isn't just packaged away into neat boxes as it is at school, or in TV programmes or popular books. It is with us constantly, evolving and shaping our lives in every second of the present. Without the Second World War, without the most horrendous unimaginable and unrepeatable moments in it, I would never have known my son.

# AFTERMATH

A few years ago, I spent a week with a friend who was taking part in an artist residency on the Finnish island of Örö, in the vast archipelago that stretches from the Baltic Sea, along the Gulf of Finland past Helsinki towards the border with Russia. Until recently, Örö was a forbidden zone, an island covered with fortifications originally built by Tsarist Russia. After Finland's independence, it was occupied by the Finnish military as part of their coastal defensive network. Frozen into the ice and carpeted with snow in the winter, the island in spring is covered with delicate flowers, tough sea kale growing on the beaches, and the air is rich with the warm scent of pine and sandy heathland. Adders sat basking on the sun-kissed concrete of old bunkers, rising to hiss at our approach. A sea eagle swooped to catch a duck off the surface of the water. I had to delve into my pal Rob's arse cheek with a special tool to try to remove a tick.

Amidst this rich fauna and flora sat the remnants of the Finnish military occupation. On one end of the island were huge 12-inch calibre guns that fired in anger during the Battle of Bengtskär between Finnish and Soviet forces on 26 July 1941. We slept in an old wooden barracks that creaked and whistled at night to the Baltic wind. There was a sandy firing range, abandoned homes that looked like they could have won mid-twentieth-century design awards for social housing, Czech hedgehog tank traps, steel doors into cliff faces, trenches hewn into the rock, concrete bunkers, metal bolts that had once secured artillery pieces rising from the ground like the stems of tall flowers. Yet this wasn't a place of decay, of abandonment in metal and concrete, a historical relic – the kind of site I had once fetishised. It wasn't an accidental memorial, like the remains of the concrete runways and decaying buildings of RAF Lissett, but a zone that felt as if it was not yet at peace.

On a tall lattice tower on the western coast, a radar span. Every morning, a Finnish gunboat appeared, gliding over the placid brackish blue of the Baltic, and opened fire with its main gun, the report echoing off the rocks and concrete. On our last night, acting on a tip-off from a local guide, we found a narrow passage in the rocks at the island's southern point, hidden down a slope and requiring a leap across a boggy ditch to access. It continued into a network of tunnels that stretched for some distance, with passageways that popped up into artillery positions. There was still electrical power in the tunnels, buzzing in boxes of circuitry. Wires sprouted from the walls, neatly sealed at the tips, as if ready to be reconnected to some communications device or computer. The oldest of the stoves might have been rusty, but there were still mattresses on the bunks, and wall-mounted racks seemed to be waiting as if with arms outstretched for deadly weapons. For all the natural beauty, Örö was a place that hummed with an expectation of violence.

I'd been on Örö on the first anniversary of the Brexit referendum and decision to leave the European Union. The subject was constantly in the news. I had gone to the island (a flight, two long bus journeys and two ferries) fully expecting that I would have a fun week with a pal running around indulging my military fantasies on our very own fortified island. Yet the strangeness of this landscape and the atmosphere of brooding tension merely connected with everything that was going on at home, and what it meant for Britain's relationship with the rest of the world. I was used to seeing the contemporary British military as a projection of power overseas, via involvement in Middle Eastern and Afghan wars or providing humanitarian assistance in times of crisis. It was often hard, with the complacency of eighty years of European peace, to see it as a defensive force in the way that the Finnish radar tower, the booming of the ship's gun, the poised readiness of those military tunnels seemed to be. Out there in the cold waters of the Baltic, war did not feel so very far away. The stirring up of nationalistic sentiment during Brexit had made my Swedish partner feel unwelcome in Britain. At the time I was over in Örö, we were trying to arrange her indefinite leave to remain. I was pleased that our love was a loud retort to the insularity that had gripped my country in recent years. She'd given me a new insight into the Second World War, which had impacted her family far more than it had impacted mine.

We have a photograph of a jovial-looking man on a motorbike in a European town square some time after the Second World War. In the sidecar, a small girl squints towards the camera. The little girl is my partner's mother, Yolande. The man is her father, Maximilian Knobel, a Jew. As I write this, his great-grandson sits in his bouncing chair, wide eyes intent on the brightly coloured smiling flower that, at five weeks old, he has just learned to hit to make it spin on its pivot.

One hundred and ten years ago, in 1912, his great-grandfather was born, probably in Pinczow, a small town to the north-east of Krakow with a then-sizeable Jewish population of 3,500. Was Maximilian even Polish? We're not sure. His family barely spoke the language but were fluent in Yiddish and German. He used to tell his daughter about his memories of family in Galicia, the province of the Austro-Hungarian Empire that vanished with its demise at the end of the First World War, part of the endless and enduring upheaval of European borders and nations. He told her how at Jewish school, they would be naughty, putting glue on the desks to trap the Rabbi's beard, and on the chair to stick the Polish teacher in her place. In the early twentieth century, some of Maximilian's family left Poland, sending him one of the other pictures we have, of a group of people on an English beach. European and British names are muddled in the key on the back. Maximilian became a tailor, so renowned for his suits that people would travel a long way to order one. In 1937, he took on the family business, making pickled cucumbers. To this day, his daughter is very particular over her pickles – the right tang of a fermented cucumber, not one preserved in vinegar or brine, is one of the few sensations that can connect her to her father's past.

Maximilian had married a Polish Catholic woman, and Yolande was born in the Polish city of Wrocław in 1948 (that is where the photograph of her sitting in the sidecar of the motorbike was taken) not long after it had been renamed from the pre-war German Breslau. The city was still largely in ruins. It was not a happy marriage. The Polish Catholic family had not liked their daughter marrying a Jew and had refused to attend their wedding. When the little girl was small, her parents divorced; her father left Poland and moved to Paris, taking her with him. Maximilian struggled to put a life back together, doing all sorts to survive – tailoring, pickling, the skills that had made his family prosperous before the war. Relatives came to visit and Yolande overheard conversations in Yiddish with words that appeared again and again, names of places like Treblinka and Auschwitz. Slowly, she became aware of the time not so many years before she had been born, of war and Nazis, of terrible things that had happened to her family, her grandparents being killed in a slave labour camp, and worse. One day, her father announced that he was moving to Germany. He would be receiving compensation from the German government and would set up a new business. Yolande didn't understand. How could he live among Germans, those hated people who built the camps into which their family had vanished?

Her father explained that one day, German soldiers came. These men, in their steel helmets and jackboots, went from door to door, forcing the Jews out into the street, loading them into trucks like cattle or cargo. One of them came to the house where Maximilian Knobel was living. The soldier was about the same age. He spoke in German, the language that, thanks to the complicated history of the region, Maximilian knew better than Polish. The soldier said, 'If I see you flee, I have to shoot you. Please, do not let me see you run.' Maximilian ran. He went straight to his motorbike, drove to where his sister was hiding – her twin daughters had already been taken – and together they rode to Soviet-occupied territory. There, they were interned in camps. The little girl remembers her auntie, who had already lost her children to who knows what horrors, describing the harsh and bitter cold.

Maximilian was conscripted into the Ludowe Wojsko Polskie, or Polish People's Army, which operated under Soviet command during the long fight west into Poland and then Germany. Tantalising hints of that story are told in four photographs. In one blurry picture, he stands in a street wearing a long military greatcoat. The large trees in the background are bare and he looks cold, pulling his gloved hands up into his sleeves. The second is a classic soldier's mugshot: Maximilian's eyes look up and to the left, he is wearing a peaked cap with the metal Polish eagle badge of the Ludowe Wojsko Polskie, a squiggle of braid sewn onto the lapels of his jacket. The third is of Maximilian with his arm around the shoulders of another man. They are looking at one another and smiling. We know that Maximilian saved this man's life. The fourth picture features the two men, joined by a third. On the back are tender messages, written in Russian. 'To Maksim, it will be so hard without you. My heart hurts that I will be without you. And you will suffer without me, too. But I think we'll definitely be together!' The second, 'I remember that day, you were angry with me.' And the third, on the back of a torn photo of Maximilian with the same man, words missing: 'How hard . . . with you. Soon we will . . . again. I want then [. . .] with you. I'm not sure you feel the same about me. But I hope we meet again. I remember one evening [. . .]. We were happy in Murom.'

We have no knowledge of why Maximilian was in Murom, a town on the banks of the Oka river, 300 kilometres east of Moscow. Yolande believes that the words were written by the man in the photograph whose life Maximilian saved. Whatever the true nature of the love affair and whoever it was with, it did not last and is lost to time and tragedy, like the full story of how he travelled from Poland to Murom and finally to Wrocław. For much of Eastern Europe, for millions of Jews, gypsies, homosexuals, conscripts from all sides, there was no fetishised veteranhood, no parades, no memorials, no memoirs, just bodies and souls disappeared into an absence.

These scant memories, these few photographs, are all we have to know of that side of our family. Maximilian's daughter was sent back to be with her mother in Warsaw. She never saw him again. Maximilian Knobel died in Paris on 19 March 1963. In Poland, Yolande faced a society that while it had been freed of German fascism, was still riddled with antisemitism – after the war, thousands of Jews returning from the camps or from their places of hiding were murdered. Her mother had a new partner, a young Polish partisan hero who had been wounded in the 1944 Warsaw uprising against the Germans and had subsequently risen through the ranks of the Communist party to become secretary to the wife of Władysław Gomułka, the Polish leader. He had little time for his stepdaughter, who looked so Jewish. When, in 1968, Yolande became involved in the student rebellion against Communist repression, he denounced her to the secret police. She was arrested, subjected to harsh interrogation and told that she was lucky, that if they'd had her twenty-five years before – the interrogator mimed and made a whispering sound – she 'would have been up the chimney'. The secret police confiscated her passport and, although she wasn't even a practising Jew, declared that, like all Jews at that time, she was effectively a non-citizen and must leave the country for Israel. Yolande had no desire whatsoever to go to Israel but had heard that the Dutch embassy was giving out exit visas to Jews who wanted to escape the country. At the embassy, officials did not believe that 'Knobel' was a sufficiently Jewish name. There was a photograph, though, that she had from her father, of one of his sisters, one who had died at Treblinka, and on the back was writing in Yiddish. This, and only this, was enough to get Yolande out of Poland and away from the bitter violence of twentieth-century history.

As a little girl in Sweden, where her mother had ended up as a refugee, my partner cut her hair short and demanded that she be called Max. When we knew that our baby was to be a boy, there was really no other name we could pick except that of his great-grandfather. To call him Maximilian was a tribute to a man who had survived the Second World War in a few seconds of chance and humanity. If another soldier had come that day, he would have joined the rest of his family in Treblinka. Our Max's middle names, Edwin and Percy, come from my grandads, the conscientious objector and the railwayman. To give him these names from men who lived through a war eighty years ago was a tribute and an act of defiance too, for an enduring love against antisemitism, against prejudice, against those who now try to push nations apart. I often open the photographs of Percy Turner and Maximilian Knobel in their army uniforms and feel moved by how similar they seem, even down to the eyes raised away from the camera in the same direction, Maximilian round-faced and Percy long, both with large noses and faces frozen in a tight, formal expression, to make sure they caught the face that the military wanted of them. They had such different wars, fighting for ideologies and reasons that concerned them far less than simply surviving, yet in these images have a strange and palpable kinship. Together, they live on in their great-grandson.

A couple of months before Maximilian was born, I idly googled to find out the roots of his name. There were Jewish heroes and Nazi monsters, Holy Roman Emperors and saints of peace. In 295AD, Maximilian of Tebessa, a Christian, was beheaded after refusing to fight in the Roman army, becoming the first con- scientious objector. When I see Maximilian, crossing his eyes and sticking out his tongue to accompany a hilarious gush into his nappy, I see in his body the proof that we can never forget the Second World War, why it was fought and what men did in it. He is a reminder that none of this is ever far away, especially as a pandemic ended only to be replaced by a major war that has its roots in the endless turmoil of Europe.

When I hold his fragility in my arms I do not think of peace, but of how to protect the vulnerable from bullies. Sometimes, the violence that has been a lifelong obsession is inevitable, is required. Maximilian is not Jewish, just as I am not gay, but both of us could have been Jewish and gay enough to end up murdered for who we were in much of occupied Europe between the years 1939 and 1945. Totalitarianism deals in absolutes and forced identity, after all. I have never been able to shake the memory of hearing a documentary on the Nuremberg trials that featured an eyewitness account of a family waiting to be led into a gas chamber. The father pointed to the sky and seemed to be explaining something to his family. The son smiled, understanding. I had thought that becoming a parent might turn me towards a kind of blind ideological pacifism, to avoid war at all costs. Yet however vulnerable my son looks in my arms, however terrible the intrusive thoughts about what happens to babies in wars, I believe that sometimes it is necessary to fight.

The discomfort and guilt that I always felt about my war obsession has not gone, and I know I will never be able to shake it. I will build my Airfix kit of Ian Gleed's Hurricane, engaging in the ritual of carefully gluing and painting so familiar to me since childhood, trying to make it a faithful representation of the aircraft he flew as a gay lover pursuing and shooting down German fighters over the skies of Britain and Europe in 1940. I plan to build a Spitfire and then add the markings of the aircraft in which Gleed died. Kits of Halifax Mk II bombers are in short supply and go for a fortune online, but I keep bidding, hoping to one day build a model of the aircraft in which Bertram Warr flew for the last time in April 1943. I already know I won't be putting the generic plastic figures into the cockpit and fuselage. I believe that it is possible to be at once revolted by war and compelled by it, to be a pacifist who also finds weapons and accounts of battle fascinating. If war is the most extreme experience of the human condition, to make a simplistic moral judgement that all war is wrong and therefore all compulsion to study it similarly tarnished, is a wish to remain in dangerous ignorance. It also allows the histories of our wars to be owned only by those who would use them for martial and nationalistic ends, especially as those who fought and remember the conflict gradually make their way into the silent majority.

\*

Maximilian was five weeks old when Russia invaded Ukraine on 24 February 2022, the latest outburst of Europe's never-ending and interwoven tapestry of violence. Over the years of his rule, Vladimir Putin has exploited his own country's concept of the 'Greatest Generation' to bolster support for his regime and to raise public sentiment against perceived enemies, both internal and external. On a work trip to Novosibirsk in Siberia in 2015, what is known there as 'the Great Patriotic War' seemed to be all over the television and local history information boards, heroic imagery emblazoned on posters and banners around the city centre.

Putin declared that his 'special military operation' was aimed at 'de-Nazifying' Ukraine, a claim deeply offensive given that the country lost as many as seven million people under the years of German occupation. There were far-right units within Ukraine's army, but the leader of the Wagner mercenary group fighting alongside regular Russian formations has SS insignia tattooed on his body.

I watched it unfold in real time on social media. Footage from Twitter, TikTok and Telegram accounts was eerily similar to those old worn newsreel clips and newspaper photographs from eighty years ago. Russian rocket barrages, columns of tanks pushing through flat, wintry agricultural landscapes and towns of blasted homes, hospitals, churches, schools and shops, over which dark columns of smoke rose. Shattered armoured vehicles flickering with lazily malevolent flames, bodies twisted on the ground, captured soldiers staring with fearful eyes into the camera. Much of the footage shot from Ukrainian armoured cars and drones or the body-mounted cameras that give a soldier's on-the-ground perspective looked just like it could have come from a computer game. Reality and fiction, myth and history, were suddenly all blurred together. The military hardware has been updated, with drones joining tanks, aircraft and infantry on and above the bat-tlefield. Conflict feels more immediate, more instantly personal in the social media age, embodied in the ease with which people were able to find a captured Russian soldier's social media account and its heartbreaking photographs of him posing with his girlfriend. The basic energies – exploitation of history to fuel ideologies that demand metal to be put against flesh – were the same now as they were in 1939, 1941 and for so many hundreds of years before. As soon as I saw those images of tanks moving through a landscape familiar from those old newsreels of the Eastern Front or the brutal horror of *Come and See*, it felt like a terrible affirmation that it was naive to assume peace in 1945 meant a lasting peace in Europe. I had always been convinced that there was very little that truthfully ought to make us believe such a war could never happen again.

I thought of Örö when a story began to circulate of a militarised island belonging to Ukraine out in the Black Sea, populated by a detachment of border guards. First reports suggested that a Rus-sian ship had demanded the surrender of the island's garrison by loudspeaker, to which the Ukrainians had replied 'Russian warship, go fuck yourself', before being killed in the bombardment that fol-lowed. It brought home the claustrophobia of those tunnels on that Finnish island and the strong sense that the men stationed in those red-painted wooden barracks would have been easily cut off, that tonnes of rock and concrete might not have protected them, that a violence might have visited that island and wiped them out amidst its natural beauty. It turned out that the men on the Ukrainian island had survived and been taken prisoner, but not before their story had become part of a national myth. Within weeks, 'Russian warship, go fuck yourself' was on a postage stamp.

For decades now, it has been the privilege of boys like Maximil-ian to be born into a Britain that has not had to face anything like the horrors that his great-grandfather knew, that forced his grandmother from her home to seek asylum in a foreign land. It is a privilege that I fear has made our society complacent, unwilling to acknowledge that summoning nationalism and martial history as an agent of change is a dangerous and insidious alchemy. Recent events have not surprised me. The thread that holds us into supposed civilisation is thin, far more fragile than the potent, simplistic narratives that are distilled by some from the memory of those who lived through the Second World War.

I look at Maximilian, smiling, content, and hope that the transgenerational trauma of what happened to his ancestors in the Holocaust will spare him. Even more than this, I hope that he will never have to face the outrageous metal of war, to be asked to kill or be killed, that he might live in a country that has quiet and tempered thoughts of its past. It is my hope, but it is a forlorn one. Imagine peace, the hippies said, from their cloud of naivety and privilege. I can't. When reading about the war it is impossible not to encounter images of atrocities, in the curious digital democracy of the internet, alongside adverts for barbecues and pop culture. One, for instance, of a flat landscape on the Eastern Front, a German soldier distinctive in his coal-scuttle helmet, rifle raised at the moment of firing. At first I thought the dark rounded form in front of him was some kind of farm animal, but then I realised it was a huddle of people and in front of them a mother, holding her child close and turning her back to the soldier and the bullets in a futile final attempt to save it – the tragedy of these photographs is the life we will never know of, even down to whether to write 'him' or 'her'.

As a child, I tried to ignore images like that. They both terrified and bothered me in the confusion about what my obsession with war machines actually meant. Now, they don't just hit my brain but my body too, rising in a sickly energy from the pit of my stomach and shivering along my limbs and across my skin, something primal and beyond real. It is the knowledge that such things have always happened through our human history, that they are happening now, that they will happen again, for they are a part of who we are.

# NOTES

All books/articles referenced within the text are listed alphabetically beneath each chapter heading.

**Never Served**

Dan Billany, *The Trap* (London: Faber & Faber, 1954), p. 87

Tom Brokaw, *The Greatest Generation* (New York: Random House, 1998)

Thomas Colley, *Always at War* (Ann Arbour: University of Michigan Press, 2019), p. 165

Dr Henry Irving, *Keep Calm and Carry On – The Compromise Behind the Slogan*, 27 June 2014 for History of Government, https://history.blog.gov.uk/2014/06/27/keep-calm-and-carry-on-the-compromise-behind-the-slogan/ Accessed online 15 October 2022

https://hansard.parliament.uk/Commons/1940-05-13/debates/8954756e-525b-448e-bb4d-5cc77d60aaf1/HisMajestySGovernment?highlight=%22blood%2C%20toil%2C%20tears%20and%20sweat%22#contribution-f03873fc-31e4-41ff-bf8c-6d1b7241ecbe

## Boys and Their Toys

British Pathe, 'Defence: Empire Day: RAF Open Day at Hendon Air Base', 1935

Winston Churchill, *My Early Life* (London: Eland, 2000), p. 19

Antonia Fraser, *A History of Toys* (London: Hamlyn, 1972), p. 61

Henry Harris, *Model Soldiers* (London: Octopus, 1972), p. 5

Richard Hillary, *The Last Enemy* (London: Macmillan & Co Ltd, 1946), p. 29

Jan Mark, *Thunder and Lightnings* (Harmondsworth: Puffin Books, 1976), p. 89, 142

Mass Observation File Report 87, 'What Children Think of the War', April 1940, reproduced courtesy of the Trustees of the Mass Observation Archive

Noel Monks, *Squadrons Up* (London: Victor Gollancz, 1940), p. 18

John Rawlings Rees, *The Shaping of Psychiatry by War* (London: Chapman & Hall, 1945), p. 80

Various Authors, *Bedtime Rhymes* (Loughborough: Ladybird Books LTD, 1977), p. 30

H. G. Wells, *Little Wars* (London: Arms & Armour Press, 1970), p. 10

https://www.rafmuseum.org.uk/research/online-exhibitions/the-polish-air-force-in-world-war-2/303-squadron

https://www.rafmuseum.org.uk/documents/collections/74-A-12-Avro-Lancaster-R5868.pdf

## Come and See

Michael Burn, *Turned Towards the Sun – An Autobiography* (Norwich: Michael Russell, 2003), p. 48, 72, 70, 74, 77, 80

Michael Burn, *Yes, Farewell* (London: Jonathan Cape, 1946), p. 388

Andrew Davies, *Conrad's War* (London: Blackie & Son, 1978), p. 53

Antonia Fraser, *A History of Toys* (London: Hamlyn, 1972), p. 230

David Holbrook, *Flesh Wounds* (London: Methuen & Co Ltd, 1966), p. 164

Patrick Wright, *On Living in an Old Country: The National Past in Contemporary Britain* (London: Verso, 1985), p. 81


**Heavy Metal**

Dan Billany, *The Trap* (London: Faber & Faber, 1954), p. 72

British Pathe, 'A Gift from the Skies', 5 November 1945

Imperial War Museum, Documents 7811 Private Papers of Flight Lieutenant T W Fox RAFVR

Nicholas Monsarrat, *The Cruel Sea* (London: The Reprint Society, 1953), p. 389

*The Times*, 10 July 1940

https://www.bmwgroup.com/en/company/history/BMW-during-the-era-of-national-socialism.html

https://britishlistedbuildings.co.uk/101390665-ze7-lippitts-hill-concrete-sculpture-of-a-man-epping-forest


**The Generation Game**

Elizabeth Bowen, *The Heat of the Day* (London: Jonathan Cape, 1954), p. 23

Michael Burn, *Turned Towards the Sun – An Autobiography* (Norwich: Michael Russell, 2003), p.19, 261

Robert Graves and Alan Hodge, *The Long Week-End: A Social History of Great Britain, 1918–1939* (London: Penguin, 1971), p. 267

Derek Jarman, *The Last of England*, (London: Constable & Company, 1987), p. 121, 179, 211, 212, 107

Julian Maclaren-Ross, *Collected Memoirs* (London: Black Spring Press, 2004), p. 3

George Orwell, *My Country Right or Left* (London: The Folio Society, 1998), p. 99

Colin Spencer, *Backing into the Light: My Father's Son*, (London: Quartet, 2013), p. 65

Peter Stanley, *Commando to Colditz* (London: Pier 9 / Murdoch Books UK Ltd, 2009), p. 29

**Private Normal**

Dan Billany, *The Trap* (London: Faber & Faber, 1954), p. 97, 145

Quentin Crisp, *The Naked Civil Servant* (London: Jonathan Cape, 1968), p. 159

David French, *Raising Churchill's Army – The British Army and the War Against Germany 1919–1945* (Oxford: Oxford University Press, 2000), p. 14, 21, 126, 152, 242

Robert Graves and Alan Hodge, *The Long Week-End: A Social History of Great Britain, 1918–1939* (London: Penguin, 1971), p. 88, 97

Willis Hall, *The Long and the Short and the Tall* (Oxford: Heineman Educational Books Ltd, 1965)

*Infantry Training: Training and War*, (London: HMSO, 1937), p. 209

*Infantry Training – Volume One. Training* (London: HMSO, 1932), p. 12

Interview with John Alcock by Paul Marshall, July 1985, Hall-Carpenter Oral History Archive, British Library, C456/03 art Tape 1 (F2068)

*The King's Regulations and Air Council Instructions for the Royal Air Force 1939* (London: HMSO, 1939), p. 466

Julian Maclaren-Ross, *Collected Memoirs* (London: Black Spring Press, 2004), p. 254

Julian Maclaran-Ross, *The Stuff to Give the Troops*, (London: Jonathan Cape, 1944), p. 54, 102

George Mosse, *Nationalism and Sexuality: Respectability and*

*Abnormal Sexuality in Modern Europe* (New York: Howard Fertig, 1985)

PRO W/O 231/8 Director of military training, General Lessons of the Italian Campaign, 18th December 1943

Valerie A. Reeves and Valerie Showan, *Dan Billany: Hull's Lost Hero* (Kingston upon Hull: Kingston Press, 1999), p. 81

*The Sun*, 'OK kids, let's see how you deal with REAL problems – like a posting to Ukraine's frontline', 15 February 2022, accessed online 9 October 2022 https://www.thesun.co.uk/ news/17662973/jane-moore-real-problems-ukraine/

## Fight or/and/or Flight

Anomaly, *The Invert and His Social Adjustment* (London: Baillière, Tindall & Cox, 1927), p. 65.

BBC, *Fawlty Towers*, 'The Germans', 24 October 1975

British Pathé archive, '1000 a Night Only the Start' https://www.britishpathe.com/video/ VLVA135FNFPCODSP8B1IA5TQVQZ2W-DEFENCE-WORLD-WAR-II-AIR-MARSHAL-HARRIS-ON-BOMBING-RAIDS) (accessed 2 September 2022)

Coventry *Evening Telegraph*, 10 January 1940.

David French, *Raising Churchill's Army – The British Army and the War Against Germany 1919–1945* (Oxford: Oxford University Press, 2000), p. 147, 153

Patrick Hamilton, *Hangover Square* (London: Penguin, 2001), p. 101

*Hansard* HC Deb. vol.270 col.632, 10 November 1932. [Online]. [Accessed 2 September 2022]. Available from: https://www. parliament.uk

*Hansard* HC Deb. vol.295 col.858, 28 November 1934. [Online]. [Accessed 2 September 2022].

Lincolnshire *Echo*, 28 May 1940.

Christopher J. Scott and Patrick Major, 'The ionospheric response over the UK to major bombing raids during World War II', *Ann. Geophys.*, 36, 1243–1254

W. G. Sebald, *On the Natural History of Destruction* (London: Penguin Books, 2004), p. 3

*The Sphere*, 8 April 1939.

Kevin Wilson, *Journey's End: Bomber Command's Battle from Arnhem to Dresden* (London: Weidenfeld & Nicolson, 2010), p. 393, 401

https://media.nationalarchives.gov.uk/index.php/untold-story-raf-black-second-world-war-fliers-europe


**Strength in Unity**

Dan Billany, *The Trap* (London: Faber & Faber, 1954), p. 75

W. R. Chorley, *In Brave Company – The History of 158 Squadron* (Taunton: Barnicotts Ltd, 1978), p. 15

Imperial War Museum: Documents.16764

Harry Lomas, *One Wing High* (Shrewsbury: Airlife Publishing, 1995), p. 98, 158

National Archives AIR 27/1050/8

Kenneth Skidmore, *Follow the Man with the Pitcher* (Wirral: Countyvise, 1996), p.83

*Times Literary Supplement*, 7 August 1943

Bertram Warr, *Acknowledgement to Life – The Collected Poems of Bertram Warr* (Toronto: The Ryerson Press, 1970), p. 16, 32, 56, 85, 91

Bertram Warr's notebook, 158 Squadron archive

Bertram Warr, *Yet A Little Onwards* (London: Resurgam, 1941), introduction

http://www.ceylonmedals.com/rohan.htm

http://www.ceylonmedals.com/book1.htm

# NOTES

## Dead's Men Beds

Martin W. Bowman, *Nachtjagd, Defenders of the Reich 1940–1943* (Barnsley: Pen & Sword Aviation, 2016), p.242

W. R. Chorley, *In Brave Company – The History of 158 Squadron* (Taunton: Barnicotts Ltd, 1978), photographs and p. 163., also Friday the 13th – Lucky for Some, the York Press, 23 March 2013, accessed online 8 October 2022 https://www.yorkpress.co.uk/news/10309839.friday-the-13th-lucky-for-some/

Peter Johnson, *The Withered Garland: Reflections and Doubts of a Bomber* (London: New European Publications Ltd, 1995), p. 246.

Harry Lomas, *One Wing High* (Shrewsbury: Airlife Publishing, 1995), p. 94.

S. P. MacKenzie, 'Beating the Odds: Superstition and Human Agency in RAF Bomber Command, 1942–1945' (*War in History*, Vol. 32 Issue 3, 2015), p. 389

Douglas A. Robinson, *Life Is a Great Adventure* (London: Janus, 1997), p. 32.

Ian Robinson, *The Unbeaten Warrior Returns – The Story of Reconstructing the Handley Page Halifax at the Yorkshire Air Museum 1983–1986* (York: Yorkshire Air Museum, 1996), p. 15.

Bertram Warr, *Acknowledgement to Life – The Collected Poems of Bertram Warr* (Toronto: The Ryerson Press, 1970)


## They Don't Like It Up 'Em

ATM no. 35, London 1940

British Pathé newsreel, 'Realism in Training', 27 October 1941

Michael Burn, *Turned Towards the Sun – An Autobiography* (Norwich: Michael Russell, 2003), p. 237

John Atkinson Hobson, *The Psychology of Jingoism* (London: Grant Richards. 1901), p. 30, 31

*Infantry Training, Training and War* (London: War Office, 1937), p. 75, 145, 176

Nella Last, *Nella Last's War – The Second World War Diaries of Housewife 49* (London: Profile Books, 2006), p. 7

George Orwell, *The Lion and the Unicorn: Socialism and the English Genius* (London: Penguin, 1941), p. 58

*Look Who's Talking*, Border Television / ITV, 1983 (accessed online 3 September 2022)


**Vile Bodies**

*Army Manual of Hygiene and Sanitation* (London: HMSO, 1940), p. 7, 20

Lord Baden-Powell, *Rovering to Success – A Book of Life Sport for Young Men* (London: Herbert Jenkins, 1938)

Dan Billany, *The Trap* (London: Faber & Faber, 1954), p. 77

Michael Burn, *Yes, Farewell* (London: Jonathan Cape, 1946), p. 311

Dudley Cave Oral History, Bishopsgate Institute, SB/19/1/8

Paul Fussell, *The Great War and Modern Memory* (Oxford: Oxford University Press, 2000), p. 298

Robert Graves and Alan Hodge, *The Long Week-End: A Social History of Great Britain, 1918–1939* (London: Penguin, 1971), p. 377

*Hansard* HC Deb. series 5 vol. 285 col. 1148, 7 February 1934. [Accessed 3 September 2022]. Available from: https://www.parliament.uk

*Health and Strength* Annual, 14 May 1938

J. H. Witte, *The One That Didn't Get Away* (Bognor Regis: New Horizons, 1983), p. 135


**The Clap Trap**

Alexander Baron, *From the City, From the Plough* (London: Imperial War Museum, 2019), p. 67.

# NOTES

Quentin Crisp, *The Naked Civil Servant* (London: Jonathan Cape, 1968), p. 154

David French, *Raising Churchill's Army – The British Army and the War Against Germany 1919–1945* (Oxford: Oxford University Press, 2000), p. 144

Herbert A. Friedman, Sex & Psychological Operations https://www.psywarrior.com/sexandprop.html

Peter Johnson, *The Withered Garland: Reflections and Doubts of a Bomber* (London: New European Publications Ltd, 1995), p 186

Norman Lewis, *Naples '44: An Intelligence Officer in the Italian Labyrinth* (London: Eland Publishing Ltd, 2002), p. 25

Harry Lomas, *One Wing High* (Shrewsbury: Airlife Publishing, 1995), p. 55, 94

Nicholas Monsarrat, *The Cruel Sea* (London: The Reprint Society, 1953), p. 331

PRO WO 163/161 'Morale Report May–July 1942' p. 3, Quoted in J. A. Crang, 'The British Soldier on the Home Front: Army Morale Reports 1940–45' in *Time to Kill*, p. 60

George Ryley Scott, *Sex Problems and Dangers in Wartime* (London: T Werner Laurie Ltd, 1940), preface, 3, 40, 43, 70

*Sydney Morning Herald* interview, 17 May 2003, [accessed 3 September 2022].

Gordon Westwood, *Society and the Homosexual* (London: Victor Gollancz, 1952), p. 22

J.H. Witte, *The One That Didn't Get Away* (Bognor Regis: New Horizons, 1983), p. 22, 51, 73, 79, 80, 83

http://www.moidigital.ac.uk/reports/home-intelligence-reports/morale-summaries-of-daily-reports-part-b-inf-1264/idm140465727534816

**Sodomy and Ignominy**

Hector Bolitho, *A Penguin in the Eyrie: An RAF Diary, 1939-1945* (London: Hutchison, 1955), p. 111

Norman Franks, *Fighter Leader: The Story of Wing Commander Ian Gleed* (London: Kimber, 1978), p. 126

Ian Gleed, *Arise to Conquer* (London: Gollancz, 1942), p. viii

The *Independent*, 27 June 1996, accessed online 10 November 2022 https://www.independent.co.uk/news/rioting-is-blamed-on-media-jingoism-1339100.html, p. 195

Interview with John Alcock by Paul Marshall, July 1985, Hall-Carpenter Oral History Archive, British Library, C456/03 art Tape 1 (F2068)

*The Kings Regulations and Admiralty Instructions for the Government of His Majesty's Naval Service* (London: HMSO, 1936), p. 224

*The London Gazette*, Friday 22 May 1942

Robin Maugham, *Somerset and all the Maughams* (London: Longmans, 1966), p. 201

*Mirror Declares Football War on Germany*, Daily Mirror, 24 June 1996, accessed online, British Newspaper Archive

Nicholas Monsarrat, *The Cruel Sea* (London: The Reprint Society, 1953), p. 237

W. Somerset Maugham, *Strictly Personal* (London: William Heineman Ltd, 1942), p. 138

National Archives, AIR 2/9485, Royal Air Force Personnel (Code B, 68

Emma Vickers, *Queen and Country: Same-Sex Desire in the British Armed Forces, 1939–45* (Manchester: Manchester University Press, 2013), p. 108.

BBC, 'It's Not Unusual, A Lesbian & Gay History', 18 May 1997

*Capital Gay*, 5 May 1995 (Bishopsgate Institute Archive)

Dudley Cave, Bishopsgate Oral History transcript, SB/19/1/8

**NOTES**

## A Flame Without a Hearth

Michael Burn, *Mary and Richard: The Story of Richard Hillary and Mary Booker* (London: Mandarin, 1989), p. 3

Michael Burn, *Poems as Accompaniment to Life* (Norwich: Michael Russell, 2006), p. 134

Michael Burn, *Turned Towards the Sun* (Norwich: Michael Russell, 2003), p. 96, 97, 98, 165, 166

Michael Burn, *Yes, Farewell* (London: Jonathan Cape, 1946), p. 51, 355

Roberta Cowell, *Roberta Cowell's Story, by Herself* (London: William Heinemann Ltd, 1954), p. 82

Quentin Crisp, *The Naked Civil Servant* (London: Jonathan Cape, 1968), p. 96, 151, 155

Sue Elliott & Steve Humphries, *Not Guilty: Queer Stories from a Century of Discrimination* (London: Biteback Publishing Ltd, 2018), p. 79, 87

Richard Hauser, *The Homosexual Society* (London: Mayflower Books, 1965), p. 75

Richard Langworth, *The Definitive Wit of Winston Churchill* (London: Ebury, 2009), p. 204

National Archives, MEPO 2/8859

Peter de Rome, *The Erotic World of Peter de Rome*, (London: Gay Mens Press, 1984), p. 32, 37, 39, 51, 56, 66, 150, 173

George Ryley Scott, *Sex Problems and Dangers in Wartime* (London: T Werner Laurie Ltd, 1940), p. 74

Gordon Westwood, *Society and the Homosexual* (London: Victor Gollancz, 1952), p. 23, 24, 51

https://kenplummer.com/resources/on-remembered-friends-a-quiet-corner-of-the-site/memoriam-michael-schofield-service

## People are People

The pronouns used in this chapter respect and reflect those used by Cowell herself in *Roberta Cowell's Story, by Herself*, where pre-transition Cowell uses 'he' and 'Robert'.

Enid Mary Barraud, *Set My Hand Upon the Plough* (Worcester: Littlebury & Co, 1946), p. 10, 66, 71

Michael Burn, *Yes, Farewell* (London: Jonathan Cape, 1946), p. 51, 355

DS Cave, Private Papers, Imperial War Museum Documents 6443

Quentin Crisp, *The Naked Civil Servant* (London: Jonathan Cape, 1968), p. 96, 151, 155

Radclyffe Hall, *The Well of Loneliness* (London: Penguin Classics, 2015), p. 298

*The Land Girl* vol. 6, no. 12. March 1946, p. 10

Ben Macintyre, *SAS Rogue Heroes* (London: Penguin, 2017), p. 25

Ben Shepherd, *A War of Nerves, Soldiers and Psychiatrists in the Twentieth Century* (Harvard: Harvard University Press, 2003), p. 183

Peter Stanley, *Commando to Colditz* (London: Pier 9 / Murdoch Books UK Ltd, 2009), p. 60

File of reports, notes, correspondence, etc., re psychiatry in the Allied armies, including a report on German national character, Wellcome Collection, RAMC/466/49

Gordon Westwood, *Society and the Homosexual* (London: Victor Gollancz, 1952), p. 23, 24, 51

J. H. Witte, *The One That Didn't Get Away* (Bognor Regis: New Horizons, 1983), p. 128

# NOTES

## Breaking the Cage

Dan Billany, *The Trap* (London: Faber & Faber, 1954), p.229, 345

Billany family archive, p. 110, 115, 117, 158

*Forbidden love: The WW2 letters between two men*, BBC News, 17 February 2017. Accessed online 8 October 2022 https://www.bbc.co.uk/news/uk-england-38932955, p. 248

James Gardiner, *A Class Apart: The Private Pictures of Montague Glover* (London: Serpents Tail, 1992), p. 81, 134, 135

Valerie A. Reeves and Valerie Showan, *Dan Billany: Hull's Lost Hero* (Kingston Upon Hull: Kingston Press, 1999), p. 140, 155

## The Democracy of Death

Michael Burn, *Turned Towards the Sun* (Norwich: Michael Russell, 2003), p. 129

Roger A. Freeman, *Bases of Bomber Command, Then and Now* (London: Battle of Britain International, 2001), p. 207

John Keegan, *Soldiers: A History of Men in Battle* (London: Hamish Hamilton, 1985), p. 36

Eric Lambert, *The Twenty Thousand Thieves* (London: Transworld Publishers, 1963)

Harry Lomas, *One Wing High* (Shrewsbury: Airlife Publishing, 1995), p. 214

Bertram Warr notebooks, 158 Squadron archives

## Mr Thwaites' Britain

Interview with John Alcock by Paul Marshall, July 1985, Hall-Carpenter Oral History Archive, British Library, C456/03 art Tape 1 (F2068)

Michael Burn, *Farewell to Colditz* (London: White Lion, 1946), p. i, vi

Michael Burn, *Poems as Accompaniment to Life* (Norwich, Michael Russell, 2006), p. 30

*Capital Gay* magazine, Bishopsgate Archive

Dudley Cave papers, Bishopsgate Institute

Thomas Colley, *Always at War* (Ann Arbor: University of Michigan Press, 2019), p. 193

Sue Elliott & Steve Humphries, *Not Guilty: Queer Stories from a Century of Discrimination* (London: Biteback Publishing Ltd, 2018), p. 109

Patrick Hamilton, *The Slaves of Solitude* (London: Abacus, 2017), p. 2

David Holbrook, Flesh Wounds (London: Methuen & Co Ltd, 1966)

Matt Houlbrook, *Queer London: Perils and Pleasures in the Sexual Metropolis* (Chicago: University of Chicago Press, 2005) p. Appendix , 236

Intergroup's Internews pamphlet, Bishopsgate Institute archive

Letter quoted in the *Bulletin of the Unitarian Social Responsibility Department*, April 1984, Bishopsgate Institute archive

Michael Powell; Emeric Pressburgr, *A Matter of Life and Death* (The Archers, 1946)

Quentin Crisp, *The Naked Civil Servant* (London: Jonathan Cape, 1968), p. 173

Peter de Rome, *The Erotic World of Peter de Rome*, (London: Gay Mens Press, 1984), p. 57, 91

Private Papers of DS Cave, Imperial War Museum Documents 6443

Siegfried Sasson, 'On Passing the New Menin Gate' *The War Poems* (London, Faber & Faber, 2006), p. 143

Ben Shepherd, *A War of Nerves, Soldiers and Psychiatrists in the Twentieth Century* (Harvard: Harvard University Press, 2003), p. 379

Liz Stanley, *Sex Surveyed 1949–1994: From Mass Observation to the National Survey and the Hite Reports* (London: Taylor & Francis, 1995), p. 199

Peter Stanley, *Commando to Colditz* (London: Pier 9 / Murdoch Books UK LTD, 2009), p. 198

Colin Spencer, *Homosexuality – A History* (London: Fourth Estate, 1995), p. 355, 360, 361

The *Sun*, front page, 3 February 2016

'War Baby', *Guardian*, 17 August 1995

Colonel Archie Cecil Thomas White, *The Story of Army Education 1643–1963* (London: George G Harrap and Co, 1963) pp. 92–98

Gordon Westwood, *Society and the Homosexual* (London: Victor Gollancz, 1952), p.20, 21

Yahoo News, [accessed 3 September 2022] https://uk.news.yahoo.com/brexit-party-nicholas-goulding-remembrance-sunday-poppy-181844812.html

https://lareviewofbooks.org/article/pandemic-narratives-and-the-historian

https://www.royal.uk/address-her-majesty-queen-75th-anniversary-ve-day

https://vintageaviationecho.com/nhs-spitfire/ pub 19 April 2021

https://www.theguardian.com/politics/2018/jan/29/german-ambassador-peter-ammon-second-world-war-image-of-britain-has-fed-euroscepticism

https://www.channel4.com/news/nigel-farage-ukip-letter-school-concerns-racism-fascism

https://www.bbc.co.uk/news/av/uk-politics-47004688

https://www.independent.co.uk/news/uk/politics/leave-eu-merkel-tweet-brexit-world-war-germany-kraut-arron-banks-a9148356.html

https://www.telegraph.co.uk/news/2016/05/14/

boris-johnson-interview-we-can-be-the-heroes-of-europe-by-voting

https://www.standard.co.uk/news/politics/matt-hancock-suspending-parliament-would-be-an-insult-to-dday-veterans-a4163511.html

https://twitter.com/Mike_Fabricant/status/1533828338493579264?s=20&t=A1aMgusqPmEYFbl2FjI0xA

http://news.bbc.co.uk/1/hi/uk/20258.stm

## Aftermath

https://www.thetimes.co.uk/article/wagner-groups-hardened-mercenaries-pictured-in-eastern-ukraine-td9jnwwsm

https://www.theguardian.com/world/2022/feb/25/ukraine-soldiers-told-russians-to-go-fuck-yourself-before-black-sea-island-death

https://www.theguardian.com/world/2022/mar/12/ukraine-reveals-russian-warship-go-fuck-yourself-postage-stamp

# ACKNOWLEDGEMENTS

Starting to write this book just as the Covid-19 lockdown began in the spring of 2020 meant that my original plans for research were blown away overnight. Museums, archives and libraries all closed, trying to connect with veterans became an impossibility and *Men At War*, by necessity, ended up becoming a very different creature to what I had intended it to be. Sincere thanks to my editor Jenny Lord and agent Natalie Galustian for guiding me through this tricky process, to my dear pals Jennifer Lucy Allan and Tim Burrows for putting up with a barrage of WhatsApp despair and, most of all, my incredible wife Milène Larsson for her constant patience, support and love to keep me on the right side of sanity. A huge thanks to my fellow Second World War geeks Neil 'Tommo' Thomson, Andrew Walker and Richard Foster for being sounding boards and suppliers of inspiration and ideas as the book unfolded. As the Covid-19 restrictions lifted, the staff at various institutions did a wonderful job of trying to help so many of us to access research materials safely – especially all at the British Library, Stefan Dickers of the Bishopsgate Institute archives, Jessica Scantlebury of The Keep/Mass Observation Archive and Elizabeth Smith of the

Imperial War Museum research room. Discovering the literary legacy of 158 Squadron, Bomber Command was a turning point in the writing of *Men At War*, and the information and advice provided by the Squadron Association's Chuck Tolley, Alan Cowland and especially Bertram Warr's nephew, Tony Frost was invaluable. The love and respect that endures down the generations has been moving to witness while writing this book and I'd like to thank John Keston, Dennis Wilson, Stephen Wilkinson and their families for their generous interviews which, though they didn't appear in the final MS, informed the spirit in which I wrote. Thank you to Ken Worpole for the last-minute introduction to the writing of Dan Billany and then to the writer's niece Jodi Weston Brake who provided invaluable research material from her family's archive. A huge appreciation to Enid Barraud's cousin David Lumsden for his permission to connect her Mass Observation reports with the wonderful *Set My Hand Upon the Plough* – I hope that Barraud's wartime writing might soon reach the wider audience it deserves. Similarly, the estate of Michael Burn were generous in their permission to quote from his wonderful legacy of books, letters and poems. My appreciation, too, to my own family for their constancy and morale boosts, as well as helping me find out more about my grandads and great-uncle. The same goes for my mother-in-law Yolande Knobel, whose family story has given my son his name. Huge gratitude to Yolande and my parents, Martin and Biddy Turner, for taking care of Maximilian while I worked on the final edits of the book. Thank you to Philip Hoare for passing on a commission that turned out to be a liberating piece of writing to undertake and Colin Spencer for the frank interview (and lunch) down on the south coast. Further thanks to John Doran, Paddy Clarke, Bobby Barry, Christian Eede, Ella Kemp and Sean Kitching of The Quietus, Lee Brackstone, Max Leonard, Peter Tatchell, Tom Braham, Major Jamie Carraher of the Army LGBT+ Forum,

## ACKNOWLEDGEMENTS

Kirsteen McNish, Tom Shankland, Ross MacFarlane, Tim Thomas, Katya Orohovsky, Tim Crook, Rebecca Sillence, Liz Dexter, James Knight, Sue George, Peter Naylor, Pippa Marland, Rob St John, Roy Wilkinson, David Taylor and Sea Power, Lynne Kaye, Peter Stanley, James Dorrian, David McGillivray, Phillip Ward and the estate of Quentin Crisp, Juliet Annan and the Trustees of the Mass Observation Archive.

That the war generation are now moving beyond living memory was always intended to be a key theme of *Men At War*. Not long after the final draft was complete, I was greatly saddened to learn of the passing of Henry Danton on 9 February 2022. Interviewing Henry in October 2020 was the moment when what I wanted to do with this book started to become clear. I hope that in these pages I have managed to do justice to his memory, and to all those others of his generation who served and fought in the Second World War.

Luke Turner, 17 October 2022

# ORION CREDITS

Luke Turner and Weidenfeld & Nicolson would like to thank everyone at Orion who worked on the publication of Men at War.

**Agent**
Natalie Galustian

**Editorial**
Jenny Lord
Kate Moreton

**Copy-editor**
Elizabeth Marvin

**Proofreader**
Kati Nicholl

**Production**
Hannah Cox
Katie Horrocks

**Contracts**
Dan Herron
Ellie Bowker
Alyx Hurst

**Editorial Management**
Jo Roberts-Miller
Jane Hughes
Charlie Panayiotou
Tamara Morriss
Claire Boyle

**Audio**
Paul Stark
Jake Alderson
Georgina Cutler

**Design**
Nick Shah
Steve Marking
Chevonne Elbourne
Joanna Ridley
Helen Ewing

**Finance**
Nick Gibson
Jasdip Nandra
Sue Baker
Tom Costello

**Inventory**
Jo Jacobs
Dan Stevens

**Marketing**
Cait Davies

**Publicity**
Virginia Woolstencroft

**Sales**
Jen Wilson
Victoria Laws
Esther Waters
Group Sales teams across
Digital, Field Sales, International and Non-Trade

**Operations**
Group Sales Operations team

**Rights**
Rebecca Folland
Ruth Blakemore
Flora McMichael
Alice Cottrell
Ayesha Kinley
Marie Henckel

LUKE TURNER is a writer and editor. He co-founded and co-edits influential music and culture website The Quietus. He has contributed to the *Guardian, Observer, New Statesman, Sunday Times, Art Review, Dazed & Confused, Vice, NME, Q, Mojo, Monocle,* and Somesuch Stories, among other publications, and has worked as a broadcaster for the BBC. He co-curated cultural programmes related to Epping Forest and radical arts group COUM Transmissions, and has collaborated with galleries and institutions including the V&A, Hayward and Serpentine. His first book, *Out of the Woods*, was shortlisted for the Wainwright Prize and longlisted for the Polari Prize for first book by an LGBT+ writer. He lives in London.